THE PRACTICAL ARCHAEOLOGIST

Second Edition

THE PRACTICAL ARCHAEOLOGIST

Second Edition

HOW WE KNOW WHAT WE KNOW ABOUT THE PAST

Jane McIntosh

Facts On File, Inc.

THE PRACTICAL ARCHAEOLOGIST
HOW WE KNOW WHAT WE KNOW ABOUT THE PAST
Second Edition

Copyright © 1999 by Jane McIntosh

Checkmark Books
An imprint of Facts On File, Inc.
11 Penn Plaza
New York NY 10001

Library of Congress Cataloging-in-Publication Data
McIntosh, Jane.
The practical archaeologist :
how we know what we know about the past / Jane McIntosh. — Second ed.
p.   cm.
Includes index.
ISBN 0-8160-3950-X. — ISBN 0-8160-3951-8 (alk. paper)
1. Archaeology. I. Title.
CC165.M37   1999
930.1—dc21   98-48595

Checkmark Books are available at special discounts when purchased in bulk quantities for businesses, associations, institutions or sales promotions. Please call our Special Sales Department in New York at (212) 967-8800 or (800) 322-8755.

You can find Facts On File on the World Wide Web at http://www.factsonfile.com

Text design by Evelyn Horovicz
Cover design by Sandra Watanabe
Illustrations on pages 134 and 141 by Jeremy Eagle

Printed in Hong Kong

CREATIVE FOF 10 9 8 7 6 5 4 3 2 1

This book is printed on acid-free paper.

CONTENTS

The Maya god Vija Tai depicted on a pottery censer found at the impressive late Postclassic city of Mayapán, Mexico, which flourished between the mid-13th century and 1451 C.E.

PART

1

WHAT IS ARCHAEOLOGY?

SWEET FOOD OF ANTIQUITY

"In the study of Antiquity," wrote the English antiquarian William Camden (1551–1623), "there is a sweet food of the mind well befitting such as are of honest and noble disposition."

In all ages and all countries, people have been fascinated by their past. Today, many people argue that it is only by studying the past that we can properly understand the present and, perhaps, learn from the errors and achievements of our ancestors. A knowledge of their past is vital, too, to the self-respect of nations, as can be seen from the relatively large proportion of national budgets that many countries allocate to archaeological research.

Archaeology and History

Archaeology is often said to be the handmaiden of history. But the relationship between the two branches of study is not simply that of master and servant.

History depends on the availability of written records. Those are usually incomplete and may well be biased or inaccurate, too. Archaeology, on the other hand, can reveal much that would ordinarily be left out of written accounts, especially the details of everyday life. It helps, therefore, to round out our view of the past, to make it more balanced.

What is more, history deals only with the past of literate societies, a tiny portion of the human story. The written records of ancient peoples such as the Greeks of classical times tell us something about their illiterate neighbors and contemporaries. But most of what we know about these less-advanced peoples comes from archaeology. And archaeology is our only source of information about the millions of years of prehistory.

A Total Study

Archaeology is a total study. It involves analyzing everything that remains from the past, with the aim of reconstructing that past as fully as possible. Although some people regard archaeology as synonymous with excavation, it is far more than that. Excavation is only one of many of its processes.

Scientists carry out complicated analyses to date archaeological finds, to provide information on the sources of archaeological material or to establish exactly how ancient artifacts were made. Field archaeologists use many scientific devices to locate and map ancient sites.

Botanists, zoologists and physicians contribute information about the diets of ancient peoples, the environments in which they lived and their state of health. Archaeologists also study contemporary societies to gain an insight into life in the past. Their investigations range from observations of the daily life of surviving hunter-gatherers to surveys of the contents of garbage cans in modern America, to try to relate people's activities to the artifacts that are the main source of archaeological evidence.

Rummaging among the rubbish of the ages may seem a long way from Camden's "sweet food of the mind." But, as the pioneer of modern archaeology A. H. Pitt-Rivers (1827–1900) pointed out, it is the study of the ordinary, everyday things that helps us to reconstruct the past, far more so than rare, valuable objects that were unusual even in their own time and place.

The amazing achievements of our ancestors astound and fascinate us—the golden treasures of Tutankhamun, the jade princess of China, the vastness of the Pyramids. But in the end it is our common humanity that exerts the greatest appeal down the millennia—the man desperately stretching out his arms to protect his family as volcanic ash engulfed Pompeii, the 4,000-year-old exercise books of Sumerian schoolboys, the crumbling remains of the flowers laid on Tutankhamun's coffin.

That is the ultimate attraction of archaeology. Through its painstaking and detailed study of people of the past, we come ever closer to understanding ourselves.

Archaeology was lifted from pure treasure hunting to a proper level of scientific study by the work of a few great men. We are indebted to General Pitt-Rivers for demonstrating the value of detailed and methodical research and on-site recording. The publication of his findings set a new standard, and Pitt-Rivers showed scholars the great knowledge of the past that could be gleaned from observation of everyday things, so often ignored in the early days of archaeology.

MUMMIFIED FOOD FOR THE KING'S "KA": TUTANKHAMEN'S "LARDER."

THE "TIMES" WORLD COPYRIGHT, BY ARRANGEMENT WITH THE EARL OF CARNARVON.

CONTAINING MUMMIFIED JOINTS OF MEAT, HAUNCHES OF GAZELLE, LIVER, AND TRUSSED DUCKS—FOOD FOR TUTANKHAMEN'S SOUL: A PILE OF WHITE ROUNDED BOXES UNDER THE HATHOR-HEADED COUCH IN THE TOMB ANTE-CHAMBER.

Imagine the amazement of Howard Carter when he peered into the long-sealed outer chamber of Tutankhamun's tomb and saw this wonderful golden couch, with its figures of the cow-headed goddess Hathor. Underneath, stored for all time, are clay containers holding mummified joints of gazelles and ducks to sustain this pharaoh, who died so young, in the afterlife where he would have taken his place among the other gods.

3

SWEET FOOD
OF ANTIQUITY

ANTIQUARIANS AND NOBLE SAVAGES

The origins of archaeology go back more than 2,500 years. Nabonidus, the last king of Babylon (he reigned from 556 to 539 B.C.E.), excavated the temple of Shamath at Sippar to try to find out who built it. Nabonidus's daughter Ennigal-di-Nanna collected local antiquities and displayed them in the world's first known museum, in the city of Ur, which was located near the Euphrates.

The Greek historian Thucydides (c. 460–395 B.C.E.) describes how the Athenians excavated ancient graves on the Aegean island of Delos and interpreted the artifacts they found in them in terms of the politics of their own day. Chinese historians, too, used ancient artifacts and the remains of ruined cities to try to build up a picture of their ancestors' way of life.

This interest in the past was common to all literate ancient societies, while even illiterate peoples maintained an oral tradition of the deeds of their forebears. So philosophers such as the Roman Lucretius (96–55 B.C.E.) and Yuan Kang, who lived in China during the 1st century C.E., drew upon some remembrance of their ancestors when they wrote about former technological epochs—the age of stone, the age of jade, the age of bronze—and contrasted those with what they saw as the degenerate age of iron in which they themselves were living.

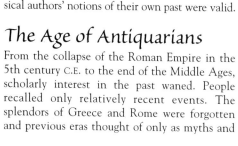

Lucretius and other writers of classical Rome and Greece were aware, too, of more primitive peoples of their own day who still used stone or bronze tools. Their existence, vigorous but barbaric to Roman and Greek eyes, showed that the classical authors' notions of their own past were valid.

The Age of Antiquarians

From the collapse of the Roman Empire in the 5th century C.E. to the end of the Middle Ages, scholarly interest in the past waned. People recalled only relatively recent events. The splendors of Greece and Rome were forgotten and previous eras thought of only as myths and legends. The Bible provided the main framework for history.

Stone tools and implements were popularly thought to be thunderbolts. Prehistoric pots dug

A clay brick (top right) found in Tell el-Muqayyar in modern Iraq, site of the ancient Chaldean city of Ur. It dates from the reign of Nabonidus, last Babylonian king to rule before the Persian conquest. The cuneiform impression records the building of a temple dedicated to Ningal, wife of the moon god Nanna.

Thucydides (bottom right) was one of the world's great historians, driven by a passion for the past of his own Greece and a desire to be as accurate as possible in recording it. He wrote of Athenian excavations on Delos and may well have seen this terrace of marble lions (middle right), which dates from the 7th century B.C.E.

4

WHAT IS ARCHAEOLOGY?

up in central Europe were believed to have been spontaneously generated in the ground.

It was the Renaissance, from the mid-15th century onward, that stimulated an upsurge of interest in classical Greek and Roman art and architecture. In turn, this aroused a passion for collecting antique objects among the well-to-do.

By the 16th century, scholars were investigating Roman ruins in Italy, helping to feed the collectors' market. Excavations at Herculaneum and Pompeii, towns buried by the eruption of Mount Vesuvius in 79 C.E., yielded a rich supply of treasures from 1709 onward.

Egyptian antiquities were transported to Europe. Mummies were particularly popular. In medieval times, powdered preparations made from mummies were believed to have formidable powers of healing, but by the 18th century that belief had waned and florid exhibitions of mummy dissection became a public entertainment. European travelers explored much of the Middle East and produced richly illustrated volumes describing its ancient monuments.

Secrets of the Stones

In northern and western Europe, the monuments of antiquity were exhaustively studied and described in scholarly fashion from the 16th century. Prehistoric megaliths, impressive structures such as Stonehenge in England, were a particular focus of interest, and their origins were the subject of learned debate. They were variously interpreted as burial chambers, memorials, altars or temples associated with human sacrifice, built by Druids, Romans or Vikings.

Some students of ancient monuments enjoyed royal patronage. In 1533, John Leland was appointed antiquary to the king of England and, as such, examined ancient documents and old buildings. Since Leland's time, many monarchs have supported antiquarians and archaeologists—perhaps because royalty has a vested interest in the past to establish its ancestry and therefore its legitimate claim to rule.

Early antiquarians did not concentrate on the monuments alone; they also focused on the general surface features of the land around. The study grew into the science of topography, and it now plays a major part in archaeology. William Camden (1551–1623) was one of its pioneers. He observed patterns of ancient streets in fields of growing corn, noting that the crop grew more thinly where the thoroughfares had once been. Today, thanks to aerial photography, such patterns are a valuable clue to archaeologists seeking ancient sites (*see pages 44–45*).

The "Childhood of Man"

The "discovery" of America in the 16th century and the exploration of Africa and the Pacific gave added stimulation to antiquarian thought.

In the optimistic climate of the Enlightenment—the 18th-century Age of Reason in Europe—the primitive inhabitants of these newly found lands were regarded as "noble savages," unspoiled examples of what humankind must have been like in its earliest days, before the biblical Fall. Their lifestyle was taken to reflect that of the inhabitants of Europe before Roman times. So it was thought that a study of their customs and way of living—part of what is now called anthropology—could illuminate the work of historians and archaeologists.

Contact between Europeans and the peoples of America and elsewhere produced one immediate and significant insight. Many of the native inhabitants still used stone tools similar to those found all over Europe and previously believed to be thunderbolts. The growing suspicion that these objects were, in fact, of human origin was thus confirmed.

From total destruction in 79 C.E. until 1594, Pompeii and its three neighboring towns (Herculaneum, Boscoreale and Stabiae) sank into oblivion. Then in the second half of the 19th century excavation began in earnest, revealing such wonders as this Temple of Apollo, unearthed from its grave of volcanic ash, and now sharing the horizon with Vesuvius, its one-time destroyer.

ANTIQUARIANS AND
NOBLE SAVAGES

ORDERING THE PAST

OPPOSITE PAGE:
Cave paintings such
as those at Lascaux,
which were discov-
ered by French
schoolboys in 1940,
revolutionized our
view of the abilities of
Paleolithic people, as
the artistic skills that
created this bison
demonstrate.

Sir John Lubbock
(right) was one of a
long line of scholars
seeking to make order
of humanity's seem-
ingly jumbled past. In
his book Prehistoric
Times (1865) he
divided the Stone Age
into two periods:
Paleolithic (Old Stone
Age), when people
used rough, chipped
stone tools, and
Neolithic (New Stone
Age), when fine pol-
ished stone tools and
weapons were in use.

Before the time of the Greeks and Romans, the past was "wrapped in a thick fog," according to Rasmus Nyerup (1759–1829), an eminent Danish antiquarian. "Everything that has come down to us from heathendom . . . is older than Christendom," he declared, but by how much "we can do no more than guess."

What was needed was a system to help dispel the fog—one that would divide the vast expanse of prehistory into workable chronological blocks, to which objects discovered by antiquarians and archaeologists could be assigned as appropriate.

The ancient Romans and Chinese had, in fact, created the basis of such a system with their ages of stone, bronze and iron. But although the theoretical significance of their approach was appreciated by some later scholars, it was not until 1819 that a coherent attempt was made to apply it to archaeological material.

In that year, the Danish National Museum reopened with a totally novel reclassification of its prehistoric exhibits. Its curator, Christian J. Thomsen (1788–1865), had arranged its collections according to the substances from which they were made, following the three consecutive ages of stone, bronze and iron that Lucretius had written about nearly 2,000 years earlier.

In 1836, Thomsen elaborated on this "three-age" scheme of prehistory in his book *Ledetraad til Nordisk Oldkyndighed* (*Guide to Nordic Antiquities*). In it, he described the objects, burial rites and tomb architecture associated with each age, drawing on his own extensive familiarity with the material.

Thomsen's study was translated into German in 1837 and into English in 1848. By the second half of the 19th century, his system had become widely accepted. It is still the foundation of archaeology's attempts to order prehistory, though it has been considerably refined.

Probing the Strata

Thomsen's assistant and eventual successor at the Danish National Museum was J. J. Worsaae (1821–1885). A meticulous and painstaking archaeologist, his work helped to show the validity of the three-age system.

Unlike many antiquarians of his day, Worsaae did not dig haphazardly into ancient sites in search of treasures. In excavating burial mounds and Denmark's peat bogs, a rich source of prehistoric objects, he worked carefully, taking note of the

distinct layers he discerned as he dug downward.

Worsaae recognized one of the fundamental principles on which archaeological investigation depends—that of stratigraphic succession. Like the geological strata laid down by the forces of nature over the ages, successive layers of archaeological material have accumulated in places frequented by people. Some are natural accumulations of soil and decayed vegetation, while others are the result of human activity. An archaeological site is therefore like a layer cake, in which the top layer is the most recent and the succeeding layers become progressively older the deeper you go. The period of time represented by each layer can vary considerably; in some burial mounds the layers may have been added within minutes of each other, while on other sites a deposit only a few centimeters deep can represent hundreds of years of human occupation.

By careful investigation, Worsaae was able to demonstrate that the Stone Age of Lucretius and Thomsen preceded an era in which most tools and implements were made of bronze. After the Bronze Age came an epoch in which everyday tools were iron, bronze being reserved for ornaments and luxury goods. This was the Iron Age that Lucretius had disparaged as degenerate.

While Worsaae conducted his pioneer investigations in Denmark, discoveries elsewhere showed that Thomsen's three-age scheme was valid for all Europe. But in France in particular, archaeologists found crudely chipped stone axes in addition to the polished ones regarded as typical of the Stone Age. This evidence led them to

conclude that there had, in fact, been two Stone Ages, for which Sir John Lubbock (1834–1913) coined new names: Paleolithic, or Old Stone Age, for the earlier period and Neolithic, or New Stone Age, for the later period.

In caves and rock shelters inhabited by Paleolithic peoples, French archaeologists such as Edouard Lartet (1801–1871) discovered breathtaking wall paintings. At first, few believed that prehistoric savages could have been capable of works of such technical skill and artistic vigor. It was not until mid-1890s that evidence emerged to win over the skeptics: Paleolithic art discovered at La Mouthe and Pair-non-Pair in France was found to be covered by undisturbed later deposits.

Four Ages of Man

As discoveries throughout Europe broadened knowledge of the artifacts of Thomsen's three ages, scholars tried to assess what the artifacts might imply about the development of human society. Researchers based their theories, at least in part, on comparisons with the lifestyles of contemporary primitive societies. One of the leading scholars in this field was another Scandinavian, Sven Nilsson (1787–1883). He proposed the idea that humankind passed or was passing through four phases. In the earliest, corresponding to much of the Stone Age, people were savage hunters and fishers. During the second phase, they herded some of the animals they had formerly hunted, but most people remained nomads. In the third phase, they settled down and turned to agriculture, creating a surplus of food that could be traded. The development of coinage to simplify such trade was, with the emergence of writing, one of Nilsson's signposts to the fourth phase—civilization.

Nilsson's ideas were adopted and modified by anthropologists such as Britain's Sir Edward Tylor (1832–1917) and Lewis H. Morgan (1818–1881) in America. Toward the end of the 19th century, it became widely accepted that all human societies everywhere were following the same general course of development, although obviously they were not all in the same phase at the same time. Believers in the theory ascribed it to what they called the "psychic unity of man." Today's archaeologists no longer accept the concept of an inevitable course of human progress, but traces of the idea of essential unity survives in the work of those who seek to discover universally applicable general laws of human behavior.

*The Lower Rhine val-
ley revealed itself to
be rich in mammal
fossils of the Pleis-
tocene epoch. This
engraving shows a
typical excavation of
the mid-19th century
at one of the many
cave sites that yielded
remains of mastodons
and other large mam-
mals dating back
more than 10,000
years. Even though no
human remains were
found in association
with these bones,
such sites provided
invaluable informa-
tion from which to
reconstruct the envi-
ronment in which our
ancestors lived.*

Until less than 200 years ago, the Bible's Old Testament version of the Creation of the world went unquestioned, at least in public, in Western nations. Thinkers and religious leaders tried to put a date to the event. In 1650, Archbishop James Ussher of Armagh in Ireland calculated from the Bible that the Creation had taken place in 4004 B.C.E.—a view subsequently widely accepted by many Christians.

Given the state of knowledge at the time, Ussher's dating did not seem unreasonable. Historical events known through biblical sources and the writers of Greece and Rome could all be encompassed within it.

First Doubts Appear

As more was learned about antiquity and as the sciences of geology and paleontology—the study of fossils—began to develop, the timetable of world events derived from a literal reading of the Bible posed increasing difficulties for those who believed in it.

The upsurge of interest in fossil hunting in 18th-century Europe revealed more and more remains of unfamiliar beasts, birds, fish and plants, often deep in the ground. The orthodox explana-

tion was that the creatures and plants had been destroyed by Noah's flood—thus reconciling them with the Bible. People who believed this came to be called "catastrophists," or "diluvianists," the latter from *diluvium*, the Latin word for flood.

However, the explanation did not satisfy everybody. Among the doubters was James Hutton (1726–1797), a geologist from Edinburgh in Scotland. Hutton is now sometimes called the father of modern geology, but in his own century and well into the following one he was vilified by many people as an atheist.

Hutton observed the natural processes that form and shape the landscape, and maintained that these processes had occurred in exactly the same way throughout the past and that they would continue to do so in the future. "We find no vestige of a beginning, no prospect of an end [in nature]," he wrote.

The theory Hutton propounded is called uniformitarianism and is now generally accepted. However, the catastrophists were not prepared to give up their case without a fight.

Faced with a steady increase in the discoveries of different species of fossil animals and plants, the catastrophists refined their ideas, still trying to reconcile them with the Bible. Perhaps, they sug-

gested, there had been another flood or similar disaster after God had created the world, but before He had created people. As all other living creatures appeared before humans in the biblical account, that would mean that some species had been destroyed even before Noah's flood.

Despite the efforts of the catastrophists, uniformitarianism gradually gained ground, as followers of Hutton expanded upon his ideas. In 1833 Sir Charles Lyell, another Scot, published his *Principles of Geology*. Lyell's masterwork was the most influential geological sourcebook of the 19th century. It gradually won scientific respectability for Hutton's thesis, establishing that the world began many millions of years before Ussher and the catastrophists said it had, and paving the way for the theory of evolutionary development of all living things.

The Diffident Iconoclast

In 1797 John Frere, an antiquarian living in Norfolk, England, wrote a description of observations he had made in a clay pit being dug at Hoxne in Suffolk. In a layer of sandy soil he had found fossilized bones of extinct animals. In the gravel layer below, there were shaped stones that, he conjectured, were primitive weapons, presumably from a distant age when metal was totally unknown.

Frere commented that the items "tempt us to refer them to a very remote period indeed; even beyond that of the present world"—a revolutionary thought in the days when he was writing, as it went against the accepted ideas of Ussher and the catastrophists.

Little notice was taken of Frere at that time. But as the geological principle of stratification (that certain types of rock are formed in layers or strata, from which it is possible to draw conclusions about their age) gained acceptance, together with the archaeological principle of stratigraphy based on it, scholars came to share Frere's opinion.

Investigations of several sites in Europe where fossils and human artifacts appeared together, particularly caves and river terraces, suggested that people had lived alongside creatures that were now extinct. This meant humankind, like the earth itself, was far older than the Bible-derived timetable would allow.

At first, the scientific establishment rejected the implications. But the turning point came in 1859, when a group of distinguished British scholars visited Abbeville in northern France to observe the work being carried out there by Jacques Boucher de Perthes (1788–1868). He had found flint tools associated with bones of extinct animals in local gravel pits. The British came away convinced of the validity of Boucher de Perthes' findings and endorsed them vigorously. As a result, most scholars came to accept humankind's great antiquity.

The Origin of Species

The revolution in 19th-century thinking in geology, started by Hutton and carried forward by Lyell and others, was accompanied by an equally massive upheaval in biology. It came to a head in 1859, when the British naturalist Charles Darwin published the book usually referred to as *On the Origin of Species*.

Since the 18th century, scholars had been speculating that fossils were earlier links in a chain of evolution in which creatures gradually adapted to changes in their environment, rather than being victims of biblical floods. To Darwin, however, belongs the credit for working out the mechanism by which evolution takes place—natural selection. Individual members of a species vary in some of their characteristics, and those with variations best suited to their environment are the most likely to survive and reproduce (i.e., "survival of the fittest"). The original variations become enhanced in succeeding generations, eventually leading to the evolution of a new species.

Various scholars quickly saw the implications the theory of evolution held for determining the origins of humankind, among them Thomas Huxley (1825–1895), who earned the nickname "Darwin's bulldog" for his vigorous championing of the idea. Darwin himself hesitated to enter the public controversy, but did so in 1871, with his book *The Descent of Man*.

In that work Darwin contended, as Huxley and others had already done, that humankind had evolved from the same ancestors as present-day apes. For the theory to hold, however, there would have to have been at some stage of prehistory a creature representing an evolutionary "bridge" between their apelike forebears and human beings themselves. The search for the fossilized remains of this creature, the so-called missing link, united naturalists, geologists and fossil-hunting antiquarians.

Charles Darwin's view of evolution challenged the traditional religious and scientific thinking of the time. People became not the unique creation of an Almighty being, but merely a particularly successful type of animal, subject to the same natural laws that governed other animals. Although the basis of Darwin's theory is still generally accepted, recent work has refined our understanding of how evolution operates. It is now clear that it is not a gradual process, operating continuously, as Darwin had surmised. Instead, there are long periods of equilibrium, punctuated by short episodes of very rapid change. Often new species emerge when a small population of a particular genus becomes isolated from the main population.

QUEST FOR THE MISSING LINK

The idea that humans are descended from the apes provoked two reactions in the second half of the 19th century. For some scholars, the search for our earliest ancestors was akin to the legendary quest for the Holy Grail in its intensity. But fundamentalist believers in the literal truth of the Bible rejected the theory of evolution.

In 1856, the skeleton of what is now known to be an early human was found in a limestone cave at Neanderthal, near Düsseldorf in Germany. It attracted great attention, but the most eminent pathologist of the day, Rudolf Virchow, declared that it came from a modern human who had suffered from arthritis and rickets.

However, in 1882 skeletons showing similar characteristics to the Neanderthal remains, associated with the bones of extinct animals, were discovered at Spy in Belgium. Scholarly opinion had changed, and these were accepted as a form of early human. Their acceptance was reinforced by subsequent finds of such skeletons from other sites in Europe, particularly in France.

Now it is known that these early humans, the Neanderthals, lived in Europe and West Asia between 200,000 and 35,000 years ago. The western European, or classic, Neanderthals developed rather different physical characteristics from their counterparts in West Asia.

The Java Apeman

The Neanderthals were too similar to modern humans to be the missing link with the apes, so the quest was still on. In 1887, a young Dutch anatomist and surgeon, Eugene Dubois, set out upon it, heading for the East Indies.

Dubois did not choose his destination at random. Some scholars, including Virchow, had already speculated that the missing link would be traced to the Tropics, home of all modern apes.

Amazingly, within four years of his arrival, Dubois found what he was looking for. In the fossil beds of Java he unearthed the skull and thighbone of a humanlike creature, with a smaller brain cavity than modern humans and a thick, bony ridge across the brows. The structure of the thighbone showed that the creature had walked upright.

The scientific world, however, was not ready to accept the Java fossil as a human ancestor. It was not until the 1930s that the German anthropologist Gustav von Koenigswald found further examples of the creature in the Java fossil beds, and the achievement of Dubois was recognized.

The Java apeman is now known as *Homo erectus* (upright man). They lived here from around 1.7 million years ago. And they were not confined to Java, as later research was to show.

From the Dragon's Teeth

For centuries, Chinese apothecaries sold what they called dragon's teeth as a sovereign remedy for illness. In fact, what they believed to be the remains of ancient dragons were fragments of fossilized animals. Many were actually teeth, and in the 1920s Western scholars concluded that some on sale in Peking could have come from apemen.

They tracked the source of the teeth to Zhoukoudian, a huge cave 28 miles (45 km) from Peking (Beijing). Excavations between 1927 and 1939 yielded the remains of 45 apemen closely resembling those previously found in Java. Similar specimens have subsequently been discovered in many parts of the Old World, including Europe and East Africa; these are now known respectively as *Homo heidelbergensis* and *H. ergaster*.

Child of the South

The scientific skepticism that greeted *Homo erectus* emerged again when the remains of a young humanlike ape were found in 1924. They were identified by Professor Raymond Dart among fossil-bearing rocks from Taung in South Africa. In modern times, no apes have lived in the region, so it did not seem a likely place in which to search for the missing link.

In addition, the skull, thought to be of a child about six years old, had teeth resembling those of a human, but a brain cavity no larger than that of modern apes. Scholars had for years reasoned that apes in the human lineage would have a large brain and apelike jaws and teeth. Their expectations had been fulfilled in 1912 by "Piltdown man," allegedly found in Sussex in England but shown in 1953 to be a hoax (*see page 129*), so the Taung child had no place in their scheme of things.

Dart named his discovery *Australopithecus africanus* (African ape of the south). By the 1940s enough specimens of *Australopithecus* had been found in Africa for scientists to accept

Peking man (Homo erectus) was the descendant of hominids (the group of primates of which modern humans are the only survivor) who had colonized East Asia more than 1.5 million years ago. They were hunter-gatherers who made stone and probably bamboo tools and had discovered how to use fire for cooking, warmth and defense against wild animals. They also used caves, like that at Zhoukoudian, to provide shelter. Homo erectus stood about 5 feet (1.56 m) tall.

them as part of our family tree. However, it now appears they were cousins, rather than direct forebears, of humans.

Today, several species of *Australopithecus* are known. *A. africanus* was small and slender and lived 2–3 million years ago. *A. robustus* was sturdier and lived 1–2 million years ago. Both species walked upright.

The Leakey Achievement

The Kenyan archaeologist and anthropologist Louis Leakey had been searching East Africa for traces of our early ancestors for 30 years when, in 1959, he was rewarded by finding the remains of a very robust *Australopithecus robustus*. He named it "Dear Boy" in understandable gratitude. The following year, he and his wife Mary made an even more important discovery—the fossil remains of another creature living at the same time as *Australopithecus* but much more human in appearance. Leakey called it *Homo habilis* (handy man). It flourished between 2 million and 1.5 million years ago.

Enter Lucy . . .

At Laetoli, near the Olduvai Gorge in Tanzania, Mary Leakey and her son Richard made one of their most exciting finds: footprints preserved in hardened volcanic ash. They show that several hominids crossed the site nearly 4 million years ago (that is, perhaps 1 million years before *Australopithecus africanus*), walking upright.

A few bones of these creatures were also unearthed at Laetoli, but Hadar in Ethiopia was the site of the most spectacular finds. There, in November 1974, a French and American team discovered nearly half of the skeleton of a hominid they nicknamed Lucy (*see page 141*). This was remarkable because fossil hominids are rarely represented by more than a few teeth or bones.

By 1981, the remains of 13 individuals like Lucy, though less complete, had been unearthed at Hadar. These hominids are called *Australopithecus afarensis* (Afar is the region of Ethiopia in which Hadar lies). *A. afarensis* is probably the direct ancestor of both early humans and their cousins, *A. africanus* and *A. robustus*.

Out of Africa

Recent work has underlined the key role of Africa in the development of humankind. *Homo ergaster* (formerly known as *H. erectus*), which emerged in Africa around 1.8 million years ago, was the ancestor of the first human inhabitants of Europe (*H. heidelbergensis*) and East Asia (*H. erectus*). While hominids in Europe and West Asia developed into the Neanderthals, *H. ergaster*'s descendants in Africa evolved into *H. sapiens sapiens*—modern humans. Most scholars now believe that the world was colonized between 100,000 and 40,000 B.C.E. by modern humans moving out of Africa, replacing the earlier Neanderthal populations in Europe and West Asia and *H. erectus* in East Asia, although some paleoanthropologists still maintain that modern humans evolved gradually over the entire inhabited region of the globe. The somewhat acrimonious debate between holders of these two opposing viewpoints shows that the search for the missing link is by no means over.

Richard Leakey and his wife, Meave, painstakingly piece together the fragments of a human skull, found near Lake Turkana, Kenya, in 1972. The skull belonged to 2-million-year-old Homo habilis, the earliest hominid to make and use tools. Richard has continued his parents' successful quest for our ancestors. In 1984 his team discovered the remarkably complete skeleton of a hominid boy at Nariokotome in East Africa. Dated around 1.6 million years old, he is the best preserved specimen of our early ancestor Homo ergaster.

FORTY CENTURIES LOOK DOWN

The civilization of Egypt was already nearly 3,000 years old when the country was conquered by Alexander the Great of Macedon in 332 B.C.E. The massive memorials of the ancient kingdom had long fascinated the Greeks, some of whom had carved their names on the Pyramids.

Egypt became a Roman province in 30 B.C.E., after the suicide of Queen Cleopatra, and it was the Romans who started the removal of the ancient treasures—a practice followed by subsequent invaders and visitors right down to the present century. The Romans took several obelisks, the tall pyramid-topped columns used as memorials.

Western European interest in Egypt flagged after the fall of Rome, but by the 16th century travelers were once again visiting the country, which had become part of the Ottoman Empire in 1517 C.E. The Pyramids aroused wild speculation. Some people surmised correctly that they were tombs. But others looked for more fanciful explanations, attributing to them mystical and magical properties. A belief in the powers of the Pyramids persisted into the 19th century, and vestiges remain today.

By the late 18th century, travelers from several nations had written detailed descriptions of many Egyptian monuments. However, one event in 1798 revived European fascination with Egypt on a grand scale, stimulating both scientific study and massive pillaging.

The French Invade

When French infantry under the command of Napoleon Bonaparte stormed ashore at Alexandria on July 2, 1798, their main aim was to emulate the army of Alexander the Great and subdue Egypt as a prelude to marching on India. But Napoleon's invasion had other purposes, too. With his troops and cannon, he brought another army—scholars excited by accounts of Egyptian antiquity and determined to record all aspects of it.

Napoleon's forces occupied Egypt for three years, until the British and Turks drove them out. In that time, the French scholars amassed enough information to fill a 19-volume work, *Description de l'Égypte*. As the volumes appeared, individual collectors and representatives of institutions such as the British Museum and the Louvre began a scramble to collect antiquities.

Many of the collectors were sincerely interested in Egypt's past, but even so they caused untold damage. One of the worst offenders was the Italian Giovanni Battista Belzoni (1778–1823), who shamelessly destroyed antiquities in his quest for papyri. "Every step I took I crushed a mummy in some part or other," he wrote of one of his forays.

A Champion Appears

The indiscriminate damage done by the Egyptologists, as the collectors came to be called, aroused the anger of the French antiquarian Auguste Mariette (1821–1881), who waged a campaign against it.

It was an uphill struggle at first. Even Said Pasha, the ruler of Egypt, could barely be restrained from joining in the pillage. But eventually Mariette persuaded the Egyptian authorities to set up a national antiquities service to control excavations and the export of relics, and, in 1857, to put him in charge of it. He acquired the sole rights to excavate in Egypt and fought long and hard to establish a museum of antiquities at Boulak, later moved to Cairo.

Mariette's policies were largely followed by his successor, Gaston Maspero (1846–1910). During

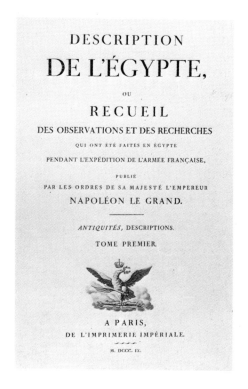

his directorship, an extraordinary cache of royal mummies was discovered near the temple of Hatshepsut at Deir el-Bahri. Maspero revoked the monopoly on excavation, and among the beneficiaries was the Englishman Sir William Flinders Petrie (1853–1942).

Petrie was employed by the Egypt Exploration Fund, set up in 1882 to promote scientific excavation and restoration of monuments and to publish the results. His meticulously recorded excavations of a large number of major sites set new standards of excellence.

Tomb of the Boy-King

The Valley of the Kings at Thebes is a dry watercourse on the west bank of the Nile and the burial place of the rulers of Egypt during the New Kingdom, from 1550 to 1069 B.C.E. The existence of the tombs was known to the Greek and Roman rulers of Egypt, but over the centuries, robbers removed most of the treasures. In 1902, an American, Theodore M. Davis, was granted the right to excavate in the valley. His team, including the Englishman Howard Carter (1873–1939), found a series of hitherto-untraced tombs, some rich in funeral ornaments.

After several successful years of exploration, Davis decided that the valley had yielded all of its secrets. But Carter was convinced there was more to find, and with the financial support of Lord Carnarvon, he continued the excavations.

For six frustrating and fruitless years, Carter systematically surveyed the valley floor. In 1922, during what was to have been his final season, an undisturbed tomb entrance was discovered. Lord Carnarvon was sent for from England, and Carter waited for his arrival before opening the tomb. His patience was rewarded, for inside was one of the most magnificent archaeological treasure-houses ever found.

The tomb was packed with precious objects, including gold figures and masks and precious jewelry. Investigation showed the tomb was that of the young, obscure king Tutankhamun, who ruled for nine years until 1352 B.C.E., dying when he was about 19 years old. Unlike the other graves in the valley, his had not been pillaged centuries before—although there was evidence that it had been entered and resealed.

The treasures from it are on display in Cairo, but the work of describing in full all the artifacts found in the tomb is still going on. Carter himself spent 10 years alone just in removing them.

Tutankhamun's tomb lay for centuries hidden and protected under the rubble created by the construction of the tomb of Rameses VI. Then, in 1922, the determined archaeologist Howard Carter discovered the entrance. Just three months later, he was looking into the burial chamber itself. At left we see Carter, arm outstretched, and Lord Carnarvon, standing, looking into the innermost of the three gilt shrines that contained the royal sarcophagus. Inside this was the young king's mummy, its face overlaid with the magnificent mask of solid gold (above) that has come to be so familiar.

VOICES FROM THE PAST

Among the discoveries that most excited antiquarians and explorers from the 17th century onward were the written records of ancient civilizations. If they could be deciphered, they would give a vivid new insight into the life and times of their authors.

Ancient, unfamiliar writing—on mud tablets, inscribed on the walls of palaces, fortresses and tombs, or on early forms of parchment or paper—present archaeologists and language experts with a problem somewhat like cracking a secret code.

The code-breakers have to look for clues. Does the language resemble any other known tongue? Do the symbols used represent letters of an alphabet, as they do in Latin and Greek and the scripts of modern Western civilization? Or do they denote syllables, as some do in modern Indian scripts, or whole words, as in the picture-writing of the earliest known scripts, found in West Asia and dated to around 3500 B.C.E.

The number of different symbols gives some guidance. If there are relatively few of them in the corpus of texts, the writing is likely to be alphabetic. But if there are hundreds or thousands, the script is probably syllabic or derived from picture-writing, or a mixture of both like various types of modern Chinese.

Some ancient writings have so far defied all attempts by scholars to decipher them—even when computers are used. The inscriptions of the Indus civilization, which flourished in southern Asia from about 2600 to 1800 B.C.E., still remain a riddle, for example. Patient detective work has unravelled other ancient scripts—of Egypt, West Asia, Homeric Greece, and the Maya civilization of Central America.

Scholars anticipated that the Maya writings would be priestly discourses on astronomy, a subject in which the Maya were known to have been expert. Instead, translation revealed a grim record of dynastic struggles, violent wars and bloody triumphs, fundamentally changing the previous view of the Maya as a peaceful theocracy.

Riddle of the Glyphs

The Rosetta Stone was the most important discovery made by the French scholars who accompanied Napoleon during his invasion of Egypt. It is a slab of basalt found in 1799, on which a decree set out by King Ptolemy V in 196 B.C.E. is inscribed.

The decree is in three scripts: two forms of old Egyptian and one of Greek. The Greek writing was, of course, familiar to the scholars, so it gave an invaluable guide toward translating the Egyptian scripts, one of which uses picture symbols called hieroglyphs. The other is cursive, a style devised for speedier writing than was possible with the ornate hieroglyphs.

Jean-François Champollion (1790–1832), a French Egyptologist, worked for 14 painstaking years to produce the first complete decipherment and translation of the Rosetta Stone—the key that unlocked the mysteries of Egyptian hieroglyphs. By matching the hieroglyphs making up the name Ptolmys (Ptolemy) to their Greek equivalents, Champollion was able to work out the sound that each symbol represented.

Egyptian hieroglyphs included over 700 signs, such as those to the right.

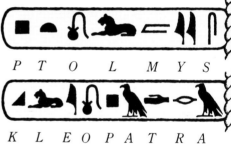

P T O L M Y S

K L E O P A T R A

Attempts at decipherment started with the proper names. In the hieroglyphs, scholars agreed, proper names would appear in cartouches, carved representations of clay seals. Some progress was made, but the scholars were considerably hampered by the mistaken assumption that the hieroglyphs were ideographic—that is, that each symbol represents a complete word. In fact, as we now know, many of these glyphs are phonetic—each symbol denotes a sound.

The man whose intuition solved the riddle

Old

With

A god

was Jean-François Champollion (1790–1832), a remarkable French-born linguist who from 1809 devoted all his available time to the study of Egyptian manuscripts and inscriptions. Champollion had an intimate knowledge of Coptic, a language derived from ancient Egyptian. He was the first person to suspect that the hieroglyphs might be phonetic.

Examining the cartouches, Champollion was able to assign phonetic values to a number of symbols, enabling him to identify many personal names. Painstakingly, Champollion built up an alphabet from the inscriptions in the cartouches. In 1823, the breakthrough came. Champollion realized that his alphabet of symbols formed the greater part of the main text outside the cartouches of the Rosetta Stone. Could it be, he wondered, that they were used phonetically there, too?

Champollion tried the theory, and it worked. Recognizable Coptic words sprang out at him from the text. He was able to produce the first full translation of the Rosetta Stone. But Champollion's work drew mixed reactions. It was fully vindicated only in 1866, more than 30 years after the Frenchman's death, when another bilingual inscription, the Decree of Canopus, was translated using his system.

Victories of Darius

High upon cliffs near Behistun in what is now western Iran is a lengthy inscription in three ancient languages. It dates from the time of Darius I, ruler of Persia from 521 to 486 B.C.E. The inscription includes an account of Darius's victory over rebels against his authority and other events in his life.

Its decipherment was largely the work of a brilliant British army officer and archaeologist, Sir Henry Rawlinson (1810–1895). Perched on a ladder 325 feet (100m) up the cliffside and aided by a helper he described as "a wild Kurdish boy," Rawlinson copied the inscription in order to try to decipher it later at his leisure.

The three languages—Old Persian, Babylonian and Elamite—are written in cuneiform (wedge-shaped) scripts typical of the ancient Near East. Old Persian resembles Avestan, the language in which the holy text of the Zoroastrian religion is written, and that had been translated by the mid-18th century.

Other scholars had already been working on Old Persian and had shown that its cuneiform symbols are alphabetic. Independently of them, Rawlinson deciphered the alphabet and was the first to translate the Old Persian text of Behistun. Armed with that, he moved on to the Babylonian inscription, which contains many more symbols and was clearly syllabic.

As with the ancient Egyptian script, work started with the proper names. By the 1850s, many scholars were successfully reading Babylonian.

Rawlinson did not decipher the third script of the inscription, Elamite, which was used by the peoples of the highland state of Elam in western Iran but was then completely unknown. It was not worked on until the early 20th century after excavations yielded tablets inscribed with bilingual syllabaries and other Elamite texts.

Forerunner of Greek

Linear B, the script on tablets found during excavations at Knossos on Crete from 1899, presented more problems for would-be translators than either ancient Egyptian or Babylonian had done. The language was completely unknown. There were no bilingual texts nor any clues from recorded history about what the tablets might contain.

An American scholar, Alice Kober (1907–1950), eventually concluded the language was inflected—that is, the word endings varied according to the case of the nouns or the tense of the verbs. She assembled an impressive array of words that looked the same except for their endings and suggested grammatical values for these.

After Kober's death, her work was continued by a Briton, Michael Ventris (1922–1956), and by the early 1950s he had built up a complete picture of the interrelationships of the different symbols. What was lacking was any idea of how they had been spoken.

Ventris eventually identified what seemed likely to be the names of Cretan towns and started trying some—Amnisos, Knossos, Tylissos. The approach worked, and it gave him the crucial key to the symbols. but it did more. To Ventris's amazement, it revealed that the language of the Linear B texts was a form of ancient Greek, an idea that scholars had firmly rejected many years before.

Sumerian picture-writing developed into cuneiform symbols in the 3rd millennium B.C.E. A stylized picture of grain (above) was drawn sideways, then reduced to four simple strokes. This cuneiform tablet (below), dating from 2050 B.C.E., is a receipt for a large number of bronze and copper tools.

Deciphering the Maya script has been a great challenge. It is highly pictorial and elaborate, as can be seen at left in these glyphs from a stone tablet at the important city of Palenque. The script allows many different "spellings" of the same word, both as single glyphs and as various combinations of other glyphs. Although the task is still incomplete, decipherment has now reached the stage where the dynastic history and public records of many of its city-states can be read.

PALACES AND ROYAL GRAVES

Claudius Rich (1787–1821) owed his appointment as British resident (diplomatic representative) in Baghdad, in his early 20s, largely to his extraordinary aptitude for languages. Although he spent most of his term of office in skillful diplomacy, he found time to collect antiquities and to make detailed surveys of some of the ruins of Iraq, including the ancient cities of Babylon and Nineveh.

Rich's early death robbed archaeology of a fine scholar. But his collection of antiquities laid the foundation of the British Museum's Oriental Department, and the tradition he established of giving hospitality and encouragement to antiquarian-minded travelers was continued for many years by his successors in Baghdad and Iraq's second largest city, Mosul.

Among those who benefited from this hospitality was the English antiquarian and explorer Sir Austen Henry Layard (1817–1894). While in Mosul in the 1840s, he met the recently arrived French scholar Paul-Émile Botta (1802–1870) and visited his excavations.

Botta was looking for Nineveh, an important city of the Assyrian Empire, which reached its height in the 8th and 7th centuries B.C.E. The ruins of Nineveh were thought to be somewhere near Mosul, on the river Tigris.

The Kuyunjik mound in Mosul, which later turned out to be part of Nineveh, was Botta's first target for excavation. However, he soon transferred his attention to nearby Khorsabad. His discovery there of the spectacular remains of the palace of Sargon II, king of Assyria from 721 to 705 B.C.E., prompted the French government to give him further generous financial support to continue excavations of the site.

Layard, meanwhile, had privately been given funds by the British ambassador in Istanbul, Sir Stratford Canning, to excavate at Nimrud, also near Mosul. There he found two Assyrian palaces, which he thought were remnants of Nineveh. But Layard continued investigating Kuyunjik, claimed by the French as "their" site.

In 1847, Layard found a corner of a building under the mound. Intensive excavations between 1849 and 1851 revealed that he had located the massive palace of Sennacherib, ruler of Assyria between 705 and 681 B.C.E., conqueror of Babylon and the man who rebuilt and extended Nineveh. Within the palace was Sennacherib's great library, providing a wealth of information about Assyrian life. Sennacherib's palace was in Nineveh itself, so Layard had succeeded where Botta had failed.

Destructive Digging

The British and French archaeologists who worked in Mesopotamia—the land between the rivers Tigris and Euphrates, now mostly in Iraq—in the 1840s and 1850s did so under a handicap. The people and institutions financing their expeditions, among them the British Museum and the Louvre in Paris, expected instant and spectacular finds.

This limestone slab comes from excavations at Nineveh, ancient capital of the Assyrian Empire. It was here that Sennacherib built his great palace. Looking at the three registers on the slab, from top to bottom, we see building materials being transported by boats on the Tigris River to the proposed site, which was surrounded by woods. In the site itself, workmen are moving a colossal bull from a quarry. The men shown atop the statue are actually alongside it and are carrying stonecutting tools. The wooden poles on the wheeled carts, above and behind, would have been used both to roll the statue and as general building material.

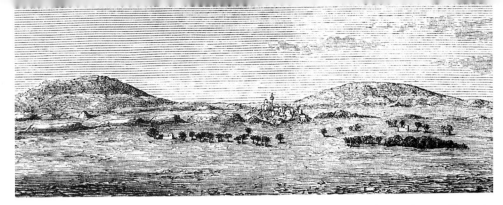

Despite any qualms among the excavators, this expectation meant that the excavations were, in effect, little more than well-documented looting expeditions. Rivalry between France and Britain made it vital to stake national claims to sites by quickly digging into them. In the process, much information was destroyed.

Matters became even worse after the outbreak of the Crimean War in 1853. The officially sponsored British and French archaeological teams were recalled, leaving the field clear for illicit plundering by independent operators who were totally unhampered by scholarly considerations and motivated by sheer greed and the desire for profit.

Even after the teams returned in 1872, the independent ransack continued. But at least, toward the end of the century, archaeologists themselves began to employ more scientific techniques in the course of their work.

Babylon Laid Bare

By 1900, American and German archaeological teams were working alongside the British and French in Mesopotamia.

Robert Koldewey (1855–1926) excavated Babylon, which became the dominant city of Mesopotamia under its great lawgiving king Hammurabi in the 18th century B.C.E. For 14 years from 1899, Koldewey carefully laid the site bare to reveal the stratigraphy and the ground plans of ancient buildings. His fellow-German Walter Andrae (1875–1956) adopted the same approach at Ashur on the river Tigris, the principal city of the Old Assyrian period.

During the early 20th century, archaeologists' attention began to shift from the relatively recent, massive and splendid cities to an earlier period in Mesopotamia's past. They sought information on the rise of civilization there and on the beginnings of agriculture.

Meanwhile, excavations continued at Nimrud, Nineveh and Khorsabad. Other ancient sites were uncovered, including Susa, capital of the Elamites and, for a time, of the Persians. At Mari in Syria, a French team discovered the remains of a palace, dating from before 2000 B.C.E.

Links with the Bible

Many episodes recorded in the Old Testament took place in Mesopotamia, and for that reason excavations there captured the imagination of scholars and the general public. This was never more so than in 1872 when a British Museum employee, George Smith (1840–1876), discovered among the museum's collection of clay tablets what appeared to be an incomplete account of the biblical Flood.

When news of Smith's discovery became public, there was great excitement. The *Daily Telegraph* newspaper sponsored an expedition to the Near East to seek the missing portion of the tablet. Smith led the expedition and, incredibly, found what he was looking for just five days after beginning his work, in the piles of debris that had resulted from previous excavations of the Kuyunjik mound.

Ur, near the river Euphrates in what is now south Iraq, is familiar to students of the Bible as the home of Abraham. The site was excavated by Sir Leonard Woolley (1880–1960), revealing royal graves and also the bodies of people sacrificed, apparently willingly, to accompany their kings and queens.

Woolley worked painstakingly to preserve the artifacts he found, and he even recovered vanished objects. Recognizing a series of small holes as traces of decayed wood, he filled them with plaster of Paris; the result was a cast of a wooden harp.

George Smith (above) was translating tablets uncovered at Nineveh (top of page) when he discovered fragments of a Babylonian account of a great flood. Similar in many details to the biblical account, this preserves a story originally recorded in 3rd-millennium-B.C.E. Sumer.

SCHLIEMANN'S ODYSSEY

The story of Heinrich Schliemann is one of a man driven by an obsession, a dream of finding Troy, the great city of legend, supposedly destroyed in antiquity. Schliemann kept his dream alive through a long, successful business career, during which he amassed the fortune that left him free to devote the remaining third of his life to archaeology— and his search. He astounded the world when he unearthed the walls of the city (below) in four periods of excavation, beginning in 1871 and continuing until his death in 1890.

The *Iliad* and the *Odyssey*, Homer's epic accounts of the siege of Troy and the wanderings of Odysseus, have enthralled people since they were composed more than 2,500 years ago. In modern times, they were widely assumed to be just myths of ancient Greece, or at least a vague, highly embroidered version of the Greek past.

Heinrich Schliemann (1822–1890), a German self-made millionaire, was an exception. For decades, he was convinced that the world so poignantly depicted by Homer was a real one, tied to actual geography and genuine historical events. Schliemann was gripped by the immediacy of Homer's tale.

His fortune made, Schliemann retired from business and set out to prove that his belief was more than just a romantic notion. He went to Turkey, followed the topographical details Homer supplied and, in 1870, dug into a mound at Hissarlik that his researches convinced him must be Troy. It was.

Schliemann's first excavation was energetic rather than scientific. But in subsequent work he was assisted by Wilhelm Dörpfeld (1853–1940), a German regarded as one of the finest field archaeologists of the day. After Schliemann's death, Dörpfeld continued the excavations.

The two also excavated Homeric sites on the Greek mainland—Mycenae, Tiryns and Orchomenos. As each spectacular find emerged, Schliemann kept the fascinated public aware of it through newspaper reports and rapid publication of results. Schliemann was in no doubt that at Troy he had located the treasures of Priam, the king killed when the city fell to the Greeks, or that graves containing exquisite gold work at Mycenae were those of Agamemnon and other semimythical Trojan War figures.

Later research has shown that many of Schliemann's finds are several centuries older than the dates he ascribed to them. Even so, his achievements were remarkable. He revealed the existence of Bronze Age civilization in the Aegean and inspired many archaeologists to investigate it. And he certainly demonstrated most dramatically the potential that archaeology possesses to illuminate the past.

Recreating the Bronze Age

From the 1890s, Schliemann's successors in the eastern Mediterranean began to build up a firm picture of the Bronze Age civilization he had identified. This was named Mycenaean, after Mycenae, and flourished from about 1600 to 1100 B.C.E.

The Mycenaeans evidently traded with ancient Egypt, and that helped in ascertaining when they had been at the height of their powers. Sir Flinders Petrie, who had done so much for Egyptian archaeology (*see page 13*), identified Egyptian pottery on a visit to Mycenae. From that, it was relatively easy to calculate the dates of the Mycenaeans. Petrie also brilliantly recognized that hitherto unfamiliar pottery that had been found in Egypt was of Aegean origin—amazingly, even before examples of an identical style had been discovered in the Aegean zone itself.

Mycenaean influence was considerable in the eastern Mediterranean, from mainland Greece to Cyprus and the islands of the Aegean, and as far west as Italy. And Mycenaean rulers were obviously wealthy as well as powerful. Bodies found by Schliemann at Mycenae were heavily decked in gold jewelry.

From about the 15th or 14th century B.C.E., chieftains lived in increasingly magnificent palaces such as those at Mycenae itself, Tiryns and Pylos. When these leaders died, they were buried in what are known as *tholos* tombs—dry stone, beehive-shaped structures with a long entrance passage.

While archaeologists fired by Schliemann's work were busy tracking down the Mycenaeans, others, including Dörpfeld at this time, were examining the classical age of Greece through excavations at Samothrace and at Olympia, home of the ancient games which were held every four years in honor of Zeus, father of the Greek gods. Meanwhile, on Crete the British archaeologist Sir Arthur Evans (1851–1941) was unearthing remnants of a civilization even older than that of the Mycenaeans.

KNOSSOS—CENTER OF THE BULL CULT

In Greek legend, Minos was a king of Crete who kept a monster called the Minotaur—half human, half bull—in a labyrinth in his palace. This creature was the offspring of the king's wife, Pasiphae, and was the result of her coupling with a white bull sent to her by the god Poseidon as a form of revenge against her family. Minos spent the final years of his reign living in a massive labyrinth, with Pasiphae and her strange love-child living at the center. Archaeological research has shown that, like Homer's tales of Troy, the story was based on vague memories of a genuine past.

Heinrich Schliemann himself had looked to Crete for the antecedents of Mycenaean civilization but did not carry out excavations there. In 1899, Arthur Evans did—digging into an ancient mound at Kephala (Knossos). He discovered the remains of a palace far older than those of the Mycenaeans.

Beautiful frescoes, a throne and a massive granary containing enormous storage jars indicated that the palace had belonged to a wealthy ruler of a highly developed civilization. Evans named this civilization Minoan, after King Minos.

An Egyptian stone figure with a dated inscription found in the great eastern court of the palace indicated to Evans that the Minoans had had contacts with Egypt long before the Mycenaeans did. Extensive work has shown the Minoan civilization to have reached its zenith between about 1950 and 1450 B.C.E. After that, Knossos and most of Crete were controlled by the Mycenaeans.

In addition to the British venture, excavations at Knossos and elsewhere on Crete were carried out by French, German, American and Greek teams. Together, they built up a vivid picture of Minoan life. Palaces, settlements and tombs were found throughout the island.

Excitingly, these provided at least part of the answer to one mystery. Stylized sculptures of bulls' horns and other depictions showed that the Minoans developed a cult of the bull—perhaps the origin of the Minotaur legend. The mazelike passages of the palace at Knossos could represent the labyrinth in which the beast was reputedly kept.

Archaeological research, however, revealed a new mystery, too. The Minoan civilization collapsed around 1450 B.C.E. No one is yet sure why, but it is probable that the Mycenaeans played some part. Around this time, many of Crete's buildings were damaged by fire; some scholars suggest this may reflect popular unrest or relate to tectonic activity to which the eastern Mediterranean is periodically subject. A massive eruption virtually destroyed the nearby island of Thera (now Thíra, formerly Santorin) at an earlier date, probably around 1628 B.C.E. The island was the home of an advanced society strongly under Minoan influence. The eruption provided a magnificent bonus. Huge drifts of volcanic ash engulfed whole areas of the island, preserving buildings (some up to three stories high) and their contents in good condition. Excavations are still going on. The exquisite frescoes in these houses have added further intimate details to our picture of life in the Minoan world.

The finds at Knossos paint a rich picture of a vibrant and prosperous civilization. The colonnaded halls and corridors of the great palace (above) are a striking feature. External colonnades would almost certainly have been surmounted by a motif of horns, recalling the bull cult that was so central to Minoan life. Scenes showing dancers with bulls (left) are common on the frescoes from Knossos and other Minoan sites.

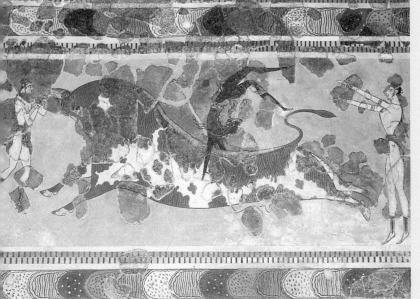

SECRETS OF THE NEW WORLD

When the Spanish and Portuguese conquered the Aztec and Inca Empires of Central and South America in the 16th century, they collected a great deal of information about the cultures of their new subjects. Despite this, the European invaders gradually came to think of the Indians of the Americas as a poor and barbaric race, incapable of great works of construction or the other hallmarks of civilization.

For that reason, the impressive ancient monuments of the Americas were attributed to a more or less unlikely collection of foreigners—the Vikings, the Welsh, the Chinese, the Phoenicians and the lost tribes of Israel. The tendency was particularly marked in North America, where many pioneers eased any qualms they might have felt about oppressing or slaughtering their victims by regarding them as unenlightened savages.

Nevertheless, as early as 1590 José de Acosta, a Spanish Jesuit, was arguing that the Americas had been colonized from Asia in prehistoric times via a land bridge that had once connected the extreme north of the continents. His contemporary Diego de Landa (1542–1579) noted a continuity of culture between the ruins of the ancient Maya civilization in Central America and the art forms of the Indians who populated the region in his day.

Native American Relics

Early European settlers noted the burial mounds and earthworks of North America. But few were investigated until the mid-19th century, when conscientious antiquarians began to create the scientific basis of American archaeology.

In 1848, Ephraim Squier and E. H. Davis published their study of the mounds of Mississippi and Ohio. It showed that there were different types of mounds—those used for burials, others in the effigy of a beast or bird and some that had been platforms for temples.

But the study revealed little about the people who had erected them, and Squier and Davis concluded that the mound-builders were not Native Americans. The antiquarians were wrong. We now know that the mounds were the work of settled farming communities hundreds of years before the arrival of Columbus and, even ear-

lier, of settled hunter-gatherers who were part of a complex trading network.

Other scholars investigated the Pueblo villages of flat-roofed stone or adobe houses in the southwestern United States, first built nearly 1,000 years ago. The villagers' predecessors in the region had lived in pit dwellings, and those were excavated, too.

The Earliest Americans

De Acosta's belief that the Americas had been colonized from Asia in prehistoric times gradually gained limited acceptance among scholars. In the 17th century, for example, the physical similarities between American Indians and the Mongoloid peoples of Asia were cited as further evidence of the theory. But it was not until the 19th century that de Acosta's view became widely held. And it was the early 20th century before solid archaeological clues to when the colonization took place started to emerge.

The search for the earliest American caught the public imagination, so much so that a whole army of tricksters claimed to have found the remains. In this climate of fraud, serious scholars had to exercise rigid scientific discipline, particularly after the most eminent physical anthropologist of the day, Aleš Hrdlička (1869–1943), declared magisterially that early humankind had not been present in America. Proof to the contrary, however, began with the discovery in 1925 of an arrowhead with the bones of an extinct type of bison, at Folsom in New Mexico.

Subsequent finds at a number of sites present-

Geometric enclosures and earthworks in the shape of birds and snakes, like the Serpent Mound in Ohio (right), were built by the inhabitants of eastern North America, who also raised impressive funerary mounds between 1000 B.C.E and 400 C.E. The precise significance of these earthworks remains a mystery, but they were probably linked to religious and mythical practices.

ed unimpeachable evidence of the existence of "Paleo-Indians" who arrived across the land bridge from Asia and gradually spread southward. But precisely when that happened is still a matter of fierce controversy. The available archaeological evidence indicates that people were living in the far north of the American continent more than 25,000 years ago and that some may have moved further south before the way was blocked by ice sheets 18,000 years ago. When the ice sheets began to retreat 4,000 years later, colonization developed on a large scale (*see page 127*).

In Search of Lost Cities

While many antiquarians of the United States were primarily concerned during the 19th century with relics of their own country, some looked further south. One of them was John Lloyd Stephens (1805–1852), who was a prominent lawyer, writer and amateur politician.

He and the talented English artist Frederick Catherwood (1799–1854) were intrigued by rumors of long-lost cities in the Yucatán peninsu-

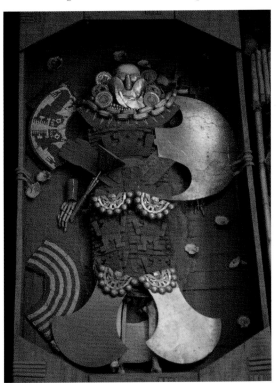

la of Mexico and Central America. Between 1839 and 1842, they braved the jungle and its suspicious or hostile inhabitants to investigate, finding five cities: Copán, Quirigua, Palenque, Uxmal and Chichén Itzá. All were virtually unknown, except to the local Indians.

Four of the cities had been built by the Maya, whose civilization reached its height from about 300 to 900 C.E. The fifth, Chichén Itzá, also bore traces of Maya building but became predominantly a city of the Toltecs, the warrior culture that flowered during the 300 or so years following the Maya's decline.

The Mystery of Tiahuanaco

European archaeologists became fascinated in the 1870s by the Inca civilization of the Andes. From 1877, they excavated sites in Peru, including the pilgrimage center of Pachacamac.

The German linguist Max Uhle (1856–1944) was in charge at Pachacamac. By studying pottery and sculpture, he identified four chronological periods in Peruvian history prior to the downfall of the Incas. The classifications, modified only slightly, are still used today, and Uhle is acknowledged as the founder of Peruvian archaeology.

Uhle also helped to prepare the first authoritative book about one of the most mysterious of the Andean ancient sites, Tiahuanaco in Bolivia. Its vast and impressive ruins include the magnificent Gateway of the Sun. The site is thought to have been a religious center and perhaps a powerful city-state, too. Local tradition says that Tiahuanaco was already in ruins when the Inca Empire was at its height, and thanks in part to Uhle's chronology, it has been shown that Tiahuanaco represents a period well before the Incas. Modern dating indicates that the site was occupied from about 1500 B.C.E., and was at its zenith between 300 and 700 C.E.

The Temple of Inscriptions, at the Maya city of Palenque, Mexico, was constructed by King Pacal the Great (603–683 C.E.) as his own funerary monument. A deep chamber beneath the temple contains his massive, elaborately carved sarcophagus and a wealth of grave goods. Palenque, like most Maya cities, was abandoned in the 9th century.

Illicit plundering of the massive burial mounds of the Moche, who flourished in northern Peru in the 1st millennium C.E., have done untold damage to our archaeological knowledge of this culture. Painted or sculptured pottery vessels depicting all aspects of daily life are frequently smashed and destroyed by tomb robbers. Recently, however, several unplundered graves have been discovered and excavated (with guards to protect them). These revealed the richly furnished burials of lords, complete with sacrificed retainers, brilliantly decorated garments of cloth and feathers, and rich personal possessions of gold and silver, as in this burial at Sipán.

LURE OF THE ORIENT

The magnificent monuments of India intrigued and impressed European travelers from the 16th century onward, and several made detailed records of them. In 1784, the foundation of the Asiatic Society of Bengal put their work on a firm footing. The society aimed to inquire widely into the arts and sciences of Asia, and its members published papers on coins and literature, as well as on ancient inscriptions and manuscripts and on archaeology.

One of the society's most eminent members was James Prinsep (1799–1840). He succeeded in deciphering the Brahmi and Kharoshti scripts of ancient India, thus making available a wealth of new background information, in particular on the empire of Ashoka, who ruled most of India in the 3rd century B.C.E.

The formation of the Archaeological Survey of India in 1861, under the direction of General Sir Alexander Cunningham (1814–1893), promoted further study of the subcontinent's history, notably of the sites associated with Buddhism, the main religion of India for many centuries. Architectural surveys by James Fergusson (1808–1886) and James Burgess (1832–1916) provided excellent, accurate and detailed reports of many of these sites.

This view of the citadel at Mohenjo-Daro, as seen from the northwest, shows the "college," one of the public building complexes, in the immediate foreground, while the mound on the skyline is a much later Buddhist stupa. Brick sizes here and throughout the Indus civilization were standardized, as were many other features of daily life. Indus cities give an impression of general affluence. Unlike other contemporary civilizations, such as that of Mesopotamia, there is no indication of warfare among the cities of the Indus.

The Great Bath at Mohenjo-Daro (shown in the foreground) was surrounded by rooms that may have housed the priests or rulers of the city. Even today, little is known about the political organization of the Indus civilization, partly because the Indus script defies decipherment.

However, it was not until the appointment of Sir John Marshall (1876–1956) as director-general in 1901 that excavation and conservation came to form an important part of the Archaeological Survey's work. Aspects of Marshall's excavation techniques have been criticized by people who subsequently investigated sites he had uncovered (*see page 25*). But he undoubtedly widened the survey's field of activities.

In the 1920s, its archaeologists began excavating the ruins of Mohenjo-Daro and Harappa, in the northwest of the subcontinent. They were the chief cities of the Indus civilization, which reached its height between about 2600 and 1800 B.C.E. The excavations dramatically revealed the unsuspected antiquity of Indian civilization, which scholars had previously thought evolved much later, well into the 1st millennium B.C.E.

One of the most remarkable attributes of the Indus peoples was their skill in town planning. Their cities and towns were laid out on two mounds. The lower mound was the residential part of the town, divided into a neat grid pattern of two-storied houses with courtyards.

On the upper mound there were municipal and religious buildings. The great bath at Mohenjo-Daro, which was probably used in religious rituals, is among the most magnificent of these.

Cleanliness was obviously extremely important to the Indus civilization. Most houses in Mohenjo-Daro and Harappa had bathrooms and latrines, from which waste was carried off by a highly developed system of covered drains running through the city.

Caravans of Silk

During the last years of the 19th century, scholars were intrigued by ancient manuscripts, some in unknown languages, originating from the desert region of Chinese Turkistan. Sir Aurel Stein (1862–1943), an archaeologist of Hungarian birth and British nationality, determined to establish their significance. Following the trail of the manuscripts, he uncovered a remarkable world in the wastes of central Asia, during three expeditions between 1900 and 1916.

In ancient times, this now-barren region lay on a great trade route linking east to west. Along it traveled merchants bringing luxuries such as Chinese silk to India and, eventually, to Rome, Greece and the Near East. In the opposite direction, Buddhist missionaries carried their faith so successfully to China, at about the same time that Christianity was spreading through Europe, that Chinese Buddhists were soon appearing as pilgrims in India.

Stein explored and excavated Buddhist caves, temples and houses, the caravanseries where travelers and their pack animals rested and the guardposts at the limit of China's Han Empire. At Miran, he found a Buddhist shrine decorated in a style reflecting the meeting of east and west, and at Dunhuang he investigated the Hall of 1,000 Buddhas. There Stein made what, to him, were his most important discoveries—a series of silk temple banners and a vast cache of sacred Buddhist manuscripts.

But at other sites the dry desert air had preserved a wealth of more ordinary artifacts. They ranged from goods made of felt to ancient wooden chopsticks and a unique form of guitar, the strings of which were broken.

China Reawakens

The Chinese developed an interest in their past during the centuries immediately before the time of Christ, studying artifacts and ruins that were ancient even then. But gradually what had been a budding science stagnated into mere hoarding of old objects. Active interest in archaeology lay dormant and was rekindled in China only around the early 1900s.

One of those responsible for the reawakening was a Swedish geologist, J. Gunnar Andersson (1874–1960). In 1921, he discovered a Neolithic village at Yangshao, in central China. Excavations showed that the inhabitants were cultivating

crops, mainly millet, more than 5,000 years ago. Stone axes and decorated pottery were also found.

Yangshao alone would have assured Andersson's place in the history of archaeology. But he was also responsible for another great discovery when, in 1926, the excavations he had initiated at Zhoukoudian yielded teeth of one of our early ancestors, Peking man (*see page 10*).

Between 1928 and 1935, teams led by Chinese archaeologists excavated a series of sites around Anyang. They were drawn to the area initially because some local farmers had found inscribed bones that were used in divination by the ancient Chinese. The work started in 1928 continues today, revealing the extraordinary wealth and technical expertise of the earliest known Chinese civilization. For Anyang was the last capital of the Shang dynasty, rulers of part of what is now China from about 1700 to 1027 B.C.E., and was a royal city for some 300 years.

Finds made there include several royal tombs containing not only the remains of the monarch, but also the skeletons of many victims of human sacrifice. There are beautiful ivory carvings and splendid weapons and ceremonial vessels of bronze. Shang craftsmen had also developed an advanced technique for casting complex bronze objects in elaborate piece molds; this was a skill that was totally unknown elsewhere in the world during that era.

The bronze works of the Shang dynasty demonstrate its high level of sophistication and artistic development. This fan ding, or sacrificial food vessel, was excavated in 1950 at Anyang, the ancient Shang capital until about 1027 B.C.E. It is approximately 9 inches (22 cm) high and the quality and detail of the relief dates it to the late Shang period, just prior to the Zhou conquest.

LURE OF
THE ORIENT

DIGGING UP THE PAST

*A poignant reminder
of the power and
influence of nature in
human history. This
cast is from Pompeii,
and the victim was
one of several beggars
who were struck
down when Vesuvius
erupted, just outside
the Nucerian gate to
the east of the city. A
bag, still full of alms,
was found next to
him. Many such casts
have been made of
the 2,000 inhabitants
who died here in 79
C.E., asphyxiated by
poisonous gases. The
images they present
give us a very clear
picture of daily life in
a typical Roman
town: the baker, Mod-
estus, with his oven
still full of bread, the
guard dog gnawing at
his chain, the gladia-
tors entertaining a
wealthy patroness.
Most citizens of Pom-
peii, however, did suc-
ceed in making their
escape in the early
stages of the eruption.*

During the latter 18th century and throughout most of the 19th century, excavation was a popular activity, combining entertainment with treasure hunting. In England, for example, the well-to-do hired laborers to dig trenches through ancient burial mounds. When the trench had almost reached the level at which finds could be expected, the gentry appeared to watch the final stage. Valuable and "interesting" artifacts were removed, and everything else was ignored or even destroyed. The site was then abandoned or plowed over.

The same was true throughout the civilized world. The kings of Naples sponsored forays into the volcanic materials covering Pompeii and Herculaneum in search of statues. European explorers—and archaeologists—dynamited their way into Egypt's pyramids and tombs. In Mesopotamia, rival expeditions sank holes into mounds simply to establish their claim to dig at the site later.

There were some lights in the darkness. Thomas Jefferson, president of the United States from 1801 to 1809, exercised great care when he excavated a burial mound in Virginia in 1784 to try to settle arguments about who built it. He did not manage to resolve the dispute, but his patient work established that it had been built in a series of stages, with six layers of bodies, buried at different times, each separated from the other by layers of soil and stones.

Half a century later, in Denmark, the young J. J. Worsaae was equally meticulous. While still in his teens, Worsaae began gaining the experience on which he based his principles of preexcavation surveys, stratigraphy and recording of all finds (*see page 6*). But Worsaae, like Jefferson, was unusual among his contemporaries, and it took many years for his approach to gain general acceptance.

Probing Pompeii

One sign of a changing trend in archaeology came in 1860, when the Italian Giuseppe Fiorelli (1823–1896) took over responsibility for the investigations at Pompeii. His immediate predecessors had already abandoned the random digging of the first statue-hunters, but Fiorelli imposed a new discipline. He was deeply interested in the everyday lives of the inhabitants of the long-buried city, and to learn as much as he could about their existence, he painstakingly excavated remains of the ancient *insulae*, the Roman tenements, block by block and layer by layer.

That was only the first of Fiorelli's innovations. He also developed a method of pouring plaster into cavities in the ash that had buried Pompeii when Vesuvius erupted in 79 C.E., and subsequently hardened. When the plaster set and the surrounding ash was removed, Fiorelli was left with a cast of the shape of the cavity itself.

The shapes were often instantly recognizable as organic material that had decayed after the ash had engulfed it—bodies of humans and animals, furniture and wooden structures. Fiorelli's casts recreated their external appearance in minute detail.

German Precision

From the 1870s, German archaeologists contributed greatly to the development of a scientific approach to archaeology. Ernst Curtius (1814–1896) carried out excavations at Olympia in Greece to an extremely high standard. One of

those who trained under him there was Wilhelm Dörpfeld, who later lent his expertise to Schliemann's work at Troy (*see pages 18–19*).

In Mesopotamia, Robert Koldewey and Walter Andrae adopted similarly rigorous methods. They were the first to succeed in tracing courses of ancient mud brick. The bricks were identical in composition to the soil surrounding them and because of this had not been detected by earlier excavators.

Andrae also pioneered the use of the deep sounding form of exploratory excavation—that is, digging deeply in a relatively small area to establish the stages in the development of a site. It enabled him to trace the history of the Temple of Ishtar in the Assyrian city of Ashur back to its origins as an early Sumerian shrine.

In Turkistan, Hubert Schmidt (1864–1933), a pupil of Dörpfeld, foreshadowed modern archaeological methods in his excavations of the mounds of Anau, the site of settlements from the later Stone Age to the Iron Age. He employed experts from other scientific fields to do detailed analyses of human and animal bones, remnants of cultivated grain and metal objects as they were uncovered.

The General's Principles

Many people of many nationalities contributed to the development of a truly scientific approach to archaeology throughout the course of the 19th century. But the man who is generally credited with taking the first real steps toward establishing archaeology on a scientific base was a British general, Augustus Henry Pitt-Rivers (1827–1900).

In 1880, Pitt-Rivers inherited a large estate including part of Cranborne Chase in Dorset, an area of England that is particularly rich in both prehistoric sites and ancient monuments. Retired from the army after a distinguished career and with a considerable fortune at his disposal, Pitt-Rivers set about excavating the monuments on his own lands.

He approached this task with rigid military discipline. Each site had to be excavated in full. The precise location of every artifact had to be recorded. Pitt-Rivers insisted that no relic was too trivial to consider; on the contrary, he asserted, for the true archaeologist, everyday objects are more valuable as a guide to the past than precious ones are.

Pitt-Rivers also developed and extended the layer-by-layer stratigraphic excavation techniques that were first used by Worsaae. He published his findings quickly and in comprehensive detail, in a four-volume study that is regarded as exemplary even today.

But Pitt-Rivers's methods were not adopted by other archaeologists overnight. Nearly 30 years after the general's death, Sir John Marshall was excavating sites in India in his capacity as the Archaeological Survey's director-general, a post to which he had been appointed because of his supposed knowledge of current excavation techniques (*see page 22*). Yet according to Sir Mortimer Wheeler (1890–1976), a major figure in the development and dissemination of scientific excavation techniques, Marshall dug the sites "like potatoes."

Wor Barrow, a late Neolithic long barrow, or burial mound, in Dorset, was excavated in 1883 by General Pitt-Rivers. Although the techniques employed were rather crude by today's standards, the carefully kept research notes are an early example of fine archaeological recording. Saxon, Roman and Bronze Age remains were uncovered in the upper levels of the ditch (left). At a depth of 8 feet (2.4 m), removal of the massive barrow revealed the underlying chalk bedrock (below). The position of each bone or artifact was meticulously indicated on a scaled plan of the site and on section drawings.

PATHS OF EVOLUTION

As archaeological knowledge has accumulated, scholars have become increasingly aware that humankind's development around the world has not followed a single evolutionary course in which progress was inevitable. Civilizations not only rose, but fell, sometimes to be replaced by others. Nor could stages be defined in which progressively more civilized features emerged. The most striking anomaly was the extraordinary cave art during the Upper Paleolithic era in Europe. It seemed inappropriate to such a primitive phase and was not subsequently built upon, but lost.

In the face of such evidence, intellectual opinion moved away from the theory of uniform stages and inevitable progress. Two contrasting views came to replace that theory and dominated the study of European prehistory until recently. The false dichotomy is gradually being dispelled.

One school of thought held that inventions and advances took place in one specially favored area of the world and then spread outward. Its most extreme exponents, the "hyperdiffusionists," were led by Sir Grafton Elliot Smith (1871–1937), a prominent Australian physical anthropologist and anatomist. His study of the processes used in Egyptian mummification convinced him that Egypt was the favored area. Such techniques, the building of megaliths, metallurgy and civilization itself had all developed in Egypt,

in Elliot Smith's opinion, and were spread by the Egyptians to areas that they visited or settled in.

At the opposite extreme were the nationalists, a school of European archaeologists who insisted that the development of humankind in Europe had been a wholly indigenous process. That led to national rivalries and, in its more chauvinistic form, to the unfortunate acceptance of several hoaxes such as Piltdown man (*see page 129*) and Glozel (*see page 139*). Both hoaxes answered a yearning for national priority in major developments—Piltdown, for the British, in the search for our earliest ancestors, and Glozel, for the French, in the origins of civilization.

At the furthest fringe of nationalism, Gustaf Kossinna (1858–1931) reversed the diffusionists' routes and distorted archaeological data to demonstrate, falsely, that a "pure master race" of Aryans was responsible for the development of civilization throughout Europe.

The Lure of Chronology

Whatever their views on the mechanisms behind cultural changes, archaeologists of the late 19th and early 20th centuries were preoccupied with establishing regional sequences of development based on changes in artifact types. The relative chronology of these types was determined from

Ebert (1879–1929) in Germany.

The American Approach

American archaeologists, in the first half of this century, were just as preoccupied with chronology as their counterparts in Europe but their approach was rather different.

Dendrochronology—the use of the annual rings of certain trees in dating (*see pages 130–131*)—enabled the age of many Pueblo villages in the Southwest to be determined quite precisely. Since many American sites had shallow deposits lacking stratigraphy, relative chronology often depended on seriation, or sequence-dating—the chronological ordering of groups of artifacts on the basis of similarities in their composition (*see pages 126–127*). But stratigraphy was not ignored and played a part, for example, in the work of Alfred Kidder (1855–1963) at Pecos in New Mexico.

Another major difference from Europe was that archaeology in the United States developed alongside anthropology, in some respects as a junior branch of it. As a result, many archaeologists focused their attention on the cultural history of groups of surviving American Indians, such as the pueblo-dwellers of the Southwest and the horse-riding Plains Indians. Little attempt was made to consider broad overall trends in American prehistory.

One exception was the "archaic hypothesis" proposed by Herbert Spinden (1879–1967). He envisaged a basic American culture, practicing farming and making pottery, that spread throughout the continent of North America from the Valley of Mexico. Although the pattern of development was later shown to be far more complex than Spinden himself had thought, his hypothesis was an important stimulus to the growth of American archaeology.

their stratigraphic relationships in excavations.

In France, rich in Paleolithic material, Gabriel de Mortillet (1828–1898) proposed a series of chronological stages based on variations in stone tools and to some extent in associated fauna. This scheme was refined by the great French Paleolithic archaeologist, the abbé Henri Breuil (1877–1961). He made particular use of "type fossils"—artifacts equivalent to the animal fossils chosen by geologists to characterize stratigraphic chronological divisions.

Other scholars subdivided the later epochs of the European past. Foremost among them was the Swedish archaeologist Oscar Montelius (1843–1921), who proposed divisions of the Neolithic period in northern Europe, each characterized by different forms of stone tools and megalithic tombs. Similar systems devised by others were based on typological changes in pottery, bronze and iron swords, stone and bronze axes, and so on.

These schemes were generally applicable only to a particular region, but some attempts were made to produce broad syntheses of European prehistory. Joseph Déchelette (1862–1914) did so in France, as did the *Reallexicon der Vorgeschichte* edited by Max

This site, Montezuma's Castle, is typical of Pueblo cliff dwellings in the southwestern United States. These remarkably sophisticated structures may have been constructed in their inaccessible locations as a defensive measure. Because the environment is hot and relatively free from rainfall, the degree of preservation both of the homes and their contents is high. As a result, modern archaeologists have been able to create a fairly complete picture of the lives of this ancient Indian people.

The views of Elliot Smith and the hyperdiffusionists remained popular for several decades. But by the 1930s, a less extreme theory of the diffusion of culture was becoming accepted among archaeologists in Europe.

The man with whom this change in attitudes is most often associated is Gordon Childe (1892–1957), an Australian who settled in Britain. Childe, who had an amazing grasp of European languages, studied both excavated material and publications from all over Europe. In 1925, he produced a major synthesis that represented the fruits of his research in his book *The Dawn of European Civilization*.

Childe introduced the important concept, already in vogue among some German archaeologists, of "archaeological cultures." Such cultures are ethnically or socially distinctive groups that can be distinguished from one another by their characteristic artifacts. Variations in the nonfunctional aspects of artifacts are taken as an expression of variations in cultural conventions. Childe's extensive body of work fostered a pan-European view of the past and counteracted the narrow preoccupation with regional chronologies. It also concerned itself with the mechanisms behind major technological and socioeconomic changes in prehistory.

Oriente Lux

Like the hyperdiffusionists, Childe believed that many innovations in human development had originated in the Near East, among them farming, metallurgy and urban life. They had spread from there to Europe and ultimately throughout the whole of the Old World. But Childe disagreed with the hyperdiffusionists about how the process of diffusion had actually taken place.

The hyperdiffusionists contended that the natives of the lands to which the Egyptians introduced the benefits of civilization had previously been existing in a condition of low savagery. Childe argued that the prehistoric societies of Europe were vigorous and independent, adapting developments and inventions that had spread from the Near East to their own cultures and needs.

Thus, according to Childe, the manifestation in Europe of new ideas and technology from the East was essentially European. This view of development came to be called "modified diffusionism" and went part of the way toward reconciling the hyperdiffusionist and nationalist schools of archaeology.

Five Thousand Years of History

Childe's modified diffusionist approach eventually gained wide acceptance among western European archaeologists. It was attractive because it offered a partial solution to the question of chronology that continued to preoccupy scholars in the years between the two world wars.

Historical records give a firm chronology for the Near East back to 3000 B.C.E. Datable Egyptian material in the Aegean had allowed Sir Flinders Petrie and Sir Arthur Evans to give historical dates respectively to the Mycenaean and Minoan

Aerial photography has provided archaeologists with a valuable tool for studying ancient sites. The technique was pioneered by O. G. S. Crawford (below), who began the interpretation of aerial photographs during World War I. Crawford was co-author of the classic work Wessex from the Air, *published in 1928. The book contains more than 300 aerial photographs, including Hod Hill (right), an Iron Age fort captured by the Romans in 63* C.E.

Bronze Age civilizations. Using the same method of cross-dating, though on less reliable ground, Childe and others attempted to date prehistoric cultures that had existed in the rest of Europe.

Two key links were perceived as being highly significant from their point of view: the megaliths of western Europe, some of which resembled

Aegean tombs, and the apparently striking similarities between the finds from sites with early metallurgy in the Balkans and those from datable Troy.

The acceptance of Near Eastern origins for many of humankind's advances made it possible for European archaeologists to date their material. If, however, the Near East had been denied its priority, for prewar archaeologists all possibility of dating European prehistory would have vanished.

Looking at the Landscape

Not every archaeologist remained obsessed by chronology during the interwar years. Some turned their attention to the factors that lay behind the Near East's emergence as a birthplace of farming and cradle of civilization, while others looked at the environmental conditions affecting patterns of prehistoric settlement.

Meanwhile, science had given archaeologists an important new tool, in the form of aerial photography. The earliest air photo had been taken from a balloon over Paris in 1858, and by the 1900s scholars were taking a bird's-eye view of many ancient sites.

The greatest pioneer of aerial photographs was O. G. S. Crawford (1886–1957). In 1928, he coauthored *Wessex from the Air*, a classic photographic study of one of England's richest archaeological areas. It revealed a host of hitherto unsuspected sites, as well as unnoticed features of known ones.

Careful Techniques

During the interwar years, excavation principles and techniques were steadily refined, in line with the growing awareness of the kinds of information that could be recovered from the soil. Massive walls and glorious artifacts ceased to be the main targets of investigation.

In particular, delicate methods were needed to uncover the prehistoric settlements of Europe, where the main traces of occupation were complicated horizontal spreads of postholes and pits. Among the pioneers was Werner Buttler (1907–1940), who excavated the great German Neolithic settlement of Köln-Lindenthal.

Not all archaeologists absorbed the lessons of such careful excavators and their predecessors. In 1954, Sir Mortimer Wheeler, the doyen of 20th-century field archaeology, denounced the incompetents in his manual *Archaeology from the Earth*. Wheeler, whose field experience spanned more than half-a-century, was particularly harsh on the then widespread practice of digging by fixed levels. He eloquently argued the case for excavation by stratigraphic deposits, the working method now generally accepted by archaeologists worldwide (*see pages 70–71*).

THE DATING REVOLUTION

In 1949, Professor Willard F. Libby (1908–1980), a chemist at the U.S. Institute for Nuclear Studies in Chicago, announced a discovery that was to win him the Nobel Prize and to precipitate a revolution in archaeology. He had found a method of determining the absolute age of organic archaeological material by measuring the level of the radioactive isotope carbon 14 it contains hence the method is called radiocarbon dating (*see pages 134–137*).

Previously, all dates for prehistoric Europe had depended on the assumption of the chronological priority of the Near East, held by diffusionists such as Gordon Childe. Now Europe could be dated independently, and previous assumptions, challenged.

The Near Eastern historical chronology, in any case, went back only to about 3000 B.C.E., and dates before then had been a matter of conjecture. Radiocarbon dating can be used to date material up to 50,000 years old.

Scholars had argued that farming communities had emerged in the Near East at around 4500 B.C.E., and that farming had reached Britain by about 2000 B.C.E. Carbon-14 dates at Jericho and at Durrington Walls in England suggested that agriculture began in the Near East at least 2,000 years earlier than originally thought, and before 2500 B.C.E. in Britain. The findings were initially greeted with disbelief. But by the 1960s, a sufficient number of consistent carbon-14 dates had been obtained to win general acceptance both for a very greatly extended Neolithic chronology and for the reliability of radiocarbon dating itself.

The technique has given archaeology a much broader perspective. Because it can provide relatively precise dates for material from all over the world, it allows archaeologists to compare the stages of human development in different regions at the same time. For instance, it has demonstrated that farming began in the millennia that followed the end of the last Ice Age in the Near East, Southeast Asia, Africa, China, and Central and South America.

The invention of the technique of radiocarbon dating by Professor W. F. Libby (above right), in 1949, radically changed the face of archaeology. Now this scientific method could accurately date objects that before could only be given a relative place in time based on assumptions proved to have been often incorrect. Here Libby is shown with the Nobel Prize he won in 1960.

Not When, but Why?

Radiocarbon dating released archaeologists from a narrow preoccupation with dating. Since the question *when* could now often be answered, other questions began to assume more importance, in particular *why*.

That had become a more urgent concern because radiocarbon dating had itself upset the generally accepted picture of the past. In particular, it showed that the period of time between the earliest farming settlements and the development of urban communities was far longer

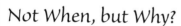

WHAT IS
ARCHAEOLOGY?

than anyone had previously thought. Recognition of that fact gave new impetus to efforts to determine how and why the transformation from village to town took place.

Similarly, scholars tried to find out why, in different regions of the world, people should have taken to farming at about the same time. Part of the cause is generally accepted to have stemmed from environmental changes that followed the end of the last Ice Age, but archaeologists are still endeavoring to assess the impact of those changes on the inhabitants of other regions where farming settlements did not emerge at that time.

In areas such as Australia and the New World that are not linked to the historical chronology of the Old World, radiocarbon dating made it possible to establish and date cultural sequences. That, for example, enabled scholars to understand for the first time the pattern of human colonization throughout the world during the last Ice Age.

A Widening Interest

Radiocarbon dating was not the only major development in archaeology in the years immediately following World War II, although it was undoubt-edly the most significant. American archaeologists, especially, began to move toward the innovative idea of carrying out regional surveys, instead of the traditional approach of simply concentrating on individual archaeological sites.

Such surveys, which document the history of human settlement within a given region, throw light on changing trends in population growth and distribution, and on the very definite impact environment has on human settlement patterns. These surveys have become a vital part of archaeological research today.

The wide-ranging and detailed aerial photography carried out for military reasons during the war also benefited archaeologists, particularly as many of them were enlisted as air photo interpreters during the hostilities. Aerial photographs of North Africa, for example, revealed the position of the Roman frontier zone, with its extensive building works. In Italy, photos showed a crowded landscape of ancient settlements in the Tavoliere region, a notoriously backward area in recent centuries. In addition, thousands of Etruscan tombs that had escaped the ravages of earlier treasure-hunters were suddenly revealed.

Postwar advances in diving equipment and marine salvage techniques have led to the development of underwater archaeology as a specialist field of research. In the 1970s and 1980s, pioneering work was undertaken on the Amsterdam, an extremely impressive and well-preserved wreck. In 1749, this Dutch East Indies ship was wrecked off Hastings, England, and sank in 20 feet (6 m) of muddy seabed. An archaeological investigation of it and legislation to ensure the protection of this and other historically significant wrecks were triggered in the 1960s by the removal of objects from it by treasure hunters. A foundation set up by the Dutch government undertook the work in earnest and has sponsored surveys of the site since 1975. Here we see Dutch scientists recording details of the structure (left, opposite page) and taking samples of wood from the ship (above).

THE DATING REVOLUTION

SCIENCE AND ARCHAEOLOGY

Radiocarbon dating was the first major breakthrough in establishing the timetable of the past, and most scholars welcomed it. But some had doubts, and those doubts increased as discrepancies between carbon-14 dates and known historical dates began to emerge.

Dendrochronology, or tree-ring dating (see pages 130–131), was used to cross-check radiocarbon techniques, and as a result the latter have now been modified and their accuracy considerably improved. The results of this cross-checking drove the final nails into the diffusionist coffin so far as Europe is concerned. The revised carbon-14 dates have definitively shown that the supposed links between the Near East and Europe, by which civilization was claimed to have spread, are chronologically impossible.

Conventional radiocarbon dating has thus been of great importance to archaeology. But it has its drawbacks. It can be performed only on organic remains, of which relatively large samples have hitherto been needed, and its range of around 50,000 years confines it to the most recent chapters of the human story.

Modern scientific equipment now allows carbon-14 dates to be obtained from smaller samples but has so far failed in its promise to extend the date-range considerably (see pages 136–137).

Other physical dating techniques have been developed, too—many of them by-products of research into radioactivity. Thermoluminescence (TL) dating, for example, is used to date pottery, ubiquitous in recent ages, as well as more ancient burnt flint (see pages 138–139). Potassium-argon, fission track, electron spin resonance and uranium series disequilibrium dating all depend on radioactive decay, and reach back into the distant past (see pages 140–141).

The result of these advances is that archaeologists now have a timescale against which human evolution can be viewed. The timescale can be stated confidently for most parts of the world. And it is far longer than had previously been imagined.

Detective Work

Aerial reconnaissance has been used by archaeologists since the turn of the century, and geophysical surveying devices have been in archaeological use since the 1940s. But like radiocarbon dating, these techniques have been considerably refined and extended. Over recent years, remote sensing has made an increasing contribution to archaeological reconnaissance (see pages 44–45).

Infrared has been added to the photographic repertoire, and a whole range of electrical, magnetic and sonic instruments have been borrowed from the earth sciences and modified, or developed specifically for archaeology. Sonic instruments have proved particularly useful in underwater detective work (see pages 52–53).

The importance of the past concealed beneath the waves has long been recognized, but until the

This aerial view clearly shows the outline of the Badbury Rings, the remains of a hillfort in southwest England, which dates back to the Iron Age. The last, or outer, ring may not have been added until just before the Roman invasion in 43 C.E. The total area of the site is just over 18 acres (7 ha).

development of the aqualung in the 1940s it could generally be investigated only in particularly favorable circumstances. Now many of the constraints have been removed, and the underwater world of ancient wrecks and submerged settlements has suddenly been opened up to view (*see pages 94–95*).

An All-Around Approach

The history of archaeology has seen a gradual broadening of interests and preoccupations. Archaeology has tended to concentrate on artifacts, human-made relics of the past. But the information artifacts are expected to yield has expanded greatly. In addition, modern scientific aids have provided much new data on ancient technology and sources of raw materials. So we can now build up a better picture of patterns of prehistoric trade, communications networks and industrial exploitation of the landscape (*see pages 114–123*).

Many advances in medical knowledge and technology have been adopted by archaeologists in their quest for information on people of the past. Bones now can be made to reveal not only the age and sex of individuals and the diseases and injuries they suffered, but even what they ate and what they looked like (*see pages 110–113*).

Attention is increasingly focused, too, on such topics as subsistence economics and the landscapes around past settlements, to find out how ancient people obtained food to support themselves. Efforts are being made to recover the remains of plants and animals that provided their diet or that can shed light on the environment in which they lived (*see pages 102–109*). One result has been a growing awareness of just how much people modified their surroundings even in remote times.

To help them in this task of relating early societies to their environment and their neighbors, archaeologists have borrowed approaches from geography. Those include site territorial analysis, to establish the economic reasons lying behind patterns of settlement, and various theoretical models of economic and political geography (*see pages 152–153*).

Geographic Information Systems (GIS), a powerful computer method of studying complex spatial relations, has also been enthusiastically adopted by archaeologists. Computers and the complex mathematical manipulations that they permit have revolutionized the way that archaeologists record, analyze and interpret their data (*see pages 168–169*).

"New Archaeology"

The borrowings of equipment and techniques from other disciplines sparked off a debate that raged in the early 1970s and has smoldered on ever since. Essentially, it asks, Can archaeology be regarded as a science?

Some people argue strongly that it cannot and that in the proliferation of scientific aids archaeologists risk losing sight of the humans behind the artifacts. Others assert that archaeologists have for too long expected their data to have self-evident meaning and that it is time their underlying assumptions were specifically stated and tested for validity.

These "new archaeologists" advocate, among other things, the scientific approach of formulating hypotheses and collecting test data. The drawback is that archaeological tests often cannot be repeated and not all of the variables can be tightly controlled. Nevertheless, a more rigorous approach to collecting and analyzing information can only be of benefit.

And some scientific techniques do lend themselves to archaeology. They include experiments with ancient forms of technology, which have provided valuable insights into, for example, manufacturing techniques, farming, building methods and navigation. Another approach is ethnoarchaeology, involving the study of present-day ethnographic groups. Their activities and the material traces these leave may give clues to the significance of ancient artifacts (*see pages 144–151*).

Science and technology may be helping, but they have also brought disadvantages. The increasingly rapid pace at which people are modifying their environment poses a growing threat to any surviving remains. Happily, many governments and private organizations have responded generously by sponsoring archaeological investigations of threatened sites and by introducing laws that make an archaeological assessment a required preliminary to development work. The burgeoning popularity of archaeology among the general public means that professional archaeologists can call upon a plentiful reserve of interested amateurs who can provide invaluable assistance in the field.

The underwater archaeologist must be as exact in recording of data as his ground-level counterpart. Here we see a scientist surveying the wreck of one of the many ships which foundered off the coast of Canada. After pinpointing the precise location of each piece of wreckage with his equipment, he then records its precise coordinates on a grid plan of the whole site.

Evidence of the past is all around us; we have only to allow ourselves
to become aware of it. Here a Bronze Age burial mound has been
preserved within a modern field of wheat in Wiltshire, England.

PART

2

THE LAY OF THE LAND

THE ARCHAEOLOGICAL LANDSCAPE

Archaeologists are frequently asked, "How did archaeological material end up underground?" There are many possible answers, stemming both from natural processes and from human activities.

When, for instance, a house is abandoned by its occupants, it gradually collapses; the roof falls in and the walls start to crumble and decay. Plants and living creatures, wind and rain, snow and frost, or intense sun all contribute to its disintegration. The slow accumulation of soil from the decay of vegetation gradually raises the ground level, and the last remnants of the house eventually become buried beneath a soil layer of increasing thickness.

Other natural forces may be involved in burying archaeological sites. Soil eroded from higher ground nearby can be deposited on them, or they can be buried by soil carried in from elsewhere by the wind or deposited by floods. In deserts or by the seashore, the site may be covered by wind-blown sand.

Sometimes, natural disasters may cause the archaeological remains to be engulfed. Ash or lava flows from volcanic eruptions can overwhelm sites—Pompeii, for example, was buried by ash from Vesuvius. Earthquakes may smother a settlement in debris.

The Human Role

Nature is not alone in covering the works of people. Humans themselves often play a part. Abandoned buildings are frequently demolished down to their foundations, and any useful material is removed. Then new buildings may be constructed on the razed debris of the old, sometimes incorporating the material saved from their predecessors.

Through this process of destruction and renewal, settlements gradually rise above the level of their earliest occupa-tion. Sometimes the results are dramatic. In the Near East, some favored sites, occupied for thousands of years, have become enormous mounds, built up gradually from the decayed remains of myriad mud-brick houses.

When a structure decays or is demolished, its foundations are the part of it most likely to survive, because they are set into the ground. Postholes, ditches, sunken floors, pits and foundation trenches are among the most common archaeo-

The twin-towered ruins of the 12th-century church of St. Egbert in Kent, England, are built upon and use many materials taken from the Roman fort of Regulbium (Reculver), which was built in 225 and occupied until the 4th century. The Roman fort gradually slipped into the sea as the cliffs were eroded.

logical finds. So are floors originally laid at ground level and the lowest courses of walls.

It would be a mistake, however, to imagine that all archaeological remains are below ground. Many structures are built of materials that resist decay or degradation, and these are likely to survive above ground for a considerable time.

Churches and castles, half-ruined but still standing, are a familiar sight in Europe, where the much older megalithic tombs and monu-ments of the Atlantic coastal region also survive. Earthen structures may also endure for millennia, as the prehistoric barrows of Europe and the impressive mounds in the shape of animals and birds in the eastern United States have done.

Forces of Destruction

The same natural processes that preserve the traces of many archaeological sites by burying them can totally destroy others. For example, sites on hilltops or slopes may be entirely obliterated by erosion. Floods, changes in the courses of rivers and the action of glaciers can have a similarly destructive effect.

Humans are even more active than nature in erasing evidence of the past, and in recent times the rate of destruction has accelerated. Modern agricultural machinery penetrates the soil to depths spared by earlier farm implements. Road building and other industrial activities in the countryside are equaled in their destructive potential by urban rebuilding and the spread of towns. The heritage of our past demands immediate investigation, before all traces of it vanish completely through the combined and uncontrollable forces of humans and nature.

Armchair Beginnings

Fieldwork usually begins in the comfort of an armchair at home or in a local library or public records office. Maps, both modern and less recent, can give clues to interesting sites. So can records of past land transfers and similar transactions, and other historical documents. It is useful to study place-names and any accounts of earlier archaeological discoveries in the locality. Aerial photographs can give details of landscapes of the past.

Once an interesting-looking site has been traced, the area should be visited and explored. If further archaeological evidence is found, detailed surveys can begin.

THE ROMANCE OF MAPS

A 17th-century map of Suffolk, England, shows the division of the county into "hundreds" and the names of the nobility. Of considerable interest for the study of the county's social geography, this map is of little use for studying the landscape. The purpose for which maps were produced determined what was shown and whether the details included were accurately mapped or, as with the woods and hills on this map, schematically represented.

Large-scale (1:10,000 or 1:10,560) modern maps contain a lot of information that is useful to archaeologists. Many features of the landscape may still survive as partial ruins—castles, churches and other old buildings, barrows, megaliths and earthworks. These are often marked on maps.

In other cases, the feature may have virtually disappeared, but its former existence may be signaled by a name. In England, for example, the word *park* associated with a piece of land can indicate that it was once a deer park or the grounds of an estate. The name *camp* may refer to Roman remains.

Maps also provide a detailed picture of modern field and parish boundaries, hedgerows and woodlands, roads and paths, and other features of the present-day landscape. Irregularities or anomalies in them may be a clue to a feature of archaeological interest. For example, an abrupt change in the line of a hedge or field boundary may have been originally to avoid a structure that has since disappeared. Small ponds or ditches may be the

last remains of a medieval moat, an old abbey fishpond or the race of a water mill. A clump of isolated trees in a field may mark the site of an ancient structure, which might be a barrow, a deserted house or even a pillow mound (an artificial rabbit warren).

Villages occupied in medieval times but later deserted can often be discovered by studying features on the map. Frequent clues are fields of unusual shape, isolated churches, and a series of paths or tracks that apparently converge nowhere in particular. Parish boundaries apparently without an associated village may also indicate an abandoned settlement.

Modern town maps are also informative, because many of the streets are likely to follow routes that date right back to the original settlement. Town streets, like rural boundaries, also contain clues to former features such as defensive walls, open markets or land once belonging to a churchyard or cemetery, manor or castle. For instance, circular castle defenses will show up as

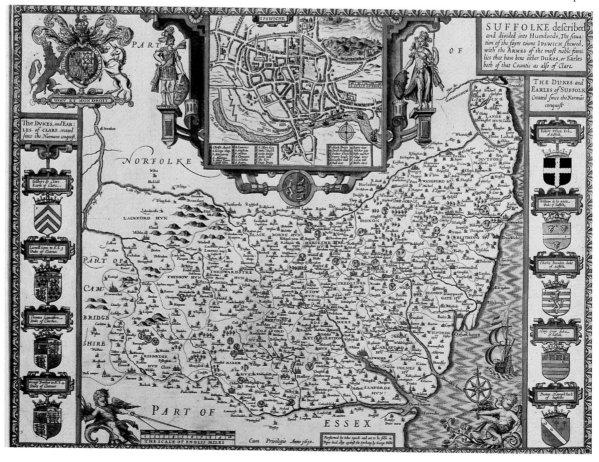

an anomaly in a basically linear street plan. Curving parallel streets may once have been separated from each other by a town wall. In ancient towns and cities, street names may indicate the occupations of those who once lived or traded there, or commemorate a former feature or a person who once owned the land.

Although many features of the present landscape reflect the past, much has also changed, particularly since the later 19th century. Earlier maps can therefore provide potentially valuable additional information. But they should be treated with caution, because their accuracy varies and they are often selective in the details they include. Large-scale estate, tithe and enclosure maps showing boundaries and land use are the most helpful.

Documentary Evidence

The reading and interpretation of old documents is the preserve of the historian. But the contents yield information of vital concern to archaeologists, either by revealing the existence of hitherto-unknown archaeological sites or, much more commonly, by assisting in the interpretation of archaeological material. For example, it may be difficult to distinguish between the earthworks constructed on medieval estates and those of later formal gardens without documentary help.

However, documents are not always easy to interpret accurately, so it is helpful to seek the advice of a historian. *The Domesday Book*, compiled in England during the 11th century, provides a good example of some of the pitfalls awaiting the incautious archaeologist. As a survey of the land conducted for William I, it seems a suitable source for studying the distribution of later 11th-century settlements. But in some instances a village name may refer to a group of settlements lumped together, or a portion of a village divided for administrative or other reasons. In other instances, villages have shifted their location or changed their name.

Despite such drawbacks, documentary sources have their place. Surveys and inquiries that give information on the economic significance of the human-made landscape are of particular interest. Land charters, some dating from before 1000 C.E., give archaeologists an additional insight into how land holdings were organized in the past. Many such documents are preserved in public records or in the archives of ancient land-owning institutions.

Although archaeologists need to rely on historians to assess ancient documents, the archaeologist may in turn be of service to the historian in dating or authenticating historical material and providing significant information about its context. Archaeological data can help to check the truth or relevance of documentary statements. For instance, the conventional picture of Vikings raping and pillaging, derived from the writings of the clerics who were their main victims, is in marked contrast to the impression from archaeological evidence of generally peaceful Viking colonization.

A page from The Domesday Book, a survey of all England compiled in 1086 and written in Latin. It recorded details of people, dwellings, land, animals and plows, and the services and dues owed to the Norman lords established recently (1066). Understanding such documents generally requires help from specialists.

39

CLUES FROM PLACE-NAMES

The names of settlements, hills, fields and other features of the landscape can provide valuable clues to the possible location of sites of archaeological interest. The principles outlined here and illustrated with examples from Europe and North America are applicable generally.

Place-names, like historical documents, are the preserve of the specialist. Superficial resemblances between words with entirely different meanings may mislead the unwary, and a grounding in philology and etymology is needed for accurate interpretation.

At the simple level, names indicate the former existence of features in the landscape, or the use to which a particular area or natural feature was put. In England, for example, field names containing the element *town* suggest that the field was once the site of a now-vanished village. Other names may derive from prehistoric monuments that are still extant or that disappeared only in historical times.

Sometimes, a name may show that the purpose of a feature was remembered, with its builders, long after it fell into disuse. *Rath*, a common component of place-names in Ireland, denotes a fort surrounded by a bank and ditch. *Wic* and its variants in several northern European languages come from the Latin *vicus* and indicate a Roman settlement.

Patterns of Settlement

At a deeper level, place-names provide vital clues to the pattern and chronology of land settlement. In Britain, the names of many towns and villages reflect the Roman presence. The most common is the suffix -*chester*, a derivation of the Latin *castra* (a fortified camp). The city of Chester itself was a major Roman fortress built in 76–78 C.E.

An interesting hybrid that reflects both Roman and Anglo-Saxon (English) settlement in an area is the place-name Wickham—a combination of the Latin *vicus* and the Old English *ham*, both of which mean "settlement" or "village." Thus West Wickham and East Wickham are both built on the site of an earlier Romano British settlement.

After the Roman period, contacts between the native Britons and English settlers are attested in the survival of Celtic names. These were mainly geographical features, including river names such as the Thames. Occasionally, English incomprehension of Celtic words led to amusing tautologies such as Bredon (Hill-hill), a compound of Celtic *bre* and English *dun*, both meaning "hill." A considerable number of place-names such as Eccles and Eccleston refer to Celtic churches (Latin *ecclesia*) surviving and being respected or noted by English settlers.

Later, the relationship between colonizing Vikings and Anglo-Saxon peasants can be gauged from the distribution of village names containing Viking elements. The most common Viking element in place-names is the suffix -*by* (farmstead or village). There are literally hundreds of names ending with the -*by* suffix in northern and eastern England. Another extremely common Viking element is the suffix -*thorp* (a small settlement that is dependent on a larger village).

In the south of England, Saxon place-names tend to be the most common. The suffix -*ham* (place or village), for instance, is widely used, as are -*tun* and -*ton*, both later Saxon words that also denote a place or village.

In some regions of England, settlement on the best lands contain Anglo-Saxon name elements, while names ending in Viking elements are generally on less favorable ground. This indicates that in these areas the Vikings peacefully colonized the second-rate land not in use by the resident Anglo-Saxon population.

The influence of European settlement in North America can be gauged to a great extent simply by examining the distribution of place-names derived from English, French, Dutch, German, Spanish and other languages. So although New York's Dutch origins are concealed by the name-change from Nieuwe Amsterdam, they are revealed in names such as Bowery (originally *Bouwerij*, from the Dutch word for farm) and Harlem (from Haarlem, the town in Holland).

The examples above give a glimpse of the way place-names can provide valuable insights into a region's history. The interrelationships between linguistic groups, the order of settlement of different topographic zones and changes in patterns of land use are the most common questions to which place-names may help provide an answer.

The area inhabited by the Picts, the descendants of the Iron Age inhabitants of much of Scotland, can be traced in place-names containing Pictish elements, such as pett (dependent estate), as in Pitcaple; caer (fort); and aber (confluence) as in Aberlemno, from which comes this fine Pictish symbol stone.

The beginning of the end for the Roman Empire came in 406 C.E., when hordes of barbarians of quite diverse tribal origins moved westward across the Rhine and started to settle in the lands on its farther shores. Some stopped only briefly in Gaul before moving on; the Vandals, for example, devastated Iberia and founded a kingdom in North Africa. Others, notably the Franks and the Burgundians, chose to stay in Gaul itself.

Another group, the Visigoths, initially settled in southern Gaul, where they founded the kingdom of Toulouse. But early in the 6th century they were defeated in a conflict with the Franks. Many migrated into what is now Spain, where the Visigoths had already established military outposts.

Much of our knowledge of these population movements and settlements comes from the study of place-names. For instance, the Alans, a group driven by the Huns from an empire on the Caspian Sea, settled on the Loire River for a time, and names such as Allaines bear witness to their former presence there. The distribution of place-names that now end in -ans or -ens (originally -ingos) chronicles Burgundian colonization of much of French-speaking Switzerland, the Jura and the plain of the Saône River in France itself. Names also support the traditional belief that the Burgundians originally came from Scandinavia—Borgund in Norway and Bornholm (once Borgundarholm), an island in the Baltic.

From the North

Increasing pressure from hostile tribes, particularly the Scots in the west and north, drove many Britons from southwest England across the sea to Brittany (Bretagne). Breton regional names such as Dumnonia (as southwest England was then known) and Cornouaille (Cornwall) show the widespread influence of the immigrants. So do names that reflect a land division into parishes around monasteries, rather than the organization by estates then practiced in the rest of Gaul.

Place-names indicating land tenure yield information about early Visigothic settlements in Spain. The invaders seized about two-thirds of the Roman landholdings there, and those became known legally as the *Sortes Gothicae* (the Gothic lot or portion), preserved in names such as Sort and Consortes. The Roman third, or *Tertiae Romanorum*, gave rise to names like Tercia. Toward the end of the 6th century, the Visigoths gained control of the whole Iberian Peninsula, but that expansion is hardly discernible from place-names, for by then the Visigoths had largely adopted Byzantine Roman language.

A Shifting Frontier

On a larger scale, place-names indicate fluctuations in the frontier between people speaking Romance, the language of Gaul, and those speaking Germanic languages. By the 7th or 8th century, the linguistic frontier more or less followed the same course that it does today. However, on either side there were enclaves where people spoke the language of the other region.

Among those was the area around Boulogne, on the Channel coast of France, which was strongly Germanic. Latin place-names there evolved differently from those in most of the rest of Gaul, where Romance was dominant. The Roman settlement name of Cessiacum became Quesques to the German-speakers, but Chessy to the French. Similarly, Gilliacum became Guelque in Germanic, but Gilly in Romance. From the 9th century onward, the Boulogne enclave was gradually reconquered by French, but the legacy of German can still be traced.

The location of the German-French language frontier can be shown to have derived from two essential factors relating to the barbarian invasions. One was distance from the borders of the original Germanic territories. The frontier runs roughly parallel to the Germanic boundaries as they existed during the 4th century, about 60 miles (100 km) beyond them. The other factor was the extent to which a given area of country was devastated during the invasions.

An area in Bavaria, in what is now southern Germany, was part of the Roman Empire until the barbarians overran it in the 5th century. Only insignificant pockets of Romance-speakers survived. Their settlements are often denoted by the element *walah* in the name. The term, in Germanic tongues, means "foreigner," and it is also preserved, for the same reason as in Bavaria, in the place-names Wales and Wallonia, the French-speaking region of Belgium.

In Gaul itself, which was predominantly Romance-speaking, the evolution of place-names subtly indicates the mingling of Roman and Germanic cultures that ultimately led to the emergence in the late 5th and early 6th centuries of the Merovingian kingdom, so-called after Merovech, the half-legendary founder of the dynasty. In particular, this can be seen in the proliferation of place-names that combine a German personal name and a Latin affix. Early examples ended in the Latin -acum or -iacas (for example, Athanacum), but by the 7th century the Latinate element was generally *ville* or *court* (for example, Villemomble and Courgains), both of which are still popular in the coining of place-names in France.

The linguistic evidence of some degree of synthesis between Roman and Germanic cultures in Gaul is borne out archaeologically by the emergence of row grave cemeteries between the 5th and 6th centuries, combining elements of both. The dead were buried with their jewelry and weapons, as was customary in the Germanic world. They were buried lying east to west in the Christian custom. Finally, many of the burials were in stone sarcophagi, a Roman feature.

KING ARTHUR—MAN OR MYTH?

The shadowy figure of King Arthur exerts a powerful fascination for people of all nationalities. The legend surrounding him and his court at Camelot first became a source of popular literature in 12th-century France, and Arthur and his ideals, in our own time, were used as a symbol by U.S. president John F. Kennedy, who inspired a whole generation with it. But did Arthur exist, and if so, how much of the legend has a basis in fact?

The full answer will never be known. Nevertheless, the quest for Arthur provides a good example of how archaeological and historical sources can complement each other to build up a picture of the past, and of how scholars in the two disciplines sift fact from fiction.

The Historian's Arthur

Scanty and dubious historical records establish the existence of Arthur, albeit not as a king, but as chief warlord of the Britons resisting invasion by Anglo-Saxons after the Roman occupation of Britain had ended in about 410 C.E. From the writings of the fiery 6th-century monk Gildas, from tables for calculating the date of Easter in which contemporary events were recorded as marginal notes and from heroic poetry with possible early 6th-century roots—all known to us only from later copies of copies—we gather that Arthur was the victor in 12 battles. They included Cat Coit Celidon, probably fought somewhere in the Caledonian Forest of the Southern Uplands in Scotland, and his last and most important victory, at Mount Badon.

There he resoundingly defeated the Anglo-Saxon (English) invaders and won a respite from their encroachment, bringing a peace that was still holding when Gildas wrote. But the penetration resumed, and the English grip on Britain was assured when they defeated the Britons at the battle of Dyrholm in 577. Arthur himself had fallen some decades after Badon in a battle between British forces at Camlann.

Documentary discrepancies make Arthur's dates uncertain. Badon could have been fought in either 490 or 518, and Camlann in 511 or 539. The exact location of neither battle is known; both Bath and Badbury Rings in Dorset have been suggested as possible locations for the site of Mount Badon.

The hillfort at South Cadbury is one of many places held to have been Camelot, where the legendary Arthur held his court. Excavations in the late 1960s found evidence that during the Arthurian period (late 5th /early 6th centuries C.E.) the old Iron Age site was strengthened and saw active use as a military base.

The Romancer's Arthur

Other elements of the Arthurian legend, we can see from the documents, are anachronisms, added in medieval times as the romantic associations of Arthur developed. His status as a warlord was transmuted into that of high king, and his mobile defensive force became medieval heavy cavalry. A court at Camelot was attributed to him as a necessary kingly base.

Camelot first appears in the romance *Lancelot, le chevalier de la charette* by the 12th-century French poet Chrétien de Troyes; where its location was remained vague. Medieval writers suggested Winchester, Caerleon and other places in the south and west of Britain. But in the early sources Arthur is not associated with any site in particular, nor is he said to have had an established base anywhere in Britain.

The Archaeologist's Arthur

What substance can archaeology add to the shadowy historical figure of Arthur? The answer is nothing to Arthur himself or to the other individuals of his age, for the information archaeology offers is generally impersonal. But to the tantalizingly incomplete historical snippets that have survived, archaeology can add a great deal, as excavations and surveys continue to reveal the remains of daily life as it existed in the aftermath of the Roman retreat from Britain.

Among the pottery finds in a number of Celtic British sites have been sherds of several types of imported ware. Fragments of redware bowls and amphorae indicate a trade linking Britain with the eastern Mediterranean, while blue-black bowls came from a somewhat closer source in France. Unlike the undistinguished native pottery, these fragments are relatively easy to date with some precision. They show that in the late 5th and 6th centuries C.E. a number of inhabitants of Britain retained some degree of contact with Europe and that they were affluent enough to be able to afford goods imported from the Continent.

So far, such pottery remains have been found in only one Roman town, Ilchester in Somerset, implying that few towns continued to be inhabited for long after the Romans left. On the other hand, the discovery of these wares in a number of long-abandoned Iron Age hillforts, the defenses of which sometimes bear indications of 5th- or 6th-century refurbishment, reinforces the picture gained from written sources of the development of petty kingdoms.

Excavations within hillforts such as Dinas Powys in Wales and Castle Dore in Cornwall have yielded remains of structures that could be chieftains' halls. Among other finds at the sites were abundant animal bones—which would seem to indicate feasting on a large scale—and some occasional evidence of metalworking and other industry. The hillfort at South Cadbury (*see pages 68–69*), while it follows the same pattern, is on a larger scale.

Although Gildas wrote of the peace that followed the battle of Mount Badon, both documentary and archaeological evidence show this to have been rather localized. Abundant finds of Germanic pottery, jewelry and other artifacts in south, north and eastern England attest to Anglo-Saxon advances and consolidation.

Nevertheless, archaeology does seem to confirm the check to the Anglo-Saxons observed by Gildas. Pottery of the type common in southeastern England in the early 6th century, as well as other Saxon material, is virtually absent from the Upper Thames valley. There is also evidence of Anglo-Saxons from Britain settling in western France and Belgium and even returning to their ancestral lands in Germany. "King" Arthur's achievement was therefore substantial, despite the ultimate failure of the Britons to stem the Anglo-Saxon tide.

The power of the legend of King Arthur has come alive and inspired people through the ages. This Dore engraving is from an illustrated edition of Vivien, one of the connected poems in the series that forms The Idylls of the King by Alfred, Lord Tennyson. The series, a modern telling of the Arthurian legends, began in 1842 and continued being released until the late 1860s. Vivien, together with Guinevere, was published in 1859; it tells the story of Vivien, whose father was killed by Arthur against whom she desires revenge. As part of her plan, she seeks out Merlin and weakens his power. It is Vivien who imprisons him inside an oak tree. Here we see the men of Arthur, depicted as a fearsome band of warriors, being led through the enchanted forests of ancient Britain.

A BIRD'S-EYE VIEW

Ancient walls, ditches and roadways continue to affect the landscape even when surface traces of their presence are not obvious. They alter the pattern of the soil below ground, causing variations in soil depth, which in turn affects plant growth. Usually even surface traces can be clearly seen only from the air.

Low bumps and shallow hollows representing relics of the past show up clearly to an aerial observer by the shadows they cast, particularly when the sun is low and shadows are elongated. The remains of the banks and ditches of ancient earthworks can be seen, as well as the last vestiges of stone structures such as demolished abbey buildings, and the house platforms and hollow streets of deserted medieval villages. Medieval strip plowing created patterns of ridges and furrows that have also survived in many areas and show up well as shadow sites.

Thin snow or frost can enhance surface variations. So can the differential melting of snow or flooding, which picks out slight depressions. The microenvironmental preferences of plants such as buttercups may give definition to low walls or shallow ditches.

Stripping and Soil Marks

Archaeological features that have left no trace above ground can sometimes be spotted from the air as soil marks, either when the topsoil is stripped, for instance in preparation for building development, or when land is deeply plowed. Stripping is similar in some respects to the actual process of excavation; the truncated remains of pits, ditches and old foundations are exposed briefly as upper layers of the soil are removed. The machinery used in stripping inevitably churns the ground, making it hard to see the soil marks when close to them. From the air, however, soil that has been recently churned is more readily distinguishable from ancient remains.

The soil marks exposed by stripping delineate the remains themselves, producing a recognizable outline. By contrast, soil marks resulting from the disturbance of underground features by plowing are far less clear-cut. The features are displaced by the turning of the earth and the dragging of the plow. That often results in quite dramatic zigzag or dogtooth effects, with material from the disturbed pit, ditch or building remains often contrasting sharply with the surrounding plow soil. But it may make the form of the underlying structure difficult to determine.

Soil marks that suggest the presence of an archaeological feature need to be investigated quickly, preferably by carefully controlled excavation. The fact that these marks exist at all shows that the buried remains are in the process of being destroyed.

Archaeological features buried below ground can still leave their mark on the landscape. Shallow ground occurs over ancient structures, such as buildings, walls and streets; deeper ground is found within pits and ditches. These variations in depth affect the growth of plants, though the patterns produced are usually only visible from above. This aerial photograph of a field of ripe wheat was shot near Petranell, southeast of Vienna, Austria. Clearly visible is the distinctive outline of a Roman encampment.

Pointers from Plants

Patterns of plant growth, visible from the air, provide a very important clue to the existence of underground remains. Cereal grains, in particular, are exceptionally sensitive to deficiencies in moisture and nutrients, especially in the early stages of the growing season. In a dry spell, they grow best over buried ditches and pits, which are deeper and retain moisture, and poorly over buried walls and stone structures, where moisture is lost and plants can take only shallow root.

Seed sown over pits and ditches germinates more rapidly than that elsewhere, and the young plants show up as patches of green against the otherwise bare earth. These precocious plants remain darker than the rest during the growing season. Their lush growth is more prolonged, and so they ripen later, remaining green while the surrounding crops turn golden. They also grow taller and therefore cast shadows that help to define buried features.

Although deep-rooted plants such as cereals produce the best crop marks, some root crops, such as sugar beets, and pulses, such as peas, may also be useful indicators. In dry years grass will become parched or die over obstacles such as walls; it will survive longest over pits, ditches and other deep-soil features. Crop marks vary widely in visibility. Whether or not they stand out clearly depends on the amount of rain in the growing season and also on when during the season it falls. Some soil types, such as gravels and chalk, produce crop marks that are more distinct than those on other soil types.

Interpreting Aerial Photographs

Two types of photographs can be taken from the air: vertical, or overhead, shots and oblique, or angled, pictures. Details observed on vertical photographs can be plotted directly onto maps, although there is likely to be some distortion of the image at the edges. Pairs of vertical shots with a 60 percent overlap can be examined using a stereoscopic viewer; the landscape relief jumps startlingly into three dimensions, emphasizing every bump and hollow.

Oblique shots, however, generally show the archaeological detail much more clearly. Computer programs are now widely used to correct and map features observed on aerial photos. Digitized and mapped information from aerial photos can also be incorporated within Geographical Information System (GIS) plots (see pages 168–169).

Interpretation of aerial photographs requires considerable skill and experience. Some modern features of the landscape, such as "envelope" plowing patterns, superficially resemble archaeological features when seen from the air. So do geological features such as frost cracks in the subsoil. A practiced eye can distinguish these from genuine archaeological remains, but the area may need to be examined.

The interpretation of archaeological remains on the ground relies heavily on a knowledge of the form of archaeological structures of many different dates. Certain distinctive features often provide clues; a short linear earthwork, for example, may be positively identified as one side of a Roman camp if its line is broken by a gateway of characteristic form.

Frequently, aerial photographs show traces of only a fraction of the remains below ground. A more complete picture may emerge by comparing several photographs of the same area under different land use, or taken at different times of the year or in varying weather conditions. Even with the most detailed aerial view, however, many features are impossible to interpret. A ring ditch, for instance, may be the remains of a Bronze Age barrow, an Iron Age hut circle, a Roman tower, a medieval windmill or an element of a more recent formal garden.

New Horizons

False-color infrared photography and thermal infrared imagery, which pick up differences in soil temperature or moisture caused by the presence of buried features, are now proving their worth, particularly when used on bare soils where no crop marks are possible.

Remote sensing is also now used: High altitude and satellite photographs can reveal interesting features, but their resolution tends to be poor. LANDSAT (Earth Resources Technology Satellites) coverage, however, has proved of great value in looking at archaeological landscapes, as has radar. Since the collapse of Communism, high resolution Russian military photographs have been released showing details as small as 6 feet (2 m) across. The value of remote sensing for detecting and mapping archaeological features can be seen in the information they have revealed in the jungles of lowland Central America.

Barbury Castle, an Iron Age hillfort in Wiltshire, England, was excavated in 1886. It was a source of great archaeological interest; finds included excellent examples of the work of Iron Age blacksmiths. It was reoccupied in Roman times: Finds from this period included a silver spoon engraved with the name of the owner, Verecunda, and an exceptionally fine ornate brooch. Its bank and ditch ramparts, typical of the defenses of Iron Age hillforts, can clearly be seen from the air, along with details of external features. Like most aerial photos, this was taken on black-and-white film; this is standard practice, partly for reasons of economy, but mainly because it usually heightens contrasts.

As knowledge of the first civilizations of the ancient world accumulated and was studied on a comparative basis, it became clear that these civilizations fitted a pattern. All depended on irrigation agriculture to sustain the needs of their populations. But there was one apparent exception to this seemingly inviolable rule: the Classic Maya civilization of the Yucatán peninsula, which reached its height more than 1,500 years ago.

The area today is cultivated by slash-and-burn agriculture, locally called *milpa*. Archaeologists assumed that the same primitive agricultural technique was used during Classic Maya times. But could *milpa*, which is capable of supporting far fewer than 100 people per square kilometer (0.4 sq. miles) of cultivated land, really be the basis of a state that appears to have had quite high population densities?

One of the first indications that it could not have been came in the 1950s, when the University of Pennsylvania surveyed the area of Tikal, the principal Maya ceremonial center in present-day Guatemala. The results of the survey showed that Tikal had been too heavily populated to have had enough room for the *milpa* plots necessary to feed all of its inhabitants. Nor, in fact, was there enough land for this purpose between Tikal and the next center of any significance, Uaxactún, 11 miles (18 km) to the north. Scholars suggested that crop rotation might have allowed more intensive farming, and that the ramon, or breadnut tree, may also have been cultivated. But even this well-thought-out explanation failed to account satisfactorily for the density of population that was indicated at Tikal, and archaeologists continued to be puzzled.

Fields and Canals

A series of startling discoveries in the 1970s provided the answer to the mystery. Archaeologists found permanent field systems on artificial terraces on hillsides in the Mexican state of Quintana Roo. These productive permanent fields were traced only in the one area, but in 1972 Dennis Puleston and Alfred Siemens noticed signs of ancient canal systems on the Candelaria River. This discovery persuaded archaeologists to survey the area from the air.

The survey covered a large portion of Yucatán and used both aerial photography and side-looking radar. New and surprising details were revealed. The canal network was found to spread over a wide area that also included swamps criss-crossed with drainage channels. Between these channels had been laid a grid of raised fields, forming the basis for a highly productive agricultural system.

Ground investigations confirmed the features noted from the air. And a new examination of the Maya centers revealed the significant fact that almost all of them were on rivers, near lakes or on swampy ground. All of the largest sites, including Tikal, were surrounded by swamps. Work over recent years has revealed further raised field systems and canals in other parts of the Maya lowlands, as well as other water-retention systems in the north.

Canals and raised fields had thus provided the agricultural base for the Classic Maya civilization. On the evidence found at one major Maya center, Mirador, such farming methods could have begun even earlier, during the late Preclassic period.

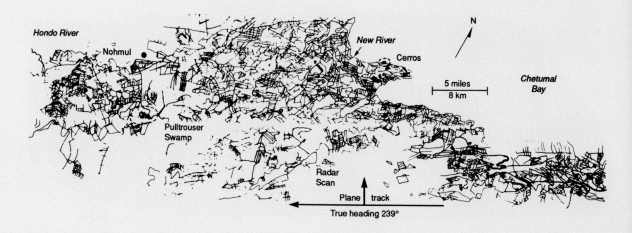

Sites in the northwest Yucatán peninsula illustrate the scale and grandeur of Maya civilization. Their temples, such as this one at Dzibilchaltún (above), are typified by the long, banked row of steps leading up to the large square structure where religious ceremonies were carried out. Recent success in the decipherment of the Maya script is providing an ever-increasing amount of information on the political, social and religious life of the Classic Maya. Remote sensing has also furnished important clues to their economic practices. This plot of features around Pulltrouser Swamp in Belize (left) was one of the first indications of the existence of the canal systems and associated raised fields that covered much of the Maya heartlands.

With the help of aerial photography, an archaeological mystery had been solved. And the theory that the rise of early civilizations depended on intensive agriculture based on water control was once more apparently vindicated.

THE VISIBLE PAST

Exposed remains of the past are often investigated by fieldwalking, a popular leisure activity among amateur archaeological groups. The best conditions for fieldwalking are, unfortunately, often uncomfortable—after rain, when objects have been washed clean and are visible, and during the winter, when vegetation is low and crops have not yet started growing.

The area to be investigated may be divided into blocks to be allocated to the participants, using field boundaries and similar features as boundaries. Ideally, large areas should be subdivided. The fieldwalkers pick up the archaeological remains they notice, or a representative sample, and note where dense concentrations of archaeological material occur. Or they may record what they have found but leave it in situ.

Typical finds include a variety of sherds of pottery, flint and stone artifacts, coins and other small metal objects, and pieces of building material, for example, brick, daub or tile. Such material often indicates that the remains of a building lie below the ground, although sometimes it may simply have been dumped on the site. Other telltale signs of disturbed occupation deposits include fragments of hewn stone and scatters of charcoal.

Dense concentrations of pottery and worked flint also suggest an occupation site, but isolated pieces more probably reached the field mixed with domestic refuse once used as manure. Dense scatters of material, such as firecrazed flint from the British Bronze Age, suggest that there are mounds of the same material underground.

Worked flint and stone may belong to any period, but they can often be dated by their form, that is, their shape and techniques of manufacture. Waste flakes and microliths (small flint tools) may be less chronologically distinctive and can at times be misleading. For example, in Cyprus fieldwalkers have on occasion been deluded into identifying archaeological sites on the basis of dense scatters of flint chips, actually made quite recently and set in threshing sledges (boards that were dragged over harvested grain).

Coins, though exciting to the finder, are not generally useful sources of archaeological information. They can be lost in any place where people walk, so finding one may not, in itself, denote an archaeological site. Similarly, small metal objects may just be evidence of ancient carelessness, although they can sometimes indicate a disturbed burial, particularly if human bones are also present.

The Sutton Hoo burial, excavated in 1939, was the richest find in Britain and a good example of how easily the past might have been lost. The barrows had been plundered, and this one had been tunneled into. Fortunately the robbers failed to locate the Saxon ship and its burial chamber in which the treasure lay (see pages 86–87). Burial mounds are a familiar sight in the landscape of many countries; often their form can indicate the period in which they were constructed.

Checking the Terrain

Fieldwalking enables archaeologists to compare the anomalies previously noted on maps or in aerial photographs with the appearance of the landscape itself. Slight undulations may be the remains of plowed-out barrows, ancient ditches or medieval villages. Variations in the color of the soil or the luxuriance of the vegetation, sudden changes in the line of hedgerows or field boundaries and curiously shaped bodies of water may also indicate the presence of archaeological features.

Sometimes the date of field boundaries can be determined by inspection on the ground. The way a wall is built may indicate how old it is. And it is possible to date hedgerows accurately by counting the number of different species of plants in a 32½-yard (30-m) stretch; a new species will colonize the hedge about every 100 years.

Walking the Streets

Plenty of information can be gained by the urban fieldworker versed in the nuances of changing architectural styles. Modifications made to a building are usually more obvious from the side or back, or inside, than from the front.

The layout of town or city streets frequently reflects elements of the original plan of the settlement, even if all or many of the buildings are relatively modern. A circular area among linear roads may once have been the bailey of a castle. Around a church, an area filled with a maze of houses without gardens is likely to represent later building over a medieval marketplace. A crack in the side of a house could be the result of subsidence that occurred because it was built over an infilled moat.

Urban reconstruction and maintenance offer opportunities for archaeologists. Trenches for drains or telephone cables, foundation holes, demolition projects and other such disturbances allow details of the past to be noted. However, sites revealed in these ways are usually glimpsed only briefly before they vanish underground again—or are destroyed completely, as is often the case—unless the developer is unusually sympathetic to archaeology and can postpone his work to allow further investigations. In an ideal world, all large-scale construction projects would be preceded by a detailed archaeological survey, using all the techniques available, to establish a record of what is likely to be destroyed. After an assessment, provision could then be made for the excavation of some of the more interesting sites. In some countries, such as the United States, such an assessment is now a legal requirement for government-funded projects.

The material collected by fieldwalkers is invaluable in providing as detailed a picture as possible of what lies underground. These pieces of pottery were gathered in 1984 from an Iron Age settlement at Kondrajanahalli, in South India, and consist mainly of diagnostic sherds—that is, ones such as base and rim sherds from which it is possible to determine the shape of the original vessels. There are also three other interesting pieces in the bottom row to the right: a grindstone and polished stone axe and, to their left, the knob of a pottery lid.

LOOKING MORE CLOSELY

Observations made while fieldwalking allow you to establish in general terms whether an area is archaeologically interesting. If it is, you will certainly want to explore further. First, however, a more detailed survey should be made, and some sort of site plan, drawn.

Any "bumps" or "hollows" you have discovered in the landscape should be carefully mapped so that their shape can be compared with known earthworks, possibly giving clues to their age and nature. With very little equipment, it is possible to make a quick but adequate record of such features.

At the simplest level, a freehand sketch plan will give a rough idea of the nature of the site. A rather more accurate method is to use a technique known as "offsetting" to draw a scale plan of landscape features (see Figures 1 and 2 on opposite page). This requires some basic items of surveyors' equipment, including ranging rods marked off in meters or feet (easy to make yourself from straight strips or poles of wood), metal or wooden pegs, several tape measures, and some balls of string.

Once all the measurements have been taken, a scale plan of the feature should be drawn.

After completing this plan, study the feature again to make sure that what you have drawn really resembles it. Record prominent landmarks such as buildings and field boundaries so that the plan can be correctly related to a map of the area. Photographs from different angles provide a valuable additional record.

A massive survey program was undertaken in the 1970s to investigate settlement patterns in the Valley of Mexico, around the three great centers of Cuicuilco (late centuries B.C.E. to c. 100 C.E.), Teotihuacán (1st millennium C.E.) and Tenochtitlán, the Aztec capital. In addition to locating villages and larger settlements, the team mapped the different environmental zones, assessing their suitability for agriculture and other economic activities, and the distribution of raw materials utilized by the people of the valley. Changes through time in the distribution of sites and exploitation of regions were noted and analyzed. This plan (opposite page) shows the situation at the height of the Teotihuacán Empire (see also page 71).

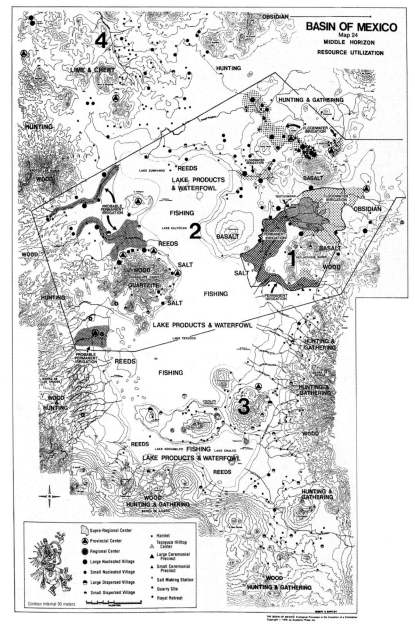

The Wider Picture

In some circumstances, a full-scale regional survey may be made. The growing appreciation of the importance of "off-site" archaeology (investigation of the whole landscape exploited in the past, not just settlements) means that such surveys are becoming more common, often in preference to excavation, which is both destructive and far more costly and time-consuming. Off-site archaeology is of particular relevance in the study of hunter-gatherer groups such as our early ancestors, since much of their time was spent in camps occupied for brief periods, rather than in year-round settlements. Investigation of the landscape through survey is likely to produce a far more balanced picture of their activities than concentration on an individual site. Similarly, when dealing with farming communities or city dwellers, a study of the landscape in which they lived is likely to reveal much that is of relevance, such as their agricultural field systems and meadows, and the sources of the raw materials that they used.

Once a thorough study of the surface remains in an area has been made, it is time to begin investigating what lies beneath the ground.

A baseline has been stretched across the site shown at top left, in preparation for taking offsets. The offset method is most useful on small sites such as this one. Tape measures are also used in a similar way to make plans of archaeological sites after excavation has begun.

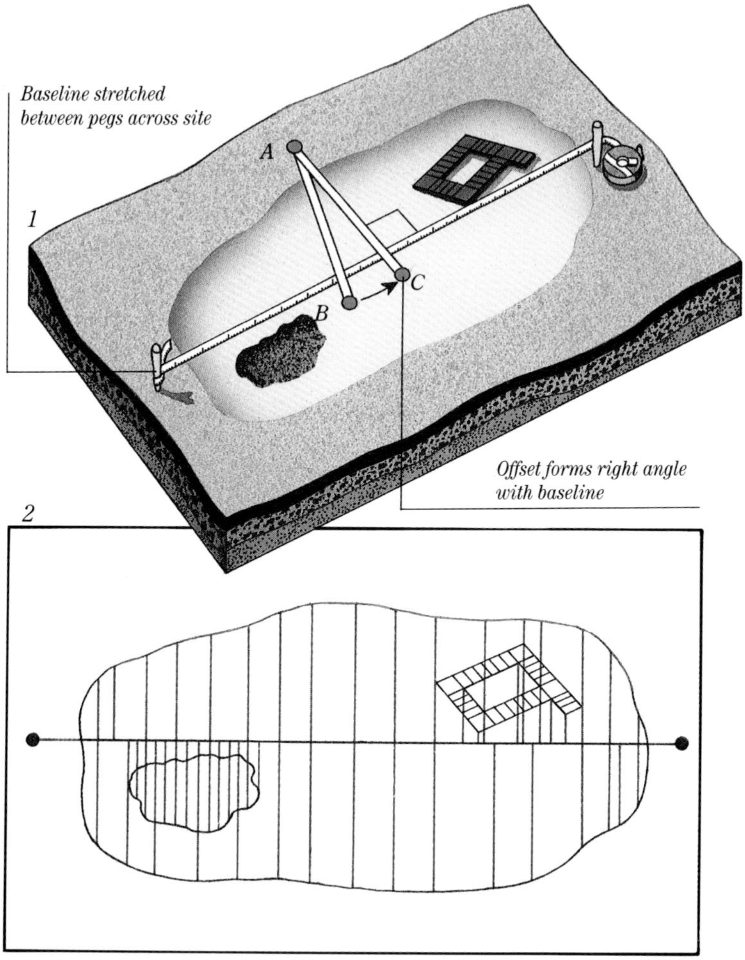

Offsetting is a quick and easy method of measuring a feature such as an earthwork in order to make a plan of it. A "baseline" is set out running along the major axis of the feature and a series of straight lines, or "offsets," are run out from the baseline to appropriate points along the edges of the feature, such as where the line of the edge changes direction. One person stands at the edge of the site (A), holding the tape; another stands at the baseline (B) and moves the other end of the tape until it forms a right angle with the baseline (C), that is, when the distance between A and the baseline is shortest. This measurement is then recorded on the plan. Offsets continue to be taken until there are enough points to produce an accurate outline of the feature. The technique is also used to make plans of small excavated areas, as in this example.

1 Baseline stretched between pegs across site

A

B

C

Offset forms right angle with baseline

2

GEOPHYSICAL SURVEY

Mechanical Aids

Many instruments, some originally developed for geophysics, can be used to help detect buried archaeological features. One category depends for its effectiveness on the fact that the electrical resistance of soil decreases if it is damp. Soil within filled-in pits or ditches retains moisture for longer periods than the earth around it does, while soil above solid stone structures, such as walls, dries out more quickly.

The electrical resistance of the soil is measured with a resistivity gauge, such as the Martin Clark meter, through probes inserted into the ground at regular intervals. A related survey technique relies on induced polarization, the physical phenomenon in which electromagnetic radiation waves are restricted to certain directions of vibration. The methods of measurement resemble those of the resistivity meter, and the results can be slightly better.

Buried features not only affect the electrical resistance of the soil, but they also produce small local variations in the strength of the Earth's magnetic field. For example, the magnetic susceptibility of pits and ditches filled with organic material is greater than that of the surrounding soil, while roads and walls have decreased magnetic susceptibility. The variations can be measured with a magnetometer, of which there are several types. They can also detect fired clay structures, such as hearths and kilns, and iron.

The most commonly used instrument is the proton magnetometer. However, it suffers background interference from electric trains and magnetic storms. This problem does not arise with the differential fluxgate gradiometer or with the proton gradiometer, which in any case is far less expensive than the other two.

Magnetic surveys are generally carried out over a previously laid out grid. They can be impeded by thick vegetation and cannot be performed at all in the vicinity of overhead cables, iron fences and built-up areas, or over igneous bedrock, so resistivity surveys have to be used in these situations. Resistivity is the more reliable of the two techniques for detecting stone structures and for tracing linear features, while magnetic surveys can more easily locate small isolated features such as pits and iron objects.

The results of such surveys should be plotted on a map of the site. One way is to draw the equivalent of contour lines linking all the points where similarly anomalous resistance or magnetic readings were obtained. Another is to use different densities of dots to denote different degrees of variation from the norm (*see illustration, page 54*).

The two main geophysical surveying instruments used for detecting buried objects—the resistivity meter and the magnetometer—are compared in the diagram at right. The black sections of the arrows represent an average background reading; diagonal stripes represent a stronger magnetic field or electrical resistance; vertical stripes indicate lower magnetism or resistance. In this example, the resistivity meter records only the pit and the wall, while the magnetometer also detects the iron ax and the hearth. Neither can pick up minor features such as the posthole.

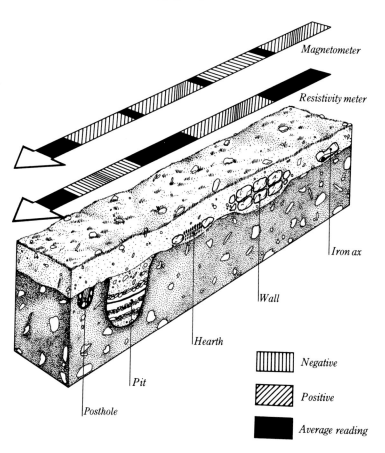

Magnetometer

Resistivity meter

Iron ax

Wall

Hearth

Pit

Posthole

	Negative
	Positive
	Average reading

Electromagnetic Devices

Electromagnetic devices, of which the simplest is the metal detector, are also helpful in detecting buried features. They identify magnetic anomalies and are a supplement to the magnetometer, but do not penetrate so deeply. The two electromagnetic devices that are most widely used in archaeology are the pulse induction meter and the soil conductivity meter.

A metal detector can be a handy survey instrument, giving quick general results. The irresponsible use of metal detectors has quite rightly been condemned by archaeologists and others; holes dug to retrieve often quite unexciting bits of metal not only remove archaeological objects from their context, but lay waste the surrounding archaeology too.

Unauthorized use of metal detectors on protected archaeological sites is illegal in many countries. Items found by people using metal detectors are unlikely to be the finder's legal property; they may belong by law to the owner of the land, or to the state, depending on national legislation.

Techniques on Trial

Advanced geophysical surveying techniques using neutron scattering or gamma rays have on occasion been tried by archaeologists, but the results have not been very satisfactory. Ground-penetrating radar seems more promising and has been used to map Etruscan tombs. Various types of echo-sounding are now in use; they have proved particularly useful in underwater reconnaissance. Sonic devices such as side-looking sonar have been employed to great effect in underwater prospecting, for example in the search for Henry VIII's long-lost warship *Mary Rose* (*see page 55*).

Simpler forms of echo-sounding include bosing (thumping the ground with a heavy object such as a wooden mallet, a lead-filled canister or even just a foot). Infilled ditches and pits should produce a more resonant sound than the surrounding undisturbed soil. Similar in principle to bosing is the standing wave technique, which has recently been successfully applied.

Dowsing—in which a hazel or other twig held above the ground is said to twitch in the presence of underground water or buried objects—is (from the author's limited experience of it) of debatable value in the detection of archaeological features.

Probing the Ground

Once an underground site has been located, further information can be obtained, at some destructive cost, by using a probe or an auger. The probe is a long metal rod with a T-bar handle, which is driven into the ground. The depth it reaches before encountering bedrock or an obstruction allows a profile to be obtained of buried structures, pits or ditches. An extension of this technique is to attach a small camera to the probe in order to photograph within buried structures such as tombs. By this means, information on their contents can be recovered without excavation. The auger is similar to the probe, but it has a corkscrew end that brings up small samples of soil.

Both devices risk damaging archaeological objects underground, and their use is therefore best confined to answering specific questions. For example, they can provide information on the depth and extent of features located by other means. An auger survey made across part of the Somerset Levels in southwest England successfully traced the course of the Abbott's Way, a late Neolithic wooden track now buried beneath peat.

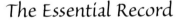

The Essential Record

Prospecting and field surveys are often carried out prior to an excavation. Not every archaeological feature of the landscape can be excavated in full, so in many cases the field survey is the only archaeological record of sites that may subsequently be destroyed. It is therefore vital that the results of these surveys are made generally available.

A brief report on what has been found should be offered to a local archaeological journal—or to a national one if the results are sufficiently interesting. At the same time, the complete details should be written into a separate, much longer report that, with the material collected, should be offered to some suitable public body for safekeeping and so that others may refer to it. The local museum is an obvious candidate, but in countries such as Britain where local government employs archaeologists to collate such material, the local government archaeologists may be more suitable recipients.

A soil sounding radar is a modern geophysical instrument that can detect archaeological remains buried under the ground by bouncing radio waves off them. The machine seen here, developed by the American Mike Gorman, was used in recent excavations at Sutton Hoo.

Painstaking preliminary research, drawing on the work of earlier investigators and on advanced technology, preceded two of the most romantic archaeological assignments to be undertaken in Britain in the last few decades. The first was at Cadbury Castle in Somerset, a spectacular Iron Age hillfort that since the 16th century had been identified with the fictional Camelot of King Arthur. The second led to the raising of the *Mary Rose,* a principal warship of Henry VIII's battlefleet, which sank in Portsmouth harbor on its maiden voyage, July 19, 1545.

The two investigations provide excellent examples of how modern archaeologists work in the field and the way in which their research puts flesh on the bones of history. They also demonstrate quite clearly that there is no real substitute for excavation.

The Fortress of Cadbury

John Leland, the king's antiquary, first linked Cadbury Castle to Camelot in 1542, apparently drawing on a strong local tradition connecting the hillfort with King Arthur. Little evidence was found to support such a link until fieldwalking in the 1950s yielded a few sherds of the imported wares characteristic of the late 5th and 6th centuries C.E. The finds rekindled interest in Cadbury, and in the 1960s Professor Leslie Alcock began excavations.

An archaeological survey of Cadbury Castle took place in the late 1960s. Here we see a detailed study of one area. The geophysical survey (A), done by testing for differences in soil magnetism and electrical resistance, indicated the possible presence of buried features. When comparing this with a diagram of what the actual excavation later revealed (B), the value of the technique is obvious. However, it is also apparent that not all features are revealed by geophysical survey and that the full interpretation (C) of the nature of the structures depends on excavation.

CADBURY CASTLE
AREA EFG

PROTON MAGNETOMETER
SOIL CONDUCTIVITY METER
GEOPHYSICAL SURVEY **A**

EXCAVATED FEATURES **B**

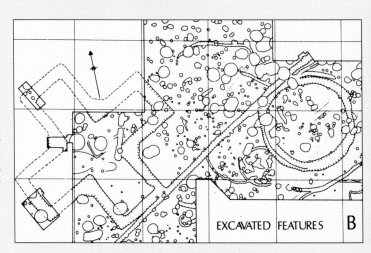

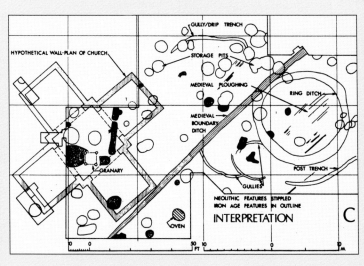

GULLY/DRIP TRENCH
STORAGE PITS
HYPOTHETICAL WALL-PLAN OF CHURCH
MEDIEVAL PLOUGHING
RING DITCH
MEDIEVAL BOUNDARY DITCH
POST TRENCH
GRANARY
GULLIES
OVEN
NEOLITHIC FEATURES STIPPLED
IRON AGE FEATURES IN OUTLINE
INTERPRETATION **C**

One of his objectives was to excavate a portion of the massive defenses to establish whether they had been strengthened or modified in Arthurian times. He also hoped to discover Arthurian structures. However, the area within the defenses was large, amounting to some 18 acres (7.2 ha), and the problem was to decide where promising remains might lie. Aerial photos of crop marks were not good enough for detailed mapping.

So a geophysical survey of the site was carried out, using magnetometers and electromagnetic instruments, including the soil conductivity meter. Results were plotted by the dot density method.

In 1967, a promising area was excavated. The results were most interesting. The large-scale features, including wide postholes, had shown up in the survey. But smaller details such as stake holes had not. The Arthurian-period timbered hall discovered in 1968 had only shallow foundations, and it was due more to good fortune than to the survey that it was found at all.

The comparison between what the survey showed and the results of actual excavation made it clear that while geophysical surveys may reveal the overall pattern of subsurface features, the relationships between those features cannot be determined without excavation. A series of parallel and transverse lines plotted in the survey were at first tentatively identified as rectangular halls. Excavation showed they were, in reality, a field ditch, a line of pits and part of the walls of an unexpected late Saxon cruciform church. (See pages 68–69.)

Search for the Mary Rose

As Henry VIII's fleet was preparing to set sail from Portsmouth, England, to do battle with the French, the Mary Rose heeled over and sank. Attempts in the following years to raise her failed. The wreck remained visible for some time but gradually became buried by silt on the seabed.

In 1836, John and Charles Deane, pioneer divers and marine salvage experts, encountered portions of the Mary Rose that were briefly exposed. They salvaged some guns and other material, but subsequently the wreck was again lost to view and its location forgotten.

In 1965, however, members of the British Subaqua Club led by the journalist Alexander MacKee, with the archaeologist Margaret Rule, renewed the search. Using a naval chart of 1841 marking the spot where the Deanes had discovered the Mary Rose, they dove and prospected with a magnetic compass and an underwater magnetometer. Disappointing results made it seem likely that the ship was too deeply buried to be detected by ordinary means.

In 1967, however, the searchers enlisted the help of Professor Harold Edgerton of the Massachusetts Institute of Technology, who conducted a survey using a sonar sidescanner and a sonic "pinger" device. These instruments detected an anomaly beneath the seabed in the search area and a slight mound above it. The following year two high-technology sub-bottom profilers were used to cross-check the site. The results were encouraging enough for excavation to begin in 1969 of what is now one of the most famous wrecks ever investigated (see page 101).

October 11, 1982, saw the culmination of years of research and a major triumph for archaeology: The Tudor warship Mary Rose (shown above) was lifted out of the waters of the Solent, near Portsmouth, where it lay buried for over four centuries. The ship is sandwiched between a carefully designed 150-ton cradle and a 60-ton lifting frame, supported by three legs (a fourth had already been removed). The ship had to drain slowly, and although the first timbers were visible at 9:03 A.M., the entire structure did not emerge until late that afternoon. Repairs were then carried out on the lifting frame and it didn't reach the harbor until 10:00 P.M.

One of the greatest urban excavations of this century took place in the 1970s, at York, England. These uncovered the remains of a Viking town, Jorvik, that flourished here about 1,000 years ago.

PART

3

EXCAVATION

THE UNDERGROUND WORLD

To understand the purpose of archaeology and archaeologists, we must project ourselves back in time, imagining the things that people are likely to have done and the traces these things will have left behind.

Burials, for instance, generally leave distinctive signs in or on the ground. In the distant past, when a grave was dug, the body buried in it was often clothed and wearing jewelry (coffins were less frequent), while around the corpse were placed a few personal possessions and other tokens for life in the afterworld. When such a grave is investigated, the archaeologist is likely to find the skeleton, jewelry (if present) and perhaps some trace of the clothes in which the corpse was buried.

There will also be the remains of grave offerings. Pieces of pottery and stone and metal tools generally survive, as do animal bones, the remains perhaps of an offering to ensure that the deceased had food for the next world.

Externally, the grave itself is usually distinguishable; the disturbed soil of what archaeologists term the grave fill normally looks different from the undisturbed soil around it. Graves are often further marked by something erected above them, from a simple headstone to the impressive barrows of antiquity.

A Wealth of Buildings

The diverse structures that peoples of all kinds have built for themselves, their animals or their gods offer a wealth of material. Stone buildings generally provide the most substantial remains. This may be simply a foundation or as much as a few courses of their walls.

Floors, too, are important. Stone structures often have well-made floors, like Roman mosaic pavements. Less imposing buildings may have floors of beaten earth, or be covered with clay or some other durable material.

Brick structures are reasonably long-lasting, though mud walls are quite difficult for the archaeologist to detect. As they are constructed of bricks made from local clay, they are often virtually indistinguishable from the surrounding earth. Spraying the area with water, however, may reveal mud bricks more clearly.

Wooden structures leave varying traces. Where the roof was supported by substantial posts, these were generally set into large postholes. Though the timbers may have long since decayed, the postholes should remain, filled with packing material that often included stones. In many instances, the soil that accumulated when the post rotted differs in appearance, so a "ghost" of the post is visible.

Other wooden structures were built using closely packed, slender uprights driven only a short way into the ground. These may remain as stakeholes, small holes whose fill often contrasts with the surrounding soil. The shallowness of such foundations means that, on a site that has been disturbed by plowing, for instance, they are unlikely to survive. The same is even more true of the remains of timber-framed structures, which were built entirely above ground with no foundations. However, with care and in favorable circumstances, their outlines may be detected by seeing how they have compacted the soil beneath them.

Where structures have left little or no detectable trace, an outline may be discovered by making a careful study of how artifacts and other remains are distributed. Establishing details of the distribution of domestic equipment—or even something as mundane as where refuse was deposited—can reveal the position of both outer walls and internal partitions.

The Purpose of Pits

Many early excavators supposed that prehistoric people often lived underground, so pits were frequently identified as "pit houses." However, most

underground structure was retained as a holy *kiva*, or "shrine."

Defending the Home

Defensive works surrounding individual houses or whole settlements were frequently composed of banks and ditches, as well as of stone or wooden walls. The impressive effects that can be achieved simply by enhancing naturally occurring features with artificial banks and ditches can be seen clearly in the many hillforts of Europe, of which Maiden Castle in southwest England is a superb example.

Time has softened the contours of these forts. The ditches have been partly filled with soil. Like many of the features already mentioned, ditches can be distinguished because their fill contrasts with the surrounding soil.

Banks seldom vanish entirely but remain as a low bump. Well-preserved examples may yield traces of a superstructure, in the form of postholes and stakeholes. Other ramparts combined stone and wood in their construction in a variety of ways, among them the timber-laced *murus gallicus* that presented such an obstacle to Julius Caesar in his conquest of Gaul.

A number of similar timber-laced ramparts have been partially preserved, particularly in Scotland, as "vitrified forts." Here, nature has come to the aid of archaeologists; the timber was destroyed in fires fanned by strong winds to such a temperature that the stonework was melted and transformed into a substance that resembles glass in appearance.

Stone fortifications, like stone-house walls, stand the ravages of time better than timber ones do, and it is not unusual to recover several of their courses, assuming they have had only the forces of nature to contend with. In many instances, both domestic and defensive walls have been exploited by later peoples as a convenient quarry for building materials. When stone or brick has been removed, the former presence of the wall may be indicated by a "robber trench."

were actually used for storage or rubbish disposal. Their sites stand out clearly in contrast to undisturbed surrounding soil.

Saxon *grubenhauser* (grub huts)—sub-rectangular hollows in the ground found in England and Germanic Europe—were for a long time accepted as pit dwellings. Now, however, it is thought that the hollow was actually an underground cellar or airspace, covered by the plank floor of an aboveground hut.

For true pit dwellings, we have to turn to the southwest United States. Here, the ancestors of the builders of great multistoried pueblos lived in semisubterranean houses with wooden superstructures. When the brick pueblos were built, the

This striking mosaic comes from Cirencester in the English Midlands, site of the ancient Roman town of Corinium, second in size only to London. The town was prosperous and yielded many finds, including examples of some of the best mosaics of the 2nd century C.E., of which this, from a substantial town house, is just one. This is, in fact, a section of a large mosaic depicting the seasons and shows Dionysus, the god of wine, in the guise of Autumn. It was made entirely from local stone: brick and tile (red), limestone (cream and white), sandstone (earth colors) and blue lias, and was crudely repaired in later Roman times. Because the mosaics are composed of hard material and lay protected some 1–2 yards (1–2 m) below ground they are exceptionally well preserved.

Maiden Castle, in Dorset, England, was fortified with bank and ditch ramparts around 700 B.C.E. The area enclosed by the hillfort was greatly expanded and the ramparts made more massive around 450 B.C.E. when it became the main center for its region. The gateway defenses were greatly elaborated, making attack difficult. In 43 C.E. it was taken by the Roman general Vespasian.

CLUES FROM THE CONTEXT

The traces of standing structures and holes in the ground together represent a large proportion of what the excavator will encounter on-site. But there are also associated material remains that in themselves may be most informative. Distinctive artifacts provide archaeologists with much of the evidence they will need for dating, and details about technology, trade and other aspects of daily life.

Another reason for the importance of material remains is perhaps less immediately obvious. It lies in the information to be obtained from the relationship between a find and its context. We have already seen that the overall distribution of material on a site can provide outlines of structures that have since vanished. Looking in more detail at how the material was actually distributed, we may hope to discover additional information about the function of particular areas within the site or within buildings on it.

Because context is so vitally significant to archaeologists, they bitterly resent destruction wrought by treasure-hunters who disturb archaeological sites. It is not, as many imagine, purely a spoilsport attitude. The removal of an object from its context means that all the information it could have yielded about that context has been lost, and the full significance of the object may never be understood.

Reading the Signs

A large jar found during excavation could have been made for one of many purposes. Its context suggests what the specific one might have been. For example, if it was discovered with several others of similar proportions in an area obviously set aside for them, it would seem likely that it was used for storage. If careful excavation reveals pollen or other plant remains, those may lend support to the conjecture.

Further support for this view would be provided if the jars were found close to the area set aside for cooking. That area could be indicated by the presence of a hearth and in some cases by more complicated cooking facilities. Around the hearth may be grouped other pieces of kitchen equipment, particularly coarse pottery vessels, their bases blackened from frequent exposure to the fire.

Another area of the house may contain a pair of small postholes, not apparently integral to the stability of the building. What might they represent? If, nearby, a number of curious triangular clay objects with a hole in the top corner is discovered, these may well be loom weights. The postholes are therefore likely to be those from the frame of an upright loom.

A find of stone or metal instruments for scraping skins, on the other hand, might lead us to identify the postholes as the remains of the uprights from a frame on which animal skins were stretched to cure. Other possibilities include that of a meat-drying rack.

Whatever the interpretation, meticulous study of associated material is vital in helping to formulate it. Thus the information that can be recovered separately from structural remains and from artifacts and other material evidence is greatly enhanced by careful observation of the relationships between them.

Sifting the Soil

Much of what the archaeologist excavates can broadly be termed "structural"—walls and floors, postholes and pits, banks and ditches. But the surrounding soil is equally important. Each layer on a site, down to the bedrock, tells something about the human activities that have taken place there in the past, or, indeed, the lack of them.

Some of the layers are natural accumulations, formed by the decay of vegetation and of any organic materials left by man, or deposits of soil introduced by wind, water or erosion. Others are human-made, such as a layer of rubble or debris where inhabitants of a settlement have razed old structures to create a flat ground surface on which to rebuild. Sites occupied at one time by settlements may become the fields or gardens of succeeding generations, in which a human-induced natural soil builds up.

In all but the earliest sites, the bedrock marks the limit of archaeological material. When investigating the extremely remote past, archaeologists rely heavily on the processes of geological upheaval to reveal the evidence that interests them. That is one of the main reasons so many early Paleolithic sites are known in the Great Rift Valley of Africa, where disturbances to Earth's crust have resulted in the exposure of enormous blocks of land once buried many tens of yards (meters) below the ground.

One of the joys of excavation is the unique experience each site offers. Houses and streets, wells and rubbish pits, roads and fortifications, fields and animal enclosures, cemeteries and megaliths—the variety of evidence of human activities is infinite.

This reconstruction of the vertical excavation of a 4th-century Roman workshop in England shows the archaeological evidence obtained from each level. The site, near Bristol, had been abandoned for some 1,500 years, although on-site evidence suggested that it had been dug into once since then, perhaps by people searching for building stone. Throughout the process of excavation, careful checks are made on the stratigraphy of the site as the various layers of soil are removed. In this, as with most digs, the bedrock marks the downward limit of investigation. Some very early sites, however, may be in or under bedrock, as a result of geological changes since they were occupied.

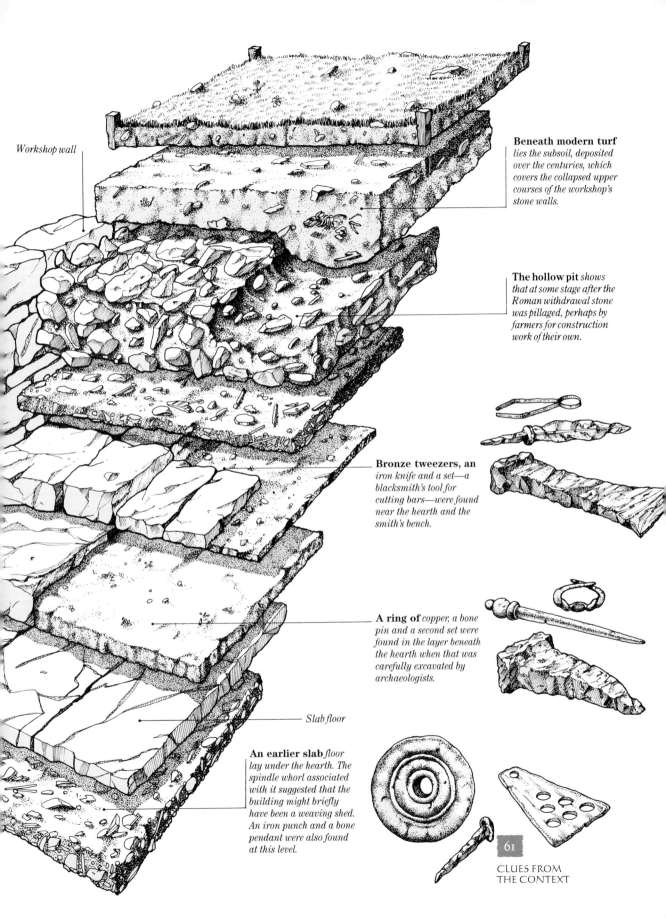

Workshop wall

Beneath modern turf *lies the subsoil, deposited over the centuries, which covers the collapsed upper courses of the workshop's stone walls.*

The hollow pit *shows that at some stage after the Roman withdrawal stone was pillaged, perhaps by farmers for construction work of their own.*

Bronze tweezers, an *iron knife and a set—a blacksmith's tool for cutting bars—were found near the hearth and the smith's bench.*

A ring of *copper, a bone pin and a second set were found in the layer beneath the hearth when that was carefully excavated by archaeologists.*

Slab floor

An earlier slab *floor lay under the hearth. The spindle whorl associated with it suggested that the building might briefly have been a weaving shed. An iron punch and a bone pendant were also found at this level.*

61

CLUES FROM
THE CONTEXT

TO DIG OR NOT TO DIG?

Why do archaeologists excavate sites? In the 19th century the answer would have been a simple, relatively straightforward one: to recover artifacts and structures, the relics of past ages. Gradually, however, the business of excavation became more skillful and its objectives more sophisticated; a mid-20th century archaeologist might well have said that he or she dug to discover the relationships between the relics of the past as much as to discover the actual relics themselves and to find out what happened and when.

Today's archaeologists, building on the foundations laid by their predecessors, will probably tell you that they dig to answer specific questions about the past. This, they will argue, requires a more thorough approach to excavation than ever before. An extreme exponent of this viewpoint will maintain that sites should be excavated only if they can be expected to answer specific questions of interest to the archaeological community.

At the opposite extreme, there are archaeologists who deplore any excavation except on threatened sites. In the frequently quoted words of Sir Mortimer Wheeler, "excavation is destruction," and the rescue excavation lobby argues that there is no justification for digging any site that is not going to be disturbed or destroyed anyway. Save other sites for future archaeologists whose techniques will be better, they say.

Who is right—the research excavator or the rescuer? Are the viewpoints indeed mutually exclusive? Surely not. The answer must lie in some compromise between the two extremes.

The Threat of Progress

Archaeological sites are today threatened to an unprecedented extent. The rate of rural and urban development and expansion is increasing due both to technological innovations and to social demands. Public funding of archaeological work has increased in many countries in an attempt to deal with this, but inevitably there are limits, even when state funds are supplemented by private generosity. Consequently, the resources can never hope to match the threat, and inevitably, some sites will be destroyed without record.

Archaeology may even be of use to contemporary planners, for it may reveal hazards below ground that the developer will be grateful to avoid. A prior knowledge of important and interesting sites may also be used to argue for the rerouting of roads or modifications in the layout of structures, to allow these sites to be preserved for the public to see. In the United States an assessment of the threat to archaeology is mandatory in advance of any construction program for which a federal permit is required. In England, developers are required to fund preliminary archaeological investigations of the areas they will be developing. In some countries, known sites are listed and given some official protection. As a result, the archaeological landscape in many countries is being intensively explored and much of it conserved.

The Unknown Factors

Another argument in favor of well-planned rescue excavations is that the contents of a site can never be entirely predicted in advance. If they could, what would be the point of excavating it?

The research archaeologist may come to his or her site with a lot of well-formulated questions about the Neolithic henge noted from an aerial photograph. But what about the unexpected Iron Age temple or the Saxon wooden church uncovered above the henge? The archaeologist is not justified in digging through those just because they are outside the immediate area of interest. It is the archaeologist's duty to excavate what he or she finds, to the best of his or her ability within the budget available, because the evidence may be of vital interest to colleagues studying the Iron Age or the Saxons. In this sense, there is no such thing as a strictly research excavation, because rescuing unwanted evidence from archaeological destruction becomes almost inevitable.

Despite the many arguments in favor of concentrating available resources on sites whose destruction is imminent, there is some justification for conducting research excavations. Certain questions can be answered only by excavating particular sites that are not threatened. Some archaeologists also believe that proper training of excavators and the advancement of excavation techniques can be satisfactorily achieved only in the unhurried atmosphere of a research excavation.

These can be extremely long-term projects. For example, the slow and meticulous open-plan excavations at Wroxeter, a Roman city in Shropshire, central England, have resulted in the discovery of traces of small timber buildings that have probably been missed on many similar sites dug at greater speed. At this rate, however, it would have taken 200 years to completely excavate Wroxeter.

RESCUING YORK

In the mid-1960s, it was recommended that inner and outer urban highways should be built around the ancient English city of York to cope with traffic problems. The threat to York's archaeology posed by the inner-city highway was obvious. The results of a preliminary investigation into its implications convinced the British government to provide full financial backing for an archaeological unit to excavate affected areas of the city.
There were also generous private contributions of time and money, and various developers made planning modifications.

York was an important settlement in Roman times, when it consisted of a legionary fortress and a civilian settlement, on opposite sides of the river Ouse. In the Viking era, it was a substantial and prosperous town, but in the later Middle Ages it declined.

Results of the York Archaeological Trust's first year of work lived up to the highest expectations. Excavation of the St. Mary's Hospital site revealed details of its evolution over the centuries from a church to a hospital for aged chaplains and finally to a school. In the low-lying Lloyd's Bank site, waterlogged Viking leatherworkers' houses were uncovered, their plank walls and floors excellently preserved, along with a wealth of fascinating organic remains.

Most exciting was the chance discovery of the remains of a Roman bathhouse, complete with a monumental sewer. Development of this site could be halted only briefly, so the archaeologists spent a frantic two weeks digging. The bathhouse was encased in the development, but the sewer can still be visited with permission.

The work of the York Archaeological Trust has gone from strength to strength. From the public viewpoint at least, the culmination was the opening of a living museum of Viking York, complete with authentic noises and smells.

Excavations at Coppergate, York (far left), in the late 1970s and early 1980s, uncovered a wealth of remains from Viking times. The site was discovered when the vaults of a bank were being deepened. A remarkably well preserved 8th-century Anglo-Saxon helmet (bottom, far left), known as the Coppergate Helmet, was among the remains.

Twenty years of excavation at York have revealed evidence of the city's long and distinguished history, often exceptionally well preserved due to waterlogging. Finds ranged from a medieval cemetery (below) and Viking tanneries to this sewer (above), a fine example of Roman engineering. From this were recovered the remains of sewer flies where two lavatories drained into the sewer and game pieces washed into it after being dropped in the bathhouse.

SELECTING THE SITE

We have already looked at some of the priorities in excavation and at the advantages of well-planned rescue excavations. In a region where a number of sites are likely to be destroyed in the near future, further decisions have to be made about which are to be excavated. The choice may involve several factors, which sometimes conflict.

Ideally, whatever the immediate priorities in selecting sites in an area, in the long term an attempt should be made to balance the investigations between sites of all periods and types—from Paleolithic to medieval or later, and including cemeteries, settlements, industrial and religious locations, and so forth. Another consideration is the relative scarcity of sites: Cases can be made for selecting both the most common types, which should give a representative picture of everyday life, and the rare or unique ones, which may have held key positions in the societies to which they belonged. Both the peasant's hut and Stonehenge deserve investigation.

The excavator may also be called upon to decide whether to excavate a few sites thoroughly, small parts of many sites, or larger areas of fewer. Such decisions will vary according to factors such as the state of local research, convenience and practicability.

Initial Considerations

Unlike our antiquarian forebears with their "speed is of the essence" approach, modern excavators do not undertake their task lightly. The work apparently entailed in digging a site is only a fraction of what is actually involved.

In addition to the obvious jobs of clearing, excavating, recording and backfilling a site, with all the attendant activities, there are many other things to do. All the material and information recovered has to be analyzed, often work for specialists in many fields. Site plans and sections need to be redrawn and labeled. The finds have to be drawn and many of them conserved. A report must be written up on everything found and what it may mean. Estimates of the effort involved range from an optimistic assessment that it will be equal to that of the excavation itself, to a probably more realistic one of four or five times as much. Excavators have to take this into consideration when they calculate the money they will require, the time entailed and any specialist assistance required. Planning for the report is essential, for unpublished sites are information lost and valuable funds wasted.

Funding for excavation may come from a variety of sources. Many countries have a state archaeological body that sponsors or organizes excavations. Frequently, local authorities also fund archaeological work by employing full-time archaeologists on their staff. Ad hoc teams may be assembled for specific projects, which may be funded either by public money or through some form of private sponsorship.

Developers often contribute generously to the cost of excavating sites in the areas they intend to develop. Other major sources of financial support are university archaeological departments, whose students participate in the excavations and gain on-site training, and privately or publicly sponsored trusts and research bodies, including a number of overseas schools and missions. Museums also provide money for many excavations, as they have done in the past, though today their aims are more than simply the collection of exhibitable material.

Permission to Dig

The prospective excavator must also obtain permission to undertake an excavation. Sometimes this involves negotiations only with the landowner and any tenants; in that case, approval will depend on agreements about compensation for the loss of crops, arrangements for access to the site, time limits for the excavation

An archaeological expedition from the University of Chicago's Oriental Institute prepares to excavate a site at Nippur in Iraq. The expedition director (at front) is supported by a team of specialists that includes a draftsperson, a surveyor, a photographer, a conservator and a finds assistant. Among the support team is a large number of Iraqis—some of them are professional laborers, descendants of workmen once employed by the great pioneer archaeologists.

work and arrangements for restoring the site to its preexcavation state. In many countries, however, all archaeological sites are regarded as the property of the nation, and official permission must be obtained from the government or other authorities.

The destination of material found during the excavation must also be agreed upon. In Britain, all finds, with the exception of gold and silver, automatically belong to the landowner, but this person is often willing to present most to a museum or at least to permit archaeologists to study them.

Laws vary considerably, and in many countries all archaeological finds are state property. This may mean that the archaeologist working abroad will have to make special arrangements to export material for a limited period for examination or to import specialists to study it in situ.

Picking the Team

Once financial support and permission for excavation have been secured, the next priority is to choose the people to do the job. A small excavation presenting no special problems will probably consist of the director and a handful of volunteers. At the opposite end of the scale, an excavation team may include a whole hierarchy of assistants and supervisors, as well as the diggers and a host of specialists, such as photographers, draftsmen and -women, conservators, finds assistants, surveyors, analysts of pollen, seeds, bones and soil, not to mention the cooks, camp commandants, night guards and even "housekeepers."

The numbers involved in the average excavation will be somewhere in between these two extremes. The director will be supported by a number of experienced assistants or supervisors, who will watch the day-to-day running of different areas of the site and who will probably do all the planning, photography and surveying. Some of these supervisors may have specialist knowledge of particular categories of evidence, and they can advise on what material should be recovered and how. By excavating certain areas themselves, they can often note details that might be missed by less-skilled diggers. A finds assistant is also likely to be included in the team, supervising the washing of pottery and other material, executing "first aid" conservation and recording the finds.

On every site, however, ordinary diggers will be found. Despite their ubiquity, they belong to a very varied species. The most common varieties in America and Europe include university students (not necessarily of archaeology) looking for an interesting and worthwhile vacation, or just addicted to digging. Others are interested amateurs, often available only on the weekends, but giving freely and generously of whatever time they have available.

In parts of Europe and increasingly in Asia and Africa, work may also be undertaken by paid laborers, often in large numbers. Generally these are local people who are interested in supplementing their income, but in some places, notably countries with a long archaeological tradition, such as Egypt and Iraq, these laborers often possess the skill and expertise of hereditary craftspeople.

Finally, many Western excavations include specimens of that curious subspecies, the itinerant digger. Bronzed and rheumatic, with clothes old and much mended, he or she has probably been digging since childhood. On leaving school or university, they have decided to spend some time on archaeological expeditions before embarking on a permanent career. When all the summer volunteers have gone home, they continue moving from dig to dig. Poorly paid, often surviving in conditions of extreme hardship, itinerant diggers provide the main labor force for winter excavations. Some will end up in full-time archaeological employment, with more comfortable winter work indoors; others will become disillusioned or physically wrecked and will turn to different work. As a rule, few itinerant diggers last many years on the hard grind of "the circuit."

WHAT KIND OF HOLE?

Excavation lays bare two dimensions of the past, the horizontal one and the vertical one. Horizontal excavation reveals the site as it was at a given time—the array of houses with their furnishings, rubbish pits, the defenses of the settlement, the arrangements for keeping animals, the areas assigned to other activities, such as crafts and administration.

The vertical dimension shows the sequence of changes within the site and the relationship of one period to those before and after it, as revealed by the stratigraphy of the various vertical sections.

The Vertical Approach

During the earlier decades of the 20th century, when archaeology was very much concerned with chronology, excavation techniques concentrated on revealing the vertical dimension.

The best-known method was Sir Mortimer Wheeler's box, or grid, system. This involved dividing the site into squares of a given size. These squares were then excavated, leaving narrower unexcavated strips, termed "baulks," between them, in which cross sections were preserved.

Although this method gives excellent vertical control, its modern opponents argue that it largely forfeits an appreciation of the horizontal dimension of the site. To some extent, this is

restored when the baulks are removed and the final plans of each layer or phase are studied. But because the evidence from each phase has never been viewed or photographed in toto, some understanding is inevitably lost and may result in some aspects of the site being misunderstood.

The Horizontal Approach

Opponents of vertically oriented methods advocate open area excavations—uncovering the site layer by layer. The technique has been particularly successful for shallow sites and for those where the horizontal picture is more important, for example, at Paleolithic or Mesolithic sites, where structural remains are rare.

Modern recording techniques ensure that the vertical dimension is recorded on paper, but it is never seen or photographed in actuality. This may be less of a disadvantage than the lack of total horizontal photographs in the rival methods, but it nevertheless may result in some aspects of the site being misunderstood.

Making the Choice

Clearly, no method can be said categorically to be the right way to dig in every case. The merits of each must be assessed, according to the site and the circumstances.

The importance of the vertical record for dating is demonstrated in this excavation of a posthole. In the past a hole (top right) was dug and a post set into it. The hole was then backfilled using the soil that had previously been removed. This contained some potsherds dated around 1300 C.E., suggesting a date for the posthole. However, the presence at the bottom of the posthole of a coin dated 1520 shows that the post was erected no earlier than this date and that the potsherds come from the soil disturbed when the posthole was dug. A second coin, dating from 1600, gives the earliest date for the disappearance of the structure.

BELOW LEFT: *In a grid* excavation, square areas are first dug out of the site, leaving "baulks" standing between them as a record of the vertical aspect. Wooden pegs at the corners of the boxes are reference points for surveying.

BELOW RIGHT: *Later, the baulks* are removed to reveal the deposits that lie below them, in this case part of a wall. The grid method of excavation is no longer commonly used.

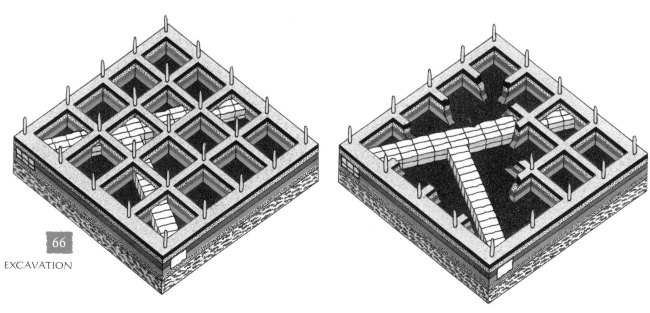

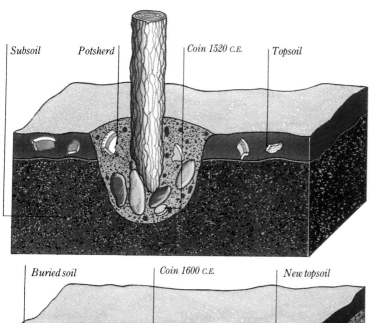

Subsoil | Potsherd | Coin 1520 C.E. | Topsoil

Buried soil | Coin 1600 C.E. | New topsoil

Often, there may be a compromise; perhaps open area excavation in a number of large trenches, whose walls preserve a visible record of the overall stratigraphy.

Laying Out the Site

Once a site has been selected and an excavation strategy decided on, the next step is usually to draw a contour survey (earthwork plan) to show in detail the topography before the first earth is removed. The height of the ground is measured at regular intervals across the site, using a level or a theodolite, and the readings are plotted on a plan that, like a map with contours above sea level, has lines joining the pieces of ground at the same heights.

The next stage is to establish a baseline from which the site is divided up into squares or rectangles, or whatever subdivisions seem appropriate—the layout. That is superimposed on the plan of the site and used in recording progress and finds. In the grid system of excavation, the baulks between each area dug become a physical reflection of the layout, but in open area excavation the boundaries between the subdivisions are hypothetical.

Whatever the excavation technique used, part of the layout must lie outside the excavation, to provide fixed reference points that cannot be disturbed. Markers on the site itself may be knocked and shifted during the digging, and it is vital to have some means of reestablishing their positions if that happens.

BELOW LEFT: **Narrow trench excavation** is particularly useful when it comes to excavating defensive banks, ditches and walls. In such cases, the sequence of construction is of particular interest.

BELOW RIGHT: **Open area excavation**, which involves uncovering the site layer by layer, is the method most commonly used today by archaeologists. Although the vertical picture is lost in the process, it can be recorded as the excavation proceeds.

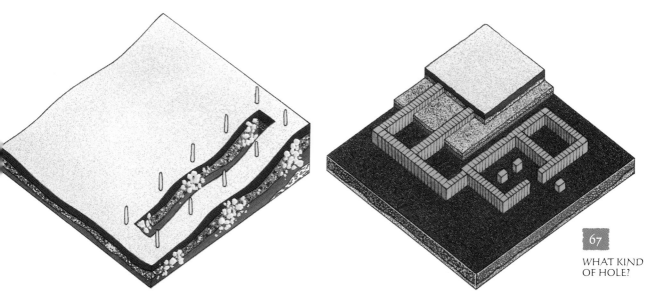

WHAT KIND
OF HOLE?

The excavations at Cadbury Castle (*see pages 54–55*) were primarily designed to test the possibility of early 6th-century C.E. "Arthurian" occupation, although evidence from other periods was also exposed and studied with equal care. The immense size of the interior, 18 acres (7.5 ha), precluded its complete excavation. Therefore, in 1966, the first season, a contour survey was made to assess which parts of the interior might have been most suitable for building. Three trial trenches were excavated, in the three main zones in which settlement seemed possible.

Below the Ramparts

In 1967, the team began investigating the ramparts. The excavation of the steep outer banks was a major undertaking, but the results were disappointing. Although they had clearly been built in several phases, there was little associated material to date these phases.

The innermost rampart was likely to be the most complex, so work started with the cutting of a machine trench across it. This machine trench was followed by a parallel hand-dug trench, 33 feet (10 m) wide. The topmost latest defense was the mortared wall of Ethelred; the third, a late Iron Age bank rebuilt to defend the hill for the last stand against the Romans—the massacred bodies of the valiant defenders were discovered later, in the 1970 excavation of the southwest gateway. Between these two was a structure dubbed the "Stony Bank." Investigations between 1967 and 1970 showed this to belong to Arthurian times. A coin built into it indicated that the structure could date from no earlier than the 5th century C.E. A cobbled road leading into the southwest gateway incorporated a 6th-century brooch, again providing a date for the Stony Bank defenses.

Excavation uncovered the face of this rampart, which was a dry-stone wall with regular gaps where upright and horizontal cross timbers had once been placed. The gateway itself had also been of timber. Dark stains showed where the massive posts supporting this had decayed.

This plan of the Cadbury site (below) shows excavations made between 1966 and 1970. First, three trial trenches were dug in the areas where settlement seemed most likely. Trenches were then cut across the ramparts, revealing the "Stony Bank" defenses and the southwest gateway. Several trenches were also dug in the interior.

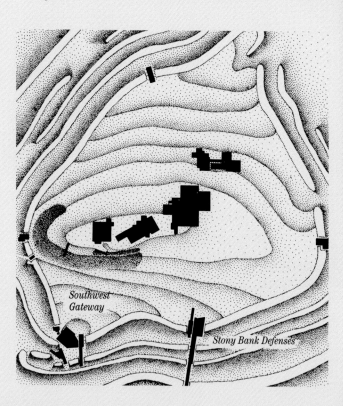

Southwest Gateway

Stony Bank Defenses

Inside the Walls

Several trenches were dug in the interior, mainly following indications of major structures from a preliminary geophysical survey. In one of these, the features uncovered included a narrow foundation trench containing a row of small postholes. Among the earth and gravel packed around these posts were two sherds of Tintagel ware, the distinctive late 5th-/early 6th-century imported pottery that had served as major dating evidence on other Arthurian period sites. The unabraded condition of these sherds indicated that they could be used to date the construction of this building closely.

The trench containing the wall was selectively enlarged to include the predicted extent of the structure, without success. So it was decided to remove the plow soil mechanically over a much wider area, a strip 16 feet (5 m) wide by 150 feet (45 m) long. Numerous features were exposed—postholes, pits, gullies and wall trenches of several periods. To pick out those that might belong to the Arthurian structure, the associated material from each had to be examined carefully and dated. After this the characteristics of the individual postholes, such as their depth and width, had to be examined to see which might belong together.

Eventually it was established that a line of postholes belonged to the 6th-century building; they ran at right angles to the original wall, which turned out to be an internal partition. Extension of the area under excavation revealed the rest of the structure, a hall more than 60 feet by 30 feet (18 m by 9 m).

Arthur's Seat?

Almost all defended hill settlements of the immediate post-Roman epoch were quite small, probably the strongholds of individual kings and their warbands. The topography of Cadbury Castle would have lent itself to building defenses around a similarly small area. The fact that a much larger area was enclosed, with considerable effort, suggests Cadbury was intended to house a much larger group—an army rather than a warband.

Thus, though the connection with Arthur can never be proved, Cadbury's location and the nature of its defenses make it a reasonable presumption that it could have served as the base for the British army that took the field against the Saxons and defeated them at the battle of Mount Badon.

A machine-cut trench (center) across the innermost rampart provided a useful picture of the stratigraphy, showing at least five main constructional phases. Although this trench proved useful, later machine trenches caused problems. It was concluded that they did not justify the potential damage to physical remains.

A sixth-century brooch (top left) found near the southwest gateway provided further evidence that Cadbury Castle was occupied in Arthurian times.

The leg of a man (bottom left) is among the remains of the much earlier massacred bodies of Cadbury's Iron Age defenders against the Romans, discovered during excavations of the southwest gateway.

SURVEYING TECHNIQUES

Taking levels involves the use of a dumpy level or a theodolite (right). Both instruments measure the height marked on a surveyor's staff at the point in an exact horizontal line from the instrument. If the height of one place—a datum point—is known, and the position of the surveying instrument remains constant, the staff can be moved to different points, and their heights determined by a simple calculation.

Surveying plays an important role in excavation. After the initial contour survey, other similar sets of measurements are made (a process generally known as "leveling") during the course of the dig to record height variations in major deposits or features—the slope of a road or the depth of a ditch, for instance. "Spot heights" are also noted. These are heights of individual features, such as the top of a pit or a posthole, or the vertical position of a small find like a coin.

The pieces of equipment most commonly used in archaeological surveying are telescope-type leveling instruments, especially the dumpy level and the theodolite. On archaeological sites, theodolites are often somewhat primitive, although the use of super-precision, self-adjusting modern instruments, which also measure distances, is becoming more common.

The principle of taking levels relies on comparing the heights of the points to be measured with that of a fixed point of known height. Officially fixed points are called bench marks. Their physical position is denoted by a symbol on a stone post, a plaque or similar object, and their precise height above sea level is recorded on official maps.

Often, however, the nearest bench mark is inconveniently far from the excavation site. In that case, it is useful to create a temporary bench mark, or datum point, on an immovable feature close to the site, such as a building. Its height can be worked out from an official bench mark, using the technique that follows.

Measuring Heights

Set the instrument up near a fixed point of known height. Get a helper to hold a surveyor's staff upright on the datum point; look through the instrument and read the height on the staff. The reading you obtain gives the vertical distance between the base of the staff and the level of the instrument's telescope. Let us say it is 1.35 meters (4 ft. 6 in.).

Now ask your assistant to move to the first point to be measured and to hold the staff on it.

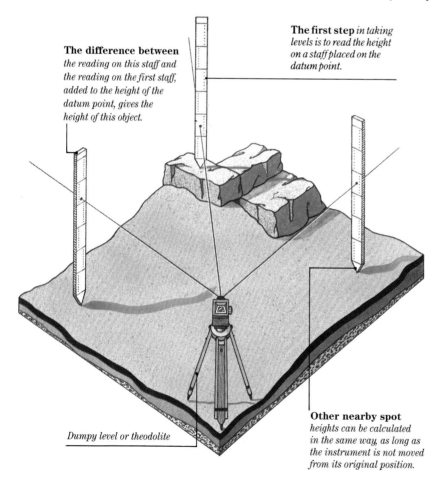

The difference between *the reading on this staff and the reading on the first staff, added to the height of the datum point, gives the height of this object.*

The first step *in taking levels is to read the height on a staff placed on the datum point.*

Other nearby spot *heights can be calculated in the same way, as long as the instrument is not moved from its original position.*

Dumpy level or theodolite

TOWN PLANNERS OF IMPERIAL MEXICO

During the 1960s, archaeologists mounted a full-scale investigation of the great Mexican city of Teotihuacán, which flourished some 2,000 years ago. A Mexican team excavated and restored much of the city center, continuing work that had begun in the 1920s.

One team from the United States undertook an intensive survey of the surrounding countryside to provide a picture of rural settlement and local ecology, while a second American team prepared a detailed map of the entire city, in which there were several thousand structures. The mapping team also made small-scale excavations to supplement its surface findings.

Although it had already been discovered that the city center was one of the world's finest examples of sophisticated early town planning, the mapping team was surprised to find that such planning had been carried out for the whole of Teotihuacán. The entire city was divided into residential blocks, generally squares of around 185 feet (57 m). These blocks presented a grim exterior of windowless walls but were arranged internally in groups of rooms surrounding open courtyards, ensuring their inhabitants both privacy and fresh air.

All the blocks were set out along a precise grid, aligned parallel and at right angles to the principal avenue of the city, the so-called Street of the Dead. This ran from the Pyramid of the Moon, past the larger Pyramid of the Sun and between the Great Compound and the Citadel, and on for a further 2 miles (3 km). The Citadel housed the Temple of Quetzalcoatl, the Plumed Serpent, an ornately decorated stepped pyramid. This temple and the pyramids of the Sun and Moon were the major religious structures in the city.

The Great Compound, on the other hand, seemed devoted to secular concerns. It includes what appear to be administrative buildings, while its enormous plaza was probably the city's main marketplace.

Teotihuacán was strategically placed to control trade between the Valley of Mexico and the adjacent Valley of Puebla and the Gulf Coast beyond, a factor in its ascendancy. Many blocks within the city seem to have been devoted to specialist crafts, such as obsidian working and pottery making.

The site was already a major settlement by the 1st century B.C.E. It rose to be the main center of the valley after the destruction of its main rival, Cuicuilco, by a volcanic eruption around 100 C.E. By the 2nd century C.E., more than 80 percent of the valley's population was living within Teotihuacán, which came to rule an empire stretching over most of highland Mesoamerica and influencing even the lowland Maya civilization (see page 50).

The ancient city of Teotihuacán was at its height in the 6th century C.E. Its center, seen here, contained a number of huge temple pyramids with a characteristic stepped profile, arranged along the main street. Palaces planned around courtyards surrounded the center, while the outskirts of town housed farmers, merchants and artisans.

Rotate the movable telescope (*not* the whole instrument) until the staff is visible and take a second reading. Say it is 1.56 meters (5 ft.); you therefore know that the second point is lower than the first by 0.21 meter (8 in.)—1.56 - 1.35 = 0.21. As you know the height of the datum point, you can calculate that of the second point by subtracting 0.21 from it.

You can probably calculate several other spot heights in this way without having to move your instrument from its starting position. Eventually, however, you may find that the next point to measure is too far away, or too high or low, and that the instrument must be shifted.

Get your assistant to "freeze" at the last point measured, with the staff in place. Move the instru-

ment to its new position, and read the height of the last point again from there. Let's say the previous reading was 2.01 meters, and the new one is 3.65 meters (these two readings are known as "foresight" and "backsight" respectively). So we know that the new position of the instrument is 1.64 meters higher than it was before, because the point on which it was focused remained constant. The next set of readings must therefore take into account the new, higher position of the instrument.

Though surveying is simple in principle, it must be very carefully performed, with strict checks to ensure accurate recording. Just one mistake will make a whole set of readings wrong, and that may often mean starting the whole job again from the beginning.

USING HEAVY MACHINERY

The use of heavy earthmoving equipment (below) is sometimes a necessary preliminary step in an archaeological excavation, where the site is buried, for instance, under subsequent layers of construction or a hard surface. Here diggers are breaking up the ground surface at the site of the Billingsgate excavation in London. The actual site to be excavated lay some 10 feet (3 m) under a surfaced parking lot and tons of postwar rubble.

Many members of the public and indeed some archaeologists are horrified at the idea of initiating excavations with earthmoving equipment. Certainly it is not a thing to be undertaken lightly. The main function of heavy earthmoving equipment on archaeological sites is to remove the soil that is of no archaeological interest and to put it back when the excavations are over. The second part is clear enough and should arouse no strong feelings, but the first is a different matter.

The deposits removed by machinery are generally either plowed soil or recent buildings and their cellars. They may also include natural layers that have accumulated on a long-abandoned site.

Archaeologists who direct the earthmover's driver have a delicate task. Their main job is to call a halt to the removal of soil at a level a little above that of the archaeological deposits. A margin is necessary because earthmoving equipment churns up and compacts soil to some depth below the level at which it is working. (Often, at sites stripped by machine, novices will excitedly discover "pottery" immediately after the earthmover has been at work. This is soil compacted so much that it becomes hard and shiny.)

On the other hand, having invested in the hire of a machine for a limited period, the director has to make sure it is used to perform as much as possible of the initial stripping. If it stops too far short of the archaeological deposits, the director could find that the team of diggers is tied up for days laboriously removing earth that the machine could have shifted in minutes.

Knowing the Depth

The archaeologist who uses an earthmoving machine needs to have in advance a good idea of the depth at which archaeological material will start to be revealed. On cultivated land, consultation with the farmer will provide information about the depth to which plowing takes place, and whether archaeological material is being turned up. A study of cuttings through the topsoil, such as streams and ditches, may also yield clues.

In towns, information may be gained by observing nearby construction sites. The records of previous excavations in the vicinity may also help.

In addition, augers and probes (*see page 53*) used at selected spots on the site will accurately indicate soil changes below ground, with minimal risk to archaeological remains. These changes, viewed in the light of what is known of local soils, are another pointer to the depth at which deposits of archaeological interest begin.

Armed with what is already known about the depth of the uninteresting deposits, the archaeologists then watch closely as the machine driver carefully removes the soil. The instant the archae-

BRONZE AGE FARM

It is often an accident that reveals unexpected evidence of some aspect of the past. Just such an accident occurred at Elp in the Drenthe province of the Netherlands. In 1960, an obvious Bronze Age barrow was being excavated, and while the site was being surveyed, the presence of what appeared to be some postholes was noticed nearby. Upon investigation, they proved to be the remains of several buildings that would have constituted a Bronze Age farm, and in 1962, these remains were investigated further.

The site was large and called for the use of heavy machinery. A bulldozer was called in, and an area 295 feet by 230 feet (90 m by 70 m)—thought to encompass the whole settlement—was laid out. The topsoil was removed in strips by the bulldozer, and the area was then cleaned. On top of the ridge along which the settlement was built, some postholes had been removed by erosion, but elsewhere enough remained to indicate several buildings.

Radiocarbon dating showed that the site had been occupied for about 400 years, between the 13th and 14th centuries B.C.E. During this period, the farmhouse and subsidiary buildings had been rebuilt five or six times, on each occasion shifting along the ridge.

The main building in each phase, on the crest of the ridge, was a large longhouse, divided into two roughly equal portions. One half was the family dwelling. The other half—the eastern half—had a row of interior postholes that were the foundations of stall partitions: This part of the building must have housed the family's herd of cattle, numbering somewhere between 20 and 30 head.

In addition, in each phase there was a smaller house situated on the west of the ridge: This may have been the home of subordinate members of the community. There were also sheds and barns in which wheat and barley were probably stored.

---

ologists notice something potentially interesting, such as a soil change or some possible archaeological material, they will call a halt and investigate. They can then decide whether the time has come to stop, or whether more soil should be mechanically removed.

Earthmoving equipment is expensive to hire and often absorbs a sizable amount of the excavation budget. Where rescue work is taking place in advance of construction, it is sometimes possible to borrow one of the contractor's machines. But the archaeologists must be well organized enough to know exactly what they want done. A contractor who has looked sympathetically on one request for a few hours' machine time is likely to be less accommodating if the request is made repeatedly.

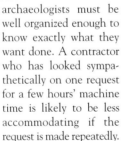

A Hard Slog

When the top layers of the site have been stripped by machine, some disturbed and compacted soil remains to be removed manually, using spades, shovels and picks. Often the amount of topsoil to be removed does not justify the use

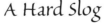

of a machine, and then the whole task must be done by hand. The topsoil and the turf, if the site was grassed, are kept separate from lower layers cleared during the excavation proper, as it usually has to be put back afterward.

As the diggers draw near to where the archaeological deposits are thought to lie, their work slows down and becomes less strenuous and more precise. The remaining topsoil is then removed in thin layers, until archaeological features begin to emerge. Sometimes this surface skimming is done with shovels or hoes, but more often it is carried out with trowels, the archaeologist's multipurpose tool. This is the stage at which volunteers begin to despair, as they trowel repeatedly over the same piece of ground and find nothing.

But at last something appears. The nature of the soil changes and "features" begin to emerge—differences in soil that show up the presence of pits, postholes and ditches, spreads of stones or other surfaces that were once house floors, courtyards or roadways. The supervisor goes around labeling these. Probably a preexcavation plan is also made, showing the locations of the features that have been spotted. Such a plan is needed because, as the site dries out, subtle differences in soil color tend to vanish, and they could easily be missed later.

Using picks, shovels and spades to remove rubble and topsoil from a site (left and above) is hard work, but it can be quite enjoyable, particularly as a way to warm up on a cold day. The monotony is often relieved by a little competition in soil-shifting and wheelbarrow-filling.

73

DISSECTING THE SITE

As we have seen, abandoned sites gradually change as a result of human activities and natural processes. The idea behind excavation is to take the site apart in the reverse order to that in which it was formed.

In some respects, the layers of an archaeological site resemble those of a layer cake, and this analogy tells something about the technique of excavation. The top coating, the icing, is removed first, followed by the first layer of cake. After that, the filling of, say, berries is removed, exposing the cake's final layer, or base. Just as the whole cake would collapse if you were to pull out only the berry filling, so would the archaeological site be ruined. They must be reached by digging down to them layer by layer.

The features of an archaeological site, however, require more thought and preplanning. They must be carefully examined to work out the order in which they were created. That can often be determined on the basis of their relationships to one another. If, for example, there are two pits close together, the relationship of their outlines should show the order in which they were dug; the outline of the earlier one will be cut by that of the later. The later one's outline will be complete.

Assessing Relationships

Although the relationships between features are clear in many cases, in others the similarity between the deposits filling them makes them much harder to distinguish. In such cases, a variety of methods is employed to try to clarify the relationship.

The surface of the features may be carefully cleaned by troweling off a tiny skim of soil in the hope that the cleaned surface will be more revealing. During the process of troweling, you may also detect some distinct textural differences between the various features.

If the site has become dry, spraying or splashing the features with water may help. One may dry out more rapidly than the other or turn a slightly

When studying an archaeological site, it is sometimes difficult to distinguish the relationship between different deposits. In this excavation, an area (middle background) has been sprayed with water to allow its different features to show up better. The results are about to be photographed.

different color when wet. This technique is also particularly useful in revealing mud bricks, which often blend completely with the surrounding soil when dry, but which frequently show up when wet.

The Art of Sectioning

In accordance with the idea that horizontal and vertical aspects of the site should be studied simultaneously wherever possible, many archaeologists advocate "half-sectioning" features, or cutting sections across larger ones. In this technique, the layers in the selected portion are removed and recorded one by one, while the rest of the feature is temporarily left unexcavated.

Once the chosen portion has been completely excavated, its vertical aspect can be studied and recorded before the rest of the feature is removed. In this way, both the horizontal nature of the layers and their vertical relationships can be carefully studied.

Some archaeologists—particularly the exponents of open area excavation—prefer to excavate each layer within a feature completely horizontally, sacrificing the vertical view for the sake of a complete horizontal one. In both methods, plans (the horizontal aspect) and sections (the vertical aspect) are recorded on paper, but the methods differ in what is actually visible to the excavators as they go along.

The debate about excavation of features is really a microcosm of the debate about excavation strategy in general, and volunteer diggers may

find themselves exposed to the advocates of both, to their confusion. Naturally, neither approach is wholly right or wrong, but one may be more appropriate than the other in particular circumstances.

Layer by Layer

Sometimes a feature is so deep or is so oddly shaped (undercut, for instance) that its complete excavation is impossible or dangerous. Then it must be excavated and recorded in stages, proceeding as the level of the surrounding deposits is lowered.

When all the features cutting or lying on the uppermost ground surface have been excavated and recorded, the surface itself is removed to reveal the deposit below.

Let us take the example of early medieval plowsoil cut by later medieval ditches, pits and house foundations. The later medieval features are excavated first. Only then is the plowsoil itself removed, perhaps revealing a Roman road beneath. Remember that while later holes cut down into a deposit, earlier structures will stick up. While removing the plowsoil, therefore, the stubs of the walls of any Roman houses that bordered the road may well be encountered.

In principle, each deposit on a site should be removed stratigraphically, dealing with a complete layer at a time. In practice, however, a deposit may be too thick to clear all in one go, for instance if it has been mixed up by centuries of cultivation. In that case, excavation proceeds in arbitrary horizontal layers called "spits." A spit of reasonable depth, perhaps 4 inches (10 cm), is removed at one time, and the process continues until the deposit is completely excavated and the next revealed.

The technique must be monitored carefully. The surface of the underlying deposits—the Roman road and houses in our example—and the depth of the deposit under excavation may both vary. Spit excavation must always be prepared to give way to stratigraphic excavation.

Half-sectioning a feature means that the horizontal nature of the layers and their vertical relationships can both be observed (left).

DISSECTING THE SITE

Most archaeological work, at least in Europe and America, relies on the trowel—not a garden trowel, but a forged mason's (pointing) trowel. There seems to be a general preference for starting with a 4-inch (10-cm) trowel, but months of excavation on hard soils gradually reduce the size so that the veteran archaeologist is often working with a blade very much shorter than it originally was. An array of trowels, in various stages of wear, is an archaeologist's status symbol.

The uses of the trowel are manifold. The main method of digging by trowel (troweling) involves scraping off a layer of soil with the edge of the blade and breaking up resistant soil with the point. Use of the trowel usually results in a clean surface on which features show up clearly, weather permitting. Experienced trowelers claim, with much justification, to be able to dig as fast with the trowel as with any of its rivals, such as a small pick, and the risk of damage is far less.

In addition, the trowel can chop through obstructive roots. It can also substitute as a scale in photographs of small finds (though it is more usual to use a calibrated scale).

Once the soil has been troweled off, it has to be removed. Hand shovels are filled with earth using the trowel, or a brush if the material is dry. The earth, or "spoil," is then taken in buckets or wheelbarrows to be dumped on the spoil heap at a safe, sensible distance from the excavation area. Before dumping, the soil may be sieved for any archaeological material that has previously been overlooked (*see page 84*).

Supplements to the Trowel

The trowel is ubiquitous, but other digging tools are sometimes required. Picks and shovels (not spades) can be used to dig out rapidly those deposits that have been tested and found to be archaeologically uninformative.

Similarly speedy operations may be appropriate for removing an archaeological feature that has been examined in detail at some point and that seems uniform throughout, such as a road or a graveled courtyard. Deeply dug modern features—Victorian cellars, in particular—merit this form of treatment.

At the opposite end of the scale, it may be necessary to use delicate tools to deal with fragile finds, though in many cases it is remarkable how delicately a trowel can be used with practice. The junction between soil and object is a natural plane of fracture, and a carefully placed trowel point can ease the soil away and make it flake off, so long as the object is tougher than the soil surrounding it, which is not always the case.

Probes, and other dental tools, come in handy when excavating delicate material—fragile bones, disintegrating metal objects, crumbling pottery and so on. Toothbrushes and a penknife are also extremely useful. Various sizes of spoons are suitable for removing the soil from small stakeholes.

In warm, dry climates, daily care of archaeological tools may not be necessary. But in wetter environments, a regular routine is observed. At rest breaks during the day, all loose soil is cleared up, the tools are neatly stacked near where each digger has been working and covered with upturned buckets or wheelbarrows. The instruction for this process to begin—"clear up your loose"—is a welcome signal to the hungry, thirsty digger that the break is only a few minutes away. At the end of the day, the tools are thoroughly cleaned of mud that has accumulated on or in them.

Coping with the Weather

A dream excavation is conducted in moderately sunny conditions, with light evening showers to

Picks and shovels can be used to dig quickly through material that is of little archaeological interest, such as Victorian cellars or a recent parking lot. Ladders are also useful for reaching down into deeply dug features—these may need to be shored up, and hard hats worn by their excavators for protection

keep the site moist and workable. In practice, the weather is seldom so obliging.

In hot climates, the site is likely to dry up, making digging difficult and obscuring archaeological features. Splashing with water, or spraying with a watering can or plant spray, is useful in such conditions. The digger can protect himself or herself from the sun by wearing wide-brimmed hats and loose, longsleeved shirts.

Wet weather, on the other hand, is harder to deal with. Where heavy rain is expected, some kind of movable shelter is usually provided. It is placed over the part of the site being dug to protect both the site and the diggers.

Although light showers may help the excavators, excessive rainfall will reduce the ground to a quagmire in which excavation is not only physically impossible for the diggers, but also damaging to the site. For this reason, if wet weather is expected, it is a good idea to cover the exposed areas of the site with plastic sheeting to protect the surface until it comes to be excavated.

A range of brushes is employed on-site, from delicate paint-brushes used to excavate fragile bones and tooth-brushes and nail-brushes for washing pottery, to hand-brushes used, as seen here, to remove dry soil from a firm surface.

The ever-present archaeologist's trowel is used for myriad purposes. Here it is being employed to scrape loose soil (spoil) into a hand shovel. The spoil is then taken by bucket to be dumped on the spoil heap. The trowel's sharp edges and point and flat blade fit it for a surprising range of tasks, including spreading butter and cutting up the diggers' sandwiches!

ESTABLISHING A RECORD

Two sets of data are accumulated as a result of excavation. One is tangible and can be examined even when the dig is over: artifacts, human, animal and plant remains, and so on. The other is destroyed as the excavation progresses and must therefore be recorded as soon as it appears. This set of data is structural and contextual: the remains of buildings and other deposits, layers and features.

Archaeological surveying (see pages 70–71), used continually during excavation, is one technique for recording structural and contextual information. There are several others used in conjunction with it to build up an accurate account of the excavation in progress, including photography and drawing.

The Role of Planning

Planning is the term used to define the recording of the horizontal aspect of the site—the distribution of layers and features and their horizontal relationships. The scale at which plans are made depends on the size of the features and their density. A site with a road, a couple of ditches and a few large pits will show up nicely on a plan at a scale of 1:20 or possibly 1:50, whereas a site covered with the stakeholes of numerous wattle-and-daub houses needs to be planned at 1:10, or even 1:5.

Plans should be made on good-quality transparent film, such as Permatrace, that will not expand or contract in any normal weather conditions. The film is stretched over a drawing board of manageable proportions and fixed down with masking tape or strong, heavy clips. Beneath this, fastened to the surface of the board, is a large sheet of metric graph paper. The planner begins by marking on the drawing paper all the relevant details—the scale at which the plan is drawn, who is doing it, the date and the name of the site and area. Then the relevant fixed points of the grid are marked in the correct position, along with an approximate indication of north (if the grid points are correctly marked, the true position of north can be ascertained later).

Few draftspeople are sufficiently confident to make their initial drawings in ink (it runs in the rain, anyway). Most planning is done with ordinary lead pencil, which is traced over in ink indoors later.

The methods used by the planner depend largely on the scale and on the prevalence of the features being plotted. On a site where there are many features, most of them small and close together, a drawing frame is essential. Where many of the features are large and the site is not very complex planning by triangulation is quicker and easier.

The Drawing Frame

The drawing frame is a rigid square of wood, whose *internal* dimensions are usually 1 meter by 1 meter (approximately 3 ft. by 3 ft.), divided by (preferably) nylon strings into 10-centimeter (0.4-in.) units. If the plan is being made at the scale 1:10, each box of the drawing frame will correspond to a 1-centimeter box on the graph paper beneath the drawing film, making planning relatively easy. At 1:20, each 1-centimeter box represents 20 centimeters on the ground.

The drawing frame is set over the area to be drawn, using its accompanying skewers to hold it in place. If the surface is bumpy, a level should be placed on two adjacent sides to check that the frame is horizontal. It is also vital to know where you have placed the grid on the plan; this can be done by triangulating the corners of the frame (see next page) from the permanent markers of the site grid.

Planning with a drawing frame requires some contortion to get a completely vertical view over what is being drawn. Yet it is a relatively easy task to transfer the image seen in the little boxes on the ground with tolerable accuracy to the tiny boxes on the drawing board, $1/10$ or $1/20$ of original size.

Techniques of Triangulation

A well-developed visual sense helps in triangulation. There is no drawing frame to provide a grid over the feature being drawn. Instead, you draw by joining up, by eye, a series of dots plotted on the site plan.

Required equipment consists of two 30-meter measuring tapes and a plumb line, a weighted line

that hangs exactly vertically when suspended. For the plotting, you need a ruler and a drawing compass. The actual technique is difficult for one person to carry out; it is usual for someone to do the mechanical side of the work while another does the plotting.

Before triangulation starts, choose a series of points on the feature to be drawn that seem to you to delineate its salient horizontal characteristics, perhaps marking them with pegs or in some other way. You can add others if necessary as you go along. The next step is to mark each point accurately on the site plan. Hook the top end of one measuring tape over one of the grid pegs inserted when the site was laid out so that the tape passes over the point you are plotting. Hook the top end of the other tape over another grid peg, chosen so that the two tapes cross each other at as narrow an angle and as near to the point being plotted as possible. Get your helper to take the unattached end of each tape and to adjust them so that they intersect exactly over the point, testing that they do so by using the plumb line. Read off the distance of the point of intersection from each grid peg on the tape attached to it.

With that information, you can now mark the point accurately on the site plan. Suppose tape A is 1.35 meters from its grid peg to the intersection, and tape B is 2.65 meters. Reduce those distances to the scale of the site plan: At 1:10, they become 13.5 centimeters and 26.5 centimeters respectively. With the compass, lightly draw an arc with a radius of 13.5 centimeters from the appropriate grid peg symbol on the site plan. Then draw another arc with a radius of 26.5 centimeters from the second grid peg symbol. The point where the two arcs cross is the position of the selected point on the site plan.

Follow the same procedure for plotting all the points you have chosen around the feature on the site itself. Once they have been recorded on the plan, join them up with freehand lines to obtain a horizontal representation of the feature.

Triangulation is a method used to record the precise find spots of "small finds" (special finds) and the exact locations of features within a given area so that they can be plotted on a scale plan, thus providing a detailed "map" of the site. The site will already have been staked out with pegs. One person carries out the function of pinpointing the feature on the site, while someone else does the actual plotting, as shown above. A tape measure is attached to each of two pegs most closely positioned to the feature (1) and a plumb line is dropped directly over the point to be marked. It is important that the tapes be taut and horizontal to minimize any distortion. The lengths of both tapes are now measured. Meanwhile, the second person positions the point of the compass (2) at the spot on the graph paper corresponding (in scale) to the exact position of one of the pegs and, setting the compass at a measure equal to the length of the tape (again, in scale), draws an arc. This is repeated at the second peg placement. Where these arcs intersect is the point to be plotted.

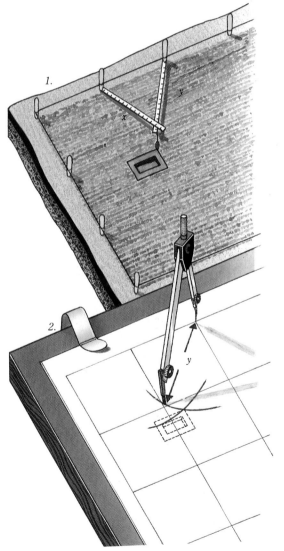

ESTABLISHING
A RECORD

SECTION DRAWINGS

A section is a vertical slice through the deposits that have accumulated in a feature or on the site in general. To make a record drawing of it, a string is set up horizontally across it, between two nails (lower right). A tape measure is attached to the nails with clothespins to provide a horizontal scale. Vertical readings are taken with a second tape at regular or appropriate intervals along it.

A line level is a small level with two hooks that allow it to be suspended from a horizontal piece of string (below). The line level must be hung at one end of the string; if it is hung in the center, its weight will cause the string to sag and give a false impression of horizontality.

Section drawings record the vertical aspect of the site and that of the features within it—in other words, the site's stratigraphy. As with plans, the scale of section drawings depends on what needs to be drawn.

A section containing a few thick deposits can adequately be drawn at 1:20, while one consisting of numerous thin layers should be recorded at 1:10. Like plans, sections can be drawn on plastic film, but they are frequently drawn directly onto graph paper, perhaps in a site notebook.

Often sections (especially long or deep ones) have been gradually exposed over a number of days. It is therefore often useful to "clean" the section by troweling a thin skim of soil off it in order to restore its color and moisture contrasts before drawing or photographing it.

To draw a short section, you need paper, pencils and erasers, two nails or surveyor's arrows, string, two tape measures, a couple of clothespins and a line level.

Set a nail at one end of the section that is to be drawn and attach the string to the nail. Hang the line level at one end of the string. You can then fix the unattached end of the string with the second nail at the other end of the section, checking from the line level that the string is absolutely horizontal.

When the string is level, vertical readings are taken along it at intervals, recording the height or depth from the string of individual archaeological deposits or features. Adjusted for scale, these provide a series of reference points that are then marked as dots on the drawing.

The dots are then joined up, looking closely at the section to make sure the drawing records it accurately. The height or depth of the section string is also measured in relation to a fixed point of known height, and the information recorded on the drawing.

Large sections, such as the side of an excavation trench, can be plotted in much the same way. But because the section string is long, the line level is not accurate enough to ensure the string is horizontal. Instead, the surveying instrument is used to insert a precisely horizontal line of steel

long views of the site, while small scales calibrated into units of 10 centimeters (4 in.) or less are used when photographing small finds and features. The scale is placed parallel to the border of the photograph (horizontally for horizontal shots and vertically for sections).

In addition to ground-level photographs, panoramic views and shots comparable to low-level aerial pictures can be taken from a suitable vantage point—a hill or tall building directly overlooking the site, the roof of a vehicle, a specially built photographic tower or a tethered balloon.

Before record shots are taken, the area or object to be photographed is carefully cleaned so that it will show up to best advantage. Cleaning is even more meticulous before photographs for publication; this may involve tedious activities like cutting the grass around the edge of the excavated area—and removing every blade of grass that has fallen on to it. Some site directors like their publication photographs to be completely free of extraneous items such as buckets and wheelbarrows, as well as volunteer diggers, but others find these enhance the shot, if neatly distributed. It is a good idea to include a person in a photograph, if possible, as this gives a much more immediate sense of scale than does a ranging rod.

Planning by Photo

A further use of photography, practiced on only a few land excavations, but in general use in underwater archaeology, is photogrammetry—planning the site by photographs. Frequent vertical record shots are taken of all the areas being excavated, from which accurate plans can then be made.

While vertical photographs can easily be taken underwater, on land it is more difficult as some means must be found of suspending a camera vertically above the area to be photographed. The framework used to support the camera must be stable, but it must also be such that it will not damage the site. Various arrangements to achieve this have been devised, of which probably the most successful is a tethered balloon. Despite its usefulness photogrammetry is still a relatively unusual recording technique, although it is now becoming more common.

pins or surveyor's arrows, and the section string will then be attached to these.

In open area excavations, where layers are totally removed one at a time, there is no section visible from which a drawing can be made. To plot the thickness of the layers and their interrelationships, measurements are made of the height of the top of each deposit as it is exposed, along a predetermined line. This is known as a "running" section.

The Use of Photography

Photographs taken of excavated areas and features have both advantages and drawbacks. The camera captures everything it sees, which means that photographs may be harder to understand than drawings in which only the relevant details have been selected and recorded. On the other hand, because photographs are complete, they can provide a cross-check on drawings and extra information if, in retrospect, a drawing proves inadequate or even inaccurate.

Shots for record purposes are usually taken in both black-and-white and color. Generally, several exposures are taken on different settings. Every shot must also contain a scale—usually a wooden or metal staff calibrated into units.

Ranging rods or other staffs are used for photographs of large things, such as major sections or

Photographs are an essential part of the basic record kept of the excavation, recording everything from overall views of the site (above left) to individual small finds in their context (above right), before they are lifted. An appropriate scale is essential to indicate the size of the object, feature or area being photographed.

Plans, sections and photographs give a picture of the features of a site and their interrelationships, but the nature of the deposits and the material found in them must obviously be recorded too. There are many different recording systems in use. On some sites, daily entries are made in a notebook, giving details of what is being excavated, the progress being made and other relevant information, such as the weather, who is in charge of the area and which volunteers are working in it.

Site notebooks allow considerable flexibility in the amount of information recorded, but on balance preprinted recording sheets are probably preferable. On a recording sheet, information is neatly presented in one place, whereas in a site notebook, it may be necessary to hunt through many pages to glean all the information that has been recorded about a particular context. One disadvantage of recording sheets is that there is little provision for expressing changes of opinion as excavation proceeds. However, the major advantage is that, because the presentation is standardized, information can readily be transferred to a computer. Many long-term excavation teams now use a computer for rapid sorting and retrieval of data. Not only is this extremely helpful on-site, but it also eases the task of preparing the final report.

The Vital Details

Whatever method is used, the information that is recorded will be much the same. First of all, there is a record of the nature of the deposit—generally, details of the color, degree of compaction, texture and particle size of the soil. The last two are usually commented on by eye and feel.

Compaction can be measured using a penetrometer, a small device that is pushed into the soil, while color is often determined with a Munsell soil color chart. This is a book in which pages show soil colors, each with a little window that is placed over a sample of the soil for comparison. Once the color has been identified, its Munsell code number can be recorded. Details of any inclusions in the deposit, such as small stones or fragments of brick, are also noted.

Next, information about the interrelationship between the deposit under consideration and the others around it is entered. On the recording sheet, there is usually a set of boxes labeled "lies above . . .," "lies below . . .," "cuts . . ." and "is cut by . . ." for this purpose. If the deposit forms a layer

within a feature, that is also noted. So are the plans and section drawings on which this deposit appears.

All such information is quite concise. By contrast, information about the excavation of the deposit and what it reveals can be lengthy. It may include some details of the material being recovered, though this is also recorded elsewhere. It is likely to contain the first germs of the archaeological interpretation. Detailed recording of impressions during excavation can be highly rewarding, so it is always useful to note all relevant thoughts, even if they are later disproved. Once a deposit has been excavated, any information not recorded will be lost; it is far better to be able to discard redundant information during the later writing-up stage than to find oneself without that little detail that could have made all the difference.

Artifacts and Other Remains

The detail in which findspots are recorded depends on the abundance of the material recovered and the importance attached to its precise context. On Roman sites vast quantities of potsherds are likely, while on some Bronze Age sites a single sherd might be an unusual occurrence. The Roman pottery will be recorded simply as deriving from a particular layer, or if it is a large one, from a grid square or spit within it. The Bronze Age sherd, on the other hand, may well be treated as what is termed a "small find" (an object of relative rarity and importance) and its three-dimensional position recorded, usually by triangulation and spot height. On a Paleolithic site, flint tools and the debris from their manufacture may be just as abundant as the pottery on Roman sites, but the laborious three-dimensional recording of every single chip of stone may reveal important details about the distribution of activities on the site.

While excavation is taking place, the volunteers are provided with finds trays in which to deposit the material they recover. Each layer will have a separate finds tray; if it is a widespread layer, a finds tray may be provided for each subdivision of it. Finds trays are always carefully labeled.

Diggers fills their trays with everything they find whose position does not have to be recorded three-dimensionally. Fragile objects, such as crumbly pottery or delicate bones are kept separate from heavy objects that are likely to crush them.

Small finds, such as coins, pieces of pottery and bronze objects, are often photographed in situ before they are removed. Their three-dimensional position is recorded and usually marked on the site plan. Human remains and associated material are also recorded in detail.

The Finds Assistant

Responsibility for the archaeological material that has been excavated then passes to the finds assistant, who supervises its cleaning and marking. Each category of material from each deposit is separately packed in well-labeled bags and boxes, ready for further treatment and analysis. A record is made of what material has been found in which archaeological contexts, the number of bags or boxes it is stored in and any other relevant details. Small finds are entered individually in the finds register, with their three-dimensional positions.

In addition to the artifacts discovered during excavation, a number of samples of other material will probably be taken. Any large amount of charcoal, for instance, may be useful for radiocarbon dating. Soil samples provide reference material if there are any later doubts about the nature of a deposit and can help to answer specific dating questions (see pages 105 and 138). Samples are also taken to obtain such organic material as pollen, seeds and insect remains (see pages 102–105).

In general, routine samples are taken from every deposit and larger ones from deposits that are expected to be particularly productive. Such samples are usually processed on-site to extract the relevant material.

Description of context includes details of its composition and of finds within it.

Site grid references, altitude and the order in which the various layers were deposited are noted.

This section provides a basis for a statistical analysis of the finds. Different categories of finds are recorded by checking the appropriate box. The amount of the find recovered is noted by entering A (all), S (some) or N (none).

When a sample is taken, the appropriate category is checked and the number of large plastic bags used is recorded in the box below.

Interpretative notes are made after all the details above have been completed and verified. Fuller notes are made at a later stage.

SIEVING ON-SITE

Volunteer diggers, after an initial period of having constantly to ask, "Is this something archaeological?" soon learn to identify and recover most of the finds from the patch they are digging. Even the most careful and sharp-eyed digger, however, is likely to miss a few things, so it is useful to sieve the excavated soil to check for further remains. Sieving is usually undertaken on or beside the spoil heap.

The simplest method of sieving is carried out with a handsieve of the kind used in grading ordinary garden soil. A more thorough method is to use a set of nested sieves in a metal-framed shaker—frequently a nest of three sieves is used—to recover objects of different sizes.

Besides objects missed due to temporary loss of concentration, sieving can also recover things too small to be noticed while digging, such as beads and tiny bones.

Where there is a convenient water source on or near the site, the process of recovery can be improved still further by wet sieving. The sieve is immersed slightly in water and gently agitated. The soil dissolves and falls through, leaving behind any objects. These show up easily among the remaining stones because they have been washed clean.

Seed Machines

Samples collected to recover plant material are usually bulky, so it is best if the material can be extracted from them on-site, rather than transporting them elsewhere for processing. Several machines have been designed to cope with the task of extraction.

Wet sieving (far right) is usually done in a tank with an outlet through which the accumulated soil can drain.

Sieving the soil before dumping it on the spoil heap (below) can turn up objects that would otherwise be lost. A seed machine (right) is used to recover seeds and plant material.

TERRA AMATA

Construction work late in 1965 near the shipyard area of Nice in France uncovered an extensive deposit containing early Paleolithic tools. The importance of the find was immediately appreciated, construction was suspended and emergency excavations were carried out in the first half of 1966.

The excavators discovered the remains of 21 "living floors," the bases of ancient and primitive dwellings. All required very careful excavation, using only trowels and brushes, and extremely detailed recording, which included making casts of the floors. The reward was a detailed picture of a few days in the life of our ancestor *Homo heidelbergensis*.

A group of these hominids built a series of oval huts on this site, known as Terra Amata, 400,000 years ago. The huts, outlined by stakes and supported by stout posts, each contained a central hearth protected from draughts by a wall of stones. Analysis of pollen from fossilized feces found around the huts showed that the visitors came here in the late spring or early summer.

They hunted large mammals, including elephant and rhinoceros, gathered shellfish and occasionally also caught fish. After a short stay, they moved on elsewhere, but they returned in successive years and rebuilt their huts on the same spots.

Among the things they left behind were the debris from making stone tools and lumps of red ocher, which they may have used for body painting. A round depression in the ground, filled with white material, may be the remains of a wooden bowl.

Because this is a site of exceptional interest, it was thought appropriate to guarantee its preservation. It is therefore incorporated in a museum that was built beneath the apartment block whose construction had sparked its discovery.

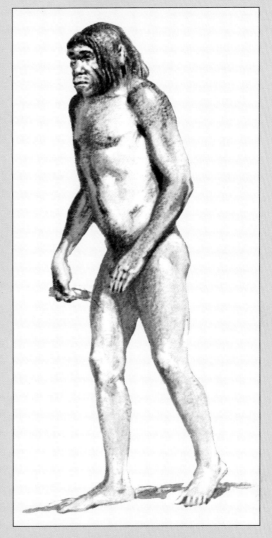

The inhabitants of Terra Amata, in the south of France, lived about 400,000 years ago. They were hunter-gatherers who used flint tools and built oval wooden huts that are among the earliest known human-made structures. Their hearths indicate that they had also mastered fire at this early date.

One uses a process called "froth flotation" borrowed from the mining industry, where it is used to obtain metal from low-grade ore. The machine consists of a small tank supported on a stand, with a narrow conical valved outlet at the bottom through which the soil can be discarded. A motor blows air through a set of nozzles in a tube set in the bottom of the tank, which is filled with water during the operation. A frothing agent and a "collector," such as kerosene, are added to the water. When small quantities of coarsely sieved sample soil are poured into the tank, seeds and other tiny organic particles attach themselves to the rising air bubbles, a tendency that is enhanced by the collector.

The froth holds the seeds in the surface water, which overflows gently through a spout into a small sieve. Any material that has been deposited is then wrapped in moistened paper towels and left for some time until it is completely dry.

Other "seed machines" operate slightly differently, but the results are much the same.

A SAXON SHIP BURIAL

The importance of appropriate conservation is extremely well demonstrated by one of the classic archaeological discoveries of the 20th century: the ship burial at Sutton Hoo in Suffolk, England. Investigations leading to the discovery began in 1938, when one of three barrows opened on the site that year yielded traces of a small ship. It was also established that the barrows held pagan Saxon burials.

The following year, excavation of the largest barrow began, revealing the first traces of a much larger ship. It had been set in a burial trench dug

the metal objects, with the exception of the goldwork, were in a sorry state. Many pieces had also been damaged when the roof of the chamber had collapsed centuries before.

The relatively stable pieces had to be carefully exposed using paintbrushes and needles, their position recorded and photographs taken. This was a key process, as it was often not clear which fragments came from which objects. In the case of the leatherwork and the fabrics, it was imperative to keep them moist, while a number of other pieces were too fragile to stand excavation. These were lifted in their sandy matrix, carefully packed (the waterlogged ones with wet moss) and sent to a laboratory for appropriate treatment.

Saxon Treasures

In addition to the difficulties of the excavation itself, the nature of the finds posed a problem. The jewelry and metalwork that were meticulously revealed included many pieces of gold and silver that were literally priceless. Although the discovery was kept as secret as possible, it was thought sensible to bring in police to guard the site at night until work was completed.

The treasures recovered from the grave are today some of the best known in the world. They include a number of silver bowls and dishes imported from the Eastern Roman Empire.

The Sutton Hoo ship has left only its imprint in the sand, so extreme care was needed during the site's excavation. Recent excavations have also uncovered many flat graves here, buried around the barrows. The bodies in them survive only as a discolored crust in the sand, making excavation extremely painstaking and difficult.

into sand that had remained moist and thus had to some extent preserved organic materials in a generally disintegrating state. A few fragments of wood remained in places.

Of the ship's timbers, however, the only traces were a series of discolorations in the sand where they had rotted and the rusted nails that had once held them together. To reveal these and to uncover the burial chamber, the sand was carefully removed in thin horizontal slices. The chamber lay in the center of the ship. Stains and fragments of the original wood showed that it was rectangular and had once had a pitched roof, made of two layers of planks set at right angles to each other.

Although the uncovering of the ship demanded great care, this was nothing compared to the problems that the excavators faced when they came to remove the contents of the burial chamber. The dampness of the sand had partly preserved several objects of leather and wood, but all

Some of the military equipment, such as an iron helmet with gilded bronze decoration and a shield, were of Swedish origin or inspiration. Other pieces were probably of native Saxon craftsmanship—gold and bejeweled buckles, strap mounts and a scabbard, and items of personal jewelry.

The most significant finds included an iron standard and a stone object bearing a bronze stag that may have been a scepter. These support the notion that the grave was that of a king. Two silver spoons carrying the names Saul and Paul may have been a christening gift, indicating that this king had been converted to Christianity.

Finally, a collection of gold coins in a beautifully decorated purse provided a date for the burial of around 613 C.E. or a little later. Based on present evidence, it seems most probable that this burial mound was erected for Raedwald, king of East Anglia and high king of England south of the Humber.

EXCAVATION

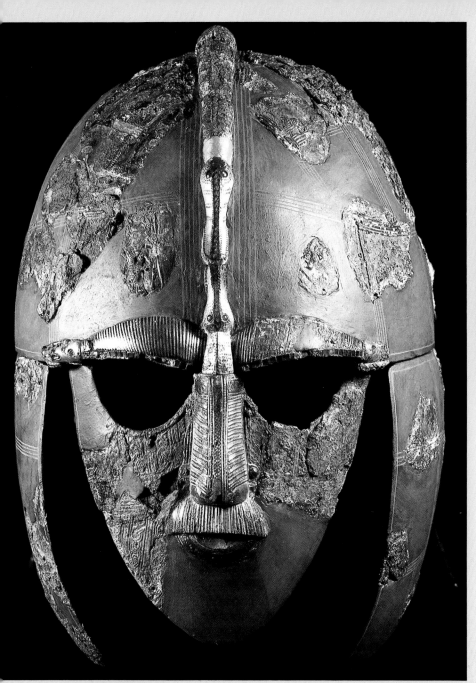

Made of solid gold, the great gold buckle (above), 5 inches (12.7 cm) long, weighs more than 14 ounces (395 g). It is covered with a design of interlaced animals and birds.

Original fragments of the decorated iron helmet (upper left) found at Sutton Hoo have been used in this reconstruction. The gilt bronze nose-piece and helmet crest are decorated with animal heads inlaid with garnets, and the helmet is covered with tinned bronze plaques with geometric decoration and scenes of warriors.

The winged dragon (left) is part of the decoration on the Sutton Hoo shield. The dragon, 11 inches (28 cm) long, is made of gilt bronze studded with garnet.

A SAXON
SHIP BURIAL

CONSERVATION IN THE FIELD

The degree to which archaeological materials are preserved depends on the conditions in which they have survived. Decay by physical action affects only those items exposed to the elements—extremes of hot and cold, wind, rain, snow, water or ice and seismic activity. The weathering of ruined buildings is an example of decay as a result of physical action. But it can also affect, for instance, long-buried ancient stone tools exposed to the air by erosion or earth movements.

The process of chemical and biological decay depends on the presence of moisture, warmth and oxygen and on the acidity or alkalinity of the environment. These types of decay are generally most rapid in humid tropical conditions but are usually negligible in desert or frozen areas. In acid soils, bone and glass will be poorly preserved, but in highly acid conditions some organic remains may survive. This is particularly so in acid bogs, from which seeds and insect remains have been recovered. In such bogs, oxidization of metal is prevented, resulting in good preservation.

In alkaline soils, organic remains decay rapidly, though bone is preserved and may become semifossilized. Glass rapidly degenerates. Insoluble salts form an encrustation on pottery, bone, stone and metals, which may cause damage. In alkaline waterlogged conditions, wood may be preserved, though weakened. Wood also survives well in seawater; so may other materials, but their chemical composition may be changed.

Safe Storage

Whatever the effects of the environment, material eventually reaches an equilibrium with it, in which further decay will not take place. Removal from its resting place may restart decay, which

must be treated at once. In general, wet objects should be stored in water, or in damp tissue paper or some similar suitable material. Dry objects should be stored dry, with a desiccating agent such as silica gel crystals if complete dryness is needed. Organic materials should be treated with a reversible fungicide to prevent molds.

Plastic bags and rigid plastic boxes are suitable for storing most materials; fragile objects must be packed with enough padding to remove the risk of damage. In the case of unstable materials, it is essential to send them to a laboratory conservator as soon as possible. Before removing a fragile object from the ground a photograph should be taken of it in case it disintegrates.

On-the-Spot Treatment

Various treatments may be necessary or desirable before an object leaves the excavation site. It is generally possible to clean stable artifacts, such as most pottery and many stone objects, without damaging them, making the task of the conservator easier. However, if it seems possible to recover microscopic traces, such as food residues or smears of blood, from the surface of pottery or stone objects, it is important not to clean the objects.

In some cases, it may be necessary to arrest any decay, such as the so-called bronze disease (cupric chloride) that exposure to the air has initiated or reactivated. Similarly, soluble and insoluble salts in the material should be removed if they are likely to cause damage. In other cases, the object may be too fragile to be removed from the ground or to survive the journey to the conservation laboratory and so must be consolidated in situ.

The golden rules when treating archaeological material in the field are not to apply any treatment unless it is absolutely necessary; to make sure that

Four stages in the process of preserving a mosaic: first, a backing cloth is covered with a latex adhesive, ready to receive the pieces of the mosaic, face downward. The mosaic, stuck to the cloth, is removed to the laboratory where the area between the tesserae is carefully cleaned before the object is set in plaster. Finally, the backing cloth is removed.

PRESERVING TOLLUND MAN

In 1950, a well-preserved Iron Age corpse was discovered by two peat cutters in a bog at Tollund, in Denmark. A curious feature of this body was the remains of a noose pulled tight around his neck indicating death by hanging. This was not the first such body to be uncovered in Europe, but it is certainly one of the best preserved.

Most of these corpses show signs of a violent death, and often several different means were employed. The bog man from Lindow Moss in England, for instance, had been strangled and hit on the head, and his throat had been cut. Most of the bodies were also virtually naked; Tollund Man wore only a skin cap and a leather belt. It is generally held that such killings were a form of ritual sacrifice.

Tollund Man was removed from the bog and taken to the National Museum in Copenhagen for thorough study in a specially constructed box that was packed with peat. However, practical considerations made it possible to conserve only the head and not the whole body. This was soaked for more than a year, first in formalin and acetic acid, then in alcohol, toluol and finally wax.

The remains of Tollund Man are now permanently on display in Denmark. He looks as if he were merely asleep; it is astonishing to think that he died 2,000 years ago.

---

any treatment given is reversible; and *not to do anything* (not even washing) to material destined for radiocarbon or other forms of dating or chemical, physical or biological analysis, as that may complicate such analyses or make them impossible.

Consolidants and Adhesives

In general, the consolidants and adhesives used in field conservation are soluble in water, alcohol, toluene or acetone. These include soluble nylon (particularly useful as it allows penetration of water, so it can be used to consolidate material before it is washed to remove salts), PVA (polyvinyl acetate), PEG (polyethylene glycol wax), polyvinyl (PV) butyral and polymethacrylate.

Benzotriazole is used to stabilize "bronze disease" until laboratory treatment is possible (silver oxide is an acceptable substitute). Cellulose nitrate (HMG) is a useful all-purpose adhesive; alternatives are PVA adhesive or rubber/resin compounds.

If an object is particularly fragile or very large, some form of structural support may be necessary. Bandages can provide simple reinforcement, while plaster of paris is widely used. It is relatively cheap, easy to apply and equally easy to remove when the object reaches the laboratory. Fiberglass sheets applied with a resin such as PV butyral are more versatile than plaster, but rather harder to remove. Other suitable supports include latex rubber

jackets, which peel off easily, and polyurethane foam, applied over a separating barrier, preferably of aluminum foil. Such foam, however, is expensive and emits toxic fumes.

Before setting an object in plaster, it is essential to protect it by covering it with a layer of damp paper, or polythene or rubber sheeting. The surface of the object may be further protected by coating it with a synthetic resin before it is wrapped in the separating material. The plaster of paris jacket should be reinforced with bandages or scrim.

Those Vital Labels

Material sent from the site for conservation or analysis should, like all other finds, be clearly labeled and recorded. The labels should carry all the relevant information, including details of any treatment given, to save the conservator's time. A copy of the full record of the find should be sent with it, too.

If possible, one label should be placed with the material inside its container and another on the outside. As a further precaution against confusion, it is helpful to put an identifying code mark on the material itself.

Use a marking pen, and put the mark in an unobtrusive place. If the surface is not suitable for marking, put on a small patch of PVA or lacquer, which can be marked when dry.

ABOVE:
The head of Tollund Man, *some 2,000 years old, is a striking testimony to the remarkable preservative powers of peat. Even the eyebrows, eyelashes and stubble on the chin are clearly visible, as is the rope with which he was garrotted.*

AS IT WAS

As the last days of an excavation approach, the pace of activities increases dramatically. Every member of the team is suddenly aware of all that remains to be done, and inevitably something unexpected will turn up, usually on the last day in the last half hour, that requires time that is not available.

At last, however, it is all over. It remains only to fill in the site and to pack up the tools. Backfilling and returning the site to its former state are a general requirement. Even if the site is to be redeveloped, it is dangerous to leave an open hole, so it will be filled in unless the redevelopment is actually in progress. On rural sites, the subsoil, topsoil and turf are replaced in the correct order. Ideally, backfilling is done by machine; it is a tedious and lengthy task replacing soil by hand, and virtually impossible to compress it sufficiently to restore it to its previous horizontal state.

The Case for Preservation

Sometimes, the structural remains excavated are impressive and interesting enough to justify the expense and effort of opening them to the public. In such a case, they must be consolidated to prevent them from collapsing.

The remains need to be made sufficiently strong to survive both the elements and the visitors who are expected to view the site. But the consolidation must be unobtrusive so that the visitor is able to see the structures, so far as possible, in something like their original state.

The degree to which restoration (as opposed to consolidation) should be undertaken is a much disputed matter. For example, when Sir Arthur Evans restored the Minoan palace of Knossos, he rebuilt and repainted much of the crumbling masonry in an effort to recreate the original appearance of the palace as closely as possible.

He has been both praised and severely criticized for this approach. The issue really is whether or not reconstruction should occur on-site, where it may perhaps obscure or destroy evidence that might later be vital in reinterpreting it.

A viable alternative is presentation of a reconstruction in a museum on-site. This allows data and interpretation to be kept separate and is academically more acceptable. However, it is unlikely

to equal the immediacy of the impression gained by actually walking around a reconstructed original site. Something of this feel can now be achieved, however, using virtual reality computer software (*see page 169*).

Obviously, there is no correct answer, but whatever is done—for instance, artifact restoration—should be carried out as accurately as possible and should also make obvious which portions are original and which have been restored.

After an excavation, if the site is not to be kept open for display to the public, it is backfilled (upper, right) and returned as closely as possible to its original state.

Knossos Palace, on the island of Crete, has been extensively reconstructed to reflect the original as closely as possible. The colonnaded staircase shown at right is one of the most striking of the reconstructed features. The palace was the center of the Minoan civilization in the 2nd millennium B.C.E.

AT THE FRINGE OF THE EMPIRE

Local politics in southeast England took on an international dimension after Julius Caesar invaded the country in 55 and 54 B.C.E. When, in 43 C.E., the Romans began their final full-scale conquest, they did so ostensibly in defense of the pro-Roman king of the Atrebates who had fled across the channel to seek their protection. The Atrebatic territory around Chichester provided the Romans with a friendly supply base from which to subdue the west of England; Togidubnus (Cogidubnus to the Romans), the client king established by the Romans in this area, enjoyed considerable Roman patronage and prosperity as a result.

In 1960, a chance find by a workman of a substantial quantity of Roman tiles led to the discovery of a large complex of buildings at Fishbourne, near Chichester. Excavations revealed several phases of construction: a substantial wooden house built in the 40s C.E., replaced in the late 60s by a series of masonry buildings. These in turn were demolished around 75 to make way for what can only be described as a palace, a vast four-winged building arranged around a central ornamental garden. The geographical location of the palace and the political history of the region make it probable that these were the successive residences of King Togidubnus.

The magnificent palace was lavishly provided with marble wall panels and moldings, colorful wall paintings and fine mosaics. The south wing, probably the private rooms of the king and his family, housed the bath suite, while the other wings contained administrative chambers, guest rooms and reception areas.

In later days the palace was modified; the addition of further bath suites suggests it may have been divided between several families. A number of new multicolored mosaics were created, as the craft of mosaic-making became established in Britain. A hypocaust, the Roman system of underfloor central heating, was installed for several rooms. While the heating was being extended to a room in the north wing, the palace was entirely destroyed by fire.

Recognition of the importance of Fishbourne—the only palace of its size outside the heartlands of the Roman Empire—led to a concentrated effort to preserve the site. Much of the north wing is now incorporated into a museum. The building is carefully designed to give an impression of the size of the wing in Roman times, but it is deliberately constructed of metal and glass to distinguish it clearly from the original Roman remains.

Traces of the garden at Fishbourne have been excavated (above), revealing trenches where box hedges once grew, planted in a rich loam that is clearly distinguishable from the surrounding poor, stony soil. The garden has now been reconstructed.

Fishbourne Roman palace, as it was in 75 C.E., is displayed in a model (left) in the Fishbourne museum. The palace was the largest and most lavish Roman residence built in Britain; it was probably the home of Togidubnus, the local king. Superb mosaic floors (lower left) are perhaps the most impressive feature of the Fishbourne remains, which are now on display in the museum.

The techniques that have been discussed so far assume the site to be more or less "normal," with some structural remains and a number of reasonably preserved finds requiring little special attention. A number of sites, however, present special problems either because of the nature of the preserved material, or because of the circumstances in which it has been preserved. These include sites on which a large amount of organic material is preserved due to waterlogging, desiccation or freezing, such as ancient tombs in Siberia where textiles, clothing and bodies are preserved in frozen layers. Others experienced a natural disaster, such as a volcanic eruption (as at Pompeii and on Thíra) or a mudslide (as at the North American site of Ozette), which engulfed houses or an entire settlement, "freezing" it in time.

Two aspects of waterlogged sites, for example, particularly affect their excavation. First, they are likely to contain a great deal of well-preserved organic material—wooden structures or artifacts, leatherwork or basketry, and plant and animal matter that can provide information on diet and on the local environment.

Many of these items, especially wooden ones, will start to deteriorate soon after exposure to the air, so care must be taken to protect them during excavation and recovery. Arrangements must also be made for their immediate treatment, on or near the site, to conserve them. In dry weather, the exposed waterlogged material that cannot immediately be lifted and taken to safety must be kept constantly wet. Drying can also be inhibited by wrapping exposed material in polyethylene.

Secondly, wooden structural remains on waterlogged sites, such as posts, stakes and trackway, are usually three-dimensional and fragile. Measures must be taken to prevent them from being compressed or otherwise physically damaged in the course of excavation.

In the early stages, before the actual remains are exposed, the weight of individual excavators is spread over a wider area by using toe boards (small planks of wood) for standing or kneeling. Later, when the remains begin to be revealed, it may be necessary to make complicated networks of planks laid across boxes set on firm ground, on which the excavators sit or lie flat to dig (*see page 105*).

The tools employed in excavating waterlogged materials must generally be more delicate than the customary trowel. Plastic spatulas and flat wooden Popsicle sticks can be used to peel off firm deposits, such as peat. Loose-textured deposits may be sprayed off with a low-pressure jet of water.

The Camp Beside the Lake

As the ice sheets began to melt and withdraw northward around 12,000 years ago, the lifestyle of the inhabitants of western Europe changed. Until then, reindeer had played a major part in their economy. Now, in the warming climate, a broader range of resources became available. More significantly for archaeologists, these early Europeans moved from the caves and rock shelters they had occupied in Paleolithic times—sites easy for modern investigators to identify—to open localities, where their camps are much harder to locate.

Between the 1920s and the 1940s, many of the tools of stone, and sometimes bone or antler, used by these Mesolithic hunter-gatherers came to light. To understand more about such people, however, a well-preserved example of one of their settlements had still to be discovered and excavated. In 1949, Professor Grahame Clark of Cambridge University examined an area in the Vale of Pickering in northeast England, where Mesolithic tools had been found. The study revealed just such a site at Star Carr. It had once stood beside a lake that subsequently became choked with peat deposits. Clark expected that the boggy soil would yield waterlogged organic remains, greatly increasing our knowledge of Mesolithic people and their environment.

Antler harpoons (below), used by Mesolithic hunter-gatherers, were discovered at Star Carr in Yorkshire in the mid-20th century. The harpoons and many other artifacts made from flint, stone, wood and bone were preserved in peat beside a lake.

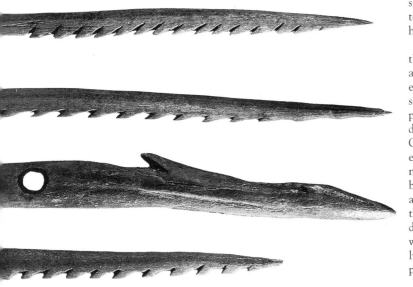

FROZEN HORSEMEN OF SIBERIA

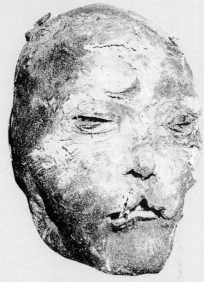

At Pazyryk in the cold Siberian steppes, richly furnished burials were made by tribes of nomadic horse-riders around 400 B.C.E., but shortly afterward, these graves were robbed of all their gold. The holes dug by the thieves filled with rainwater that froze, preserving all the remaining grave goods, as well as the bodies of the dead and their horses, which had been ritually killed and buried with them.

The graves at Pazyryk were rediscovered in 1924. One was excavated in 1929 and four more between 1947 and 1949. Nineteenth-century excavations of other such tombs had proceeded by lighting fires on top of the tombs to penetrate the frozen ground. The Pazyryk excavators, however, poured buckets of boiling water over the graves. The resulting slush made it necessary to shore up the site to ensure the safety of the excavators.

What was revealed, however, entirely compensated for the difficult excavating conditions. Each burial had been made in a wooden chamber at the bottom of a shaft, above which a cairn of earth and stones had been erected. Several bodies had been remarkably well preserved in the ice. One of them was elaborately tattooed with motifs of fabulous monsters like griffins, as well as animals such as deer and mountain goats (*see page 112*). These animal designs were echoed on the colorful textiles and carpets that were discovered—tigers killing their prey were particularly popular. Other fabrics bore geometric designs.

The excavators also found articles of wood, metal and horn, fur and leather. Among them were items of saddlery, all-important to these mounted tribespeople: bridles similar to those of today and simple saddles consisting of two cushions.

Brightly colored textiles, such as this felt wall-hanging showing a nomadic horseman, were among the finds at Pazyryk.

Hunters of the Swamp

Excavations of Star Carr took place over three seasons from 1949 to 1951, entirely uncovering what proved to be a Mesolithic camp. The lake's bank had been swampy, so the camp-dwellers had made a firm platform by covering part of it with branches and twigs of birch, as well as with other debris at hand. Large lumps of moss were placed on top of the platform, probably so that it would be more comfortable.

The distribution of flints and other tools on the platform was carefully recorded by the excavators. The information helped to define the area that had been settled; outside it the number of tools found dropped sharply. Clark estimated that the camp could accommodate three or four families, at most around 20 people.

Clearly, toolmaking was one of the main activities at Star Carr. Tools were made from flint and deer antlers, but surprisingly, not from animal bones, although there were plenty of those—mostly red deer, with roe deer, elk, ox and pig.

Deer Skull Masks

Many of the antlers and attached skull frontal portions found at Star Carr seem to have been modified for human wear. The most likely explanation is that they were masks worn as primitive camouflage when stalking deer.

Other remains recovered from the site included rolls of birch bark, which was perhaps a source of resin with which to fix spear and arrow heads to their shafts, and pieces of bracket fungus, possibly for tinder. A wooden paddle suggests the camp-dwellers had boats. Pollen studies of the lake deposits and radiocarbon dating suggest that the camp was in use in about 7500 B.C.E. There were also indications that the site had been occupied more than once.

The excavation of Star Carr is now regarded as a landmark of modern archaeology. Clark and his team conducted a pioneering study of an economic community within its environment—a far cry from the artifact-oriented approach prevalent in the mid-20th century.

ABOVE LEFT:
The mummified head of a tribal chief, preserved in ice for more than 2,000 years, was among several frozen bodies discovered in burial mounds at Pazyryk in the Siberian steppes. The skull has been damaged by a blow from a battle-ax.

UNDERWATER ARCHAEOLOGY

When recording the position of objects and features underwater, archaeologists rely heavily on tapes and measuring rods (bottom right), since the poor visibility rules out the use of ordinary surveying instruments. As many details as possible are recorded during the dive (below left), using specially adapted slates with a clear mylar surface or pre-cut sheets of plastic drawing film.

The principles applied to underwater archaeology are, in theory, exactly the same as those applied on land. But the environment imposes obvious restrictions. With standard equipment and in the most favorable conditions, a diver can stay underwater for only about four hours in the day, a period of time that decreases rapidly with cold and depth. The need to stay alert to the hazards inherent in diving reduces concentration on the archaeological task in hand, and powers of memory reportedly weaken too. So detailed and meticulous recording is normally carried out on-the-spot, rather than being left until the return to the surface.

Underwater surveying used to be difficult, having to rely largely on measuring rods and on tapes that, annoyingly, were often shifted by currents. Recently, however, surveying underwater has been revolutionized by the use of GPS (Global Positioning Systems). These use receivers to pick up signals from a set of satellites that regularly orbit the Earth: The position of these at a given time is known, so the time interval between the signal and its reception allows the three-dimensional position (latitude, longitude and elevation) of the receiver to be established to an accuracy of within 3 feet (1 m) or even 2 inches (10 cm).

Poor visibility limits the scope of photography. Single-photograph views of the whole site are often impossible to obtain, although an overall picture can be built up with a mosaic of photos of individual areas. On the other hand, photogrammetric planning is far easier underwater than on land and saves the valuable diving time conventional planning would require.

Some underwater archaeologists do make conventional plans, however, with the same pencils and plastic drawing film that their land-based counterparts use.

Not All Drawbacks

Despite the difficulties, there are some advantages in working underwater. Excavation is often easy, involving no tools, but just a gentle fanning movement of the hand. The sediments displaced in this way can be removed with a low-power dredge or a large-bore airlift. The latter also helps keep the excavation area free of silt, while the dredge can be used as an excavation tool comparable to the pickax on land. Stones can be carried away with the aid of airlifting bags.

Underwater sites have the added attraction of preserving many materials that would have perished at most land-based excavations. The warship *Mary Rose* (see pages 55 and 101), for instance, was substantially preserved and in addition contained a whole range of fascinating objects.

Underwater video cameras are also widely used for recording. Coupled with computers, they can be used for photogrammetric planning and 3-D recording: the results can be incorporated into GIS (see page 168).

Many settlements in Neolithic Europe were built by the shores of lakes, usually on platforms supported by piles. Often, the water level of the lake has subsequently risen, submerging the buildings and protecting them from biological decay.

Charavines, in Paladru lake in France, is one such village. It first appeared above the surface of the lake in 1921, during a particularly dry spell; normally it lies in 6–12 feet (2–4 m) of water. The investigation involved a number of amateur divers whose first task was to map the forest of piles still standing.

The site was divided into a grid of triangles, instead of the more usual squares or rectangles. Measurements were then recorded from three points, improving their accuracy in the poor visibility of the murky lake waters. The excavators cleared the site with

their bare hands, and soil and artifacts were removed in buckets and boxes.

The lake's water had preserved a remarkable range of material undisturbed, giving a fascinating insight into the life of this little village. Tree-ring studies of timbers revealed that they had been left to season for a year before the first house was built. A second house was added a year later.

Two Periods of Occupation

Pollen cores from Charavines show that the site had two short periods of occupation. Settlers arrived and cleared the forest nearby to plant crops. After 20–30 years, they left and the forest regenerated. The village was reoccupied some 30–40 years later, when the forest was cleared again and wheat, barley and flax were cultivated. The inhabitants also made use of many of the wild fruits, berries and nuts that were locally available.

After another 20–30 years, rising lake levels forced the villagers to abandon the settlement again. Behind them they left many traces of their daily activities. Many of these, such as butchering animals and weaving flax and wool, took place outside their houses.

Basketry and pottery were abundant and on occasion contained the remains of food. Other finds included dugout canoes in which the villagers ventured out on the lake and bows and arrows, as well as wooden spoons and weaving combs, even a half-eaten apple.

The remains of a massive wall (above) at Amnisos, the port of the Minoan palace of Knossos in northern Crete, extend several yards into the sea. It was probably some sort of jetty, but its function has never been properly explained.

Excavations of a merchant ship wrecked in the 14th century B.C.E. at Uluburun off the coast of Anatolia have yielded a treasury of Bronze Age objects. These included many copper ingots from Cyprus; Canaanite, Cypriot and Mycenaean pottery; and a unique book, made out of two wooden panels, that originally contained sheets of wax.

95

INDUSTRIAL ARCHAEOLOGY

The economies of many countries of the world have been transformed within the last four or five generations from predominantly rural to predominantly industrial. What is termed industrial archaeology applies itself to the study of these transformations, not only in terms of technology, but in human terms too.

The pursuit of industrial archaeology is still sufficiently new for its aims and methods not to be clearly defined. Like conventional archaeology, however, it encompasses much more than just excavation.

At present, its main concern is the detailed recording, preferably in situ, and understanding of the physical remains of our recent past. These include factories, mills and mines, communications systems such as canals, roads and railways, domestic and public architecture, and machinery and equipment.

Beyond this, however, there is a deeper intention: to make us aware of the immediate past, of which we are the direct heirs, to which our grandparents belonged, and which has shaped our present. To build a complete picture of this past, the industrial archaeologist may dip deeply into many other fields: geography, social and economic history, sociology and anthropology.

One of the sources such investigators can tap is the memory of survivors who can recall recently vanished ways of life, and this ability to communicate directly is the one thing that divides industrial archaeology sharply from other branches of the discipline. In other respects, however, the division is more felt than real; the methods of historical archaeology, including the study of documentary sources and of details of the urban and rural landscape as well as excavation, are equally applicable to industrial archaeology, despite the immense technological differences in the physical remains being studied.

The Hay inclined plane at Coalport, England, built in 1792, was used to raise and lower canal boats over a steep incline on the Shropshire Canal. The boats were winched on cradles that ran on rails; a pair of 5-ton boats could be passed in four minutes, compared with about three hours using a conventional lock system. The incline remained in operation until 1894; after closing, it quickly became overgrown. In the 1970s it was partially restored and is now part of the Ironbridge Gorge Museum.

ROGERS LOCOMOTIVE WORKS

In the early 1970s, plans for construction work in the historic Great Falls area of Paterson, New Jersey, led to a large-scale industrial archaeological investigation. Paterson was America's first planned industrial city, in the early 19th century.

By the 1830s iron and machinery were the city's chief products; shortly afterward the manufacture of railway locomotives became predominant. The locomotive works established in the Great Falls area by the pioneer and innovative engineer Thomas Rogers were among the most important in America.

Initial investigations in 1973–1975 established that a considerable number of historic buildings, representative of all periods in Paterson's industrial history, remained, many of them in good repair and some still in use. As a result of this preliminary study, the city's Department of Community Development decided to rehabilitate them and to encourage modern companies to use them.

An Industrial Museum

The surviving buildings of the Rogers Locomotive Works, many of them dating from the 1870s, were deemed to be of particular historic importance. It was agreed that part of the works should be converted into an industrial museum.

During 1978 and 1979, these buildings were thoroughly investigated by archaeologists. Their job was to assess the potential damage that reconstruction would inflict and, where possible, to recommend alternative locations. When the work began, the archaeologists watched and if necessary halted the operations to examine features of particular interest. Their investigations supplemented the picture already created from historical records.

Because the area had been swampy before the first buildings were put up in the 1830s, the ground level had been raised with layers of yellow clay, silt, rubble and any debris that came to hand. Over the next 40 or so years, the factories and workshops occupied a relatively small area. But in the 1870s they were demolished and replaced by a much larger complex. Locomotive production ceased around 1915. Some buildings were knocked down, while others were turned over to light manufacturing.

The excavations uncovered a large portion of a blacksmith's shop from the 1870s, with the foundations of a number of powerful steam hammers and the brick bases of several gantry cranes. Animal bones, which were probably the remains of meals, were also found; recorded memories of workers of the era indicated that they often ate while they toiled because no meal breaks were allowed.

The Rogers locomotive, built in 1882 for the Long Island Railroad, was a product of the Rogers Locomotive Works, the most important of three companies in Paterson, New Jersey, producing locomotives in the late 19th century. The works were founded by the great pioneering engineer, Thomas Rogers, who built the Sandusky, one of America's first steam locomotives, in 1837, only eight years after the triumph of Englishman George Stephenson's Rocket. Rogers based the Sandusky on a locomotive imported from Stephenson's works but introduced many important advances of his own design.

This coin, a brass sesterce bearing the image of the emperor Trajan (reigned 98–117 C.E.), was unearthed during excavations at Lime Street, in London, and is evidence of the city's Roman occupation.

PART

PROCESSING THE FINDS

CONSERVATION AND ANALYSIS

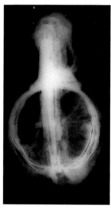

Conservators can employ a battery of scientific tools and techniques to examine in detail every fragment they receive. Before analysis, this piece of corroded iron (uppermost) was unrecognizable. X-ray analysis (above) revealed the shape and size of an object that after cleaning, was found to be a 14th-century barrel padlock (opposite page).

The excavation has been completed, and all the volunteer diggers have gone home. The director and site supervisors are left surrounded by boxes and plastic bags full of soil samples, animal bones, potsherds or pieces of stone and heaps of notebooks, drawings and photographs. How will all this be miraculously transformed into a detailed, informative report of the team's findings?

Three groups of people are likely to be involved in this task. First there are the conservators, whose task is twofold. They must ensure that all the material that has been recovered is preserved in as near a pristine state as possible. They must also treat the material in such a way as to make it suitable for further study. The first task is of key importance since, although some conservation "first aid" may have been done on-site, it is probable that many of the finds will require specialized laboratory treatment.

The material that has been collected from the excavation will, it is hoped, yield the answers to a whole series of questions: When was the site occupied? What did the people eat? What did their dwellings and environment look like? Where did they obtain their raw materials? And how did they manufacture things from them?

The job of extracting many of the answers falls to the scientific researchers. Among their number are biologists who study human, animal and plant remains and specialists in the analysis of stone, pottery, metal and other artifacts. An important group of researchers, who may devote their time entirely to archaeological work, perform the analyses that establish the age of some of the finds.

Finally, there is the archaeological director and his or her team, which also often includes various specialists, such as pottery analysts. Using typology, they sort and identify the mass of sherds, stone and metal tools, and other material, drawing conclusions about the activities that took place on the site and the relationships of the site's inhabitants to other groups. The director draws together all the strands of evidence provided by the specialist analyses in the project report. This summarizes the discoveries made in the survey or excavation and sets out the site's place in the archaeology of the region in which it lies, or the period into which it falls.

Conservation in the Laboratory

Conservation is as vital a part of modern archaeology as is the careful and patient excavation of the site itself. The archaeological conservator has a number of important tasks. In many archaeological sites, particular conditions exist that have allowed objects to be preserved; these objects must be stabilized and consolidated by the conservator to prevent deterioration. Waterlogged wood, for example, shrinks and warps as it dries out, so the water must be replaced with wax to preserve the original shape and size. Other objects may require only skillful cleaning so that the archaeologist will be able to study them in detail. In addition, the conservator may be asked to repair and restore artifacts, particularly for museum display.

Obviously, any conservator's aim is to do the best job possible with the tools and techniques available. Since, however, the pace of technical development means that new and more effective methods are constantly being devised, the conservator aims to use only treatments that can be reversed, choosing, for instance, adhesives and consolidants that can be removed with appropriate solvents. Sometimes, though, this principle and the need to preserve effectively are in conflict, as happened in the case of the *Mary Rose* cannons.

Artifacts can best be appreciated if restored as closely as possible to their original appearance. Yet it must always be possible to distinguish between the original parts of the object and the restored portions. What the conservator must do is strike a balance between these conflicting requirements, and, here, of course, much depends on individual viewpoints. Some conservators completely restore objects so that their work can be detected only when the object is examined closely. Others make it easy to distinguish between original and restoration by deliberately using different materials.

Cleaning the Finds

Most well-preserved specimens of pottery, bone, leather, wood, glass, textiles and stone can be gently washed in clean soft water. Although gold can also be washed, other metals generally must be mechanically cleaned using dental tools and fine blades. So, too, must ivory, tortoiseshell, antler, horn and objects made from unfired clay.

Most materials can be left to dry naturally in the air, but some, such as glass, could be damaged. In such cases, the water is removed by soaking in alcohol and then ether before drying. Alternatively, objects can be dried and consolidated—a process that involves removing the water and

CONSERVING THE MARY ROSE

One of the greatest problems posed by the raising of the Tudor warship *Mary Rose* has been the sheer number of fragile wood and leather objects it has produced, especially as many of them, such as the bundles of arrows and chests of longbows, are unique. Like so many finds, removal of these from their stable underwater environment meant that deterioration would begin.

To combat this problem, a special laboratory was established, with two main aims—to conserve as much as possible of the material recovered and to experiment with various ways of treating the material to find out which gave the best results. Wood and leather were first washed to remove soluble sea salts and then soaked in a chemical bath to get rid of insoluble iron salts from the disintegrated iron fittings of the ship. Wood was then consolidated by soaking in successively more concentrated baths of polyethylene glycol, while the leather was soaked in a Bavon solution. These objects were then freeze-dried.

The conservation of the ship's wrought iron and cast iron cannons presented a major challenge. Various techniques were tried, but only one proved to be reliable. It involved heating the iron in a specially constructed hydrogen furnace, which converted the oxidized iron to metallic iron. As the process is irreversible once it is under way, its use has come under criticism by some conservators. But when faced with the risk of the finds themselves actually deteriorating, the *Mary Rose* team was forced to adopt this less-than-satisfactory approach. To meet the anticipated criticism, some samples of iron that had not been conserved were set aside for any future analyses that might be required.

Members of the Mary Rose team use electrical engravers to restore fine detail to the ship's cannons.

simultaneously replacing it with wax or polyethylene glycol (PEG).

Removing Salts from Nonmetals

Potentially damaging soluble salts are generally removed from pottery, bone or stone by repeated soaking in clean water. If the surface of the specimen is flaking or decorated, it is consolidated first with permeable soluble nylon. Ivory requires extremely delicate treatment. It can be soaked only for a few seconds and must be dried immediately in alcohol and ether.

Encrusted insoluble salts should be removed by hand if possible. They can be softened first with drops of near-concentrated acid, but this must be washed off immediately after application.

Treating Metals

Before treating any metal object, it must be examined carefully to assess the thickness of the corroded layer and the strength of the metal under it, as well as ascertaining whether it is decorated. This initial examination is often done with X rays, but it can be carried out by physical probing with needles. If there is decoration, preserving it is a priority, especially if it is thin and easily damaged. A variety of acids are used to remove corrosion from silver, copper and bronze, while some commercial rust solvents can be employed on iron.

Occasionally, in seawater the shape of a cast iron object may be preserved inside a coating of calcareous matter—even though the object itself has rusted away completely. The coating can be cut into pieces, cleaned and used as a mold to produce a replica of the original.

Mending and Restoration

Most materials can be mended with various adhesives. Epoxy and polyester resins and soluble nylon are particularly suitable, as they do not shrink appreciably when dry. Small uncorroded metal objects may also be soldered.

When reconstructing pottery, a sand tray is used to hold the pieces together while the adhesive sets. Missing pieces of the pot are restored using plaster of paris appropriately colored with paint or a dough made from a mixture of alvar, jute and kaolin. A lump of plasticine molded to the correct shape is placed behind the hole, on the inside of the vessel. The edges of the hole are coated with polyvinyl acetate and the gap carefully filled.

PROCESSING ORGANIC REMAINS

The study of organic remains can give archaeologists two broad types of information. The first enables scholars to construct a picture of the prehistoric environment and people's impact on it, while the second shows the workings of ancient economies.

Examination of plant and animal material, including fish and mollusks, helps to determine what our forebears ate, while insect, parasite and other microorganic remains are valuable aids in determining details of such things as the storage of grain and crop and animal pathology. In addition, archaeologists look for evidence of seasonal exploitation of particular resources—an important facet of prehistoric economies.

In addition, organic remains may have had interesting secondary economic functions. Shells and feathers, for example, were sometimes used for personal ornaments, while bones and antlers were carved into tools.

Speed of Decay

All organic material is subject to decay, but the speed at which that takes place depends on the nature of the material itself and on its environment. In some circumstances, ancient organic matter can remain remarkably well preserved. For example, prehistoric grain is often found carbonized, turned to charcoal accidentally or deliberately by fire, but readily identifiable.

Bone and shell survive well in alkaline or neutral soils; acid soil destroys them, although it also inhibits or prevents the activity of the organisms responsible for biological decay. Therefore, acid soils are likely to yield pollen grains and other plant material occasionally. The same characteristic is shared by heavy clay soils, which may inhibit decay by excluding air.

A rich collection of human and animal bones (right) has been recovered from the Aegean volcanic island of Thira (known in ancient times as Thera and until recently as Santorin), which erupted about 1628 B.C.E., preserving houses up to three stories high beneath the volcanic ash.

Frozen in time, this exquisite portrait of a bison (below) was shaped from reindeer antler by a Stone Age artisan in the Dordogne, France, some 14,000 years ago. Art is a valuable source of information about many aspects of life in the past.

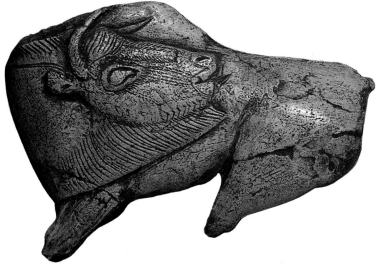

Climatic extremes deter the processes of biological decay. In dry, hot regions, in freezing conditions and in completely waterlogged marshlands preservation may be virtually total. All parts and types of plants, from pollen to trees, soft tissue of animals and humans, insects and even microorganisms can survive, although acid bogs totally destroy both bone and shell. It is because of this that bodies that are recovered from bogs are sometimes found without any bones at all, but with skin that is in an excellent state of preservation.

Arid sites, particularly in the Americas, frequently yield preserved or fossilized feces, called coprolites. They have also been recovered from waterlogged deposits, especially cesspits, and provide extremely valuable information on diet.

Analyzing the Material

Analysis of organic remains begins with the identification of the family, genus or species of the material in each category. Sometimes that can be relatively easy, but often it is difficult.

Mammal bones are generally identifiable to species or genus. Fish, on the other hand, are much harder to identify, partly because the range of species likely to be present on a site is greater than that of mammals.

Although identification keys, drawings, photographs and descriptions can be helpful, for most types of material a reference collection of specimens is virtually essential. Ideally, reference collections should include a variety of specimens of each species.

Seeking the Source

Organic remains found on an archaeological site may be evidence of what the local environment was like in the past or of the ecological influence of people. For that reason, it is essential to distinguish between their possible sources. Wood used in building or in making tools, for example, is usually chosen carefully and may have been brought to the area from a considerable distance away. Firewood, on the other hand, is normally gathered nearby, so it can be more relevant to the reconstruction of the local ecology.

People are generally responsible for the presence of large animals on a site and their remains provide only a broad indication of climate or environment. Small creatures such as rodents are much less wide-ranging and can suggest quite specific ecological conditions.

The evidence from mollusk and insect remains is particularly useful. Most species of land and freshwater snails have distinct preferences in their habitats, so those recovered should give a good picture of the local environment. Insects—particularly beetles, whose harder portions survive well in the absence of oxygen—are even more specific, as many of them are restricted to a single type of host plant.

Roman letters written on thin leaves of lime wood have, remarkably, survived due to waterlogging at the Roman fort of Vindolanda along Hadrian's Wall. The writing on them has apparently vanished but can be revealed using infrared photography. Some of the letters are official correspondence, giving, for example, an interesting picture of what the soldiers had to eat. But there are also private letters, such as this invitation for the commandant's wife to attend a birthday party and one to a soldier perhaps from his mother: "I have sent you [some] pairs of socks . . . and two pairs of underpants, two pairs of sandals . . ."

103

PROCESSING
ORGANIC REMAINS

POLLEN ANALYSIS

The microscopic grains of pollen produced by flowering plants and dispersed by insects, birds, the wind and other agencies come in a wide variety of shapes and sizes. Most can be identified to their genus and a few to their species (though grass is an exception—its pollen is identical throughout the whole family of grasses). The spores of nonflowering plants can be similarly identified.

Different trees and plants produce different amounts of pollen, and not all types preserve well. However, to a large extent, the pollen spectrum—the range of pollen types that settle in a deposit—reflects the general vegetation of the region. Studies of modern pollen spectra and their comparison with modern regional vegetation form the basis for interpreting pollen spectra of the past.

Cores are taken through ancient lake sediments and peat bogs, and the types and amounts of the different pollens present in each layer within this core are counted. Usually 200–500 grains are counted from each sample. The results of this are depicted in a pollen diagram, showing the changing proportions of the pollen of different plants (the pollen profile).

Pollen analysis was first developed as a dating technique in northern Europe. Changes in vegetation, particularly of the forests, owing to climatic shifts, were reflected in the changing nature of the pollen spectra. By establishing the sequence of vegetational periods (pollen zones), a relative chronology for much of northern and western Europe could be produced. Following this, absolute dates for the pollen zones were established using varve (a layer of glacial sediment deposited yearly in lakes and fjords) chronology (*see page 131*).

Landscape Changes

Since the development of radiocarbon dating, pollen zone dating has become less important, but pollen analysis is a major source of information about the environment and about human activities. As investigations continue, it becomes increasingly apparent that many changes in vegetation were due to humans.

One of the first examples of this to be recognized was what is known as the "landnam" (landtaking) phase in early Neolithic Europe. A substantial decrease in tree pollen associated with an increase in the pollen of cereals, weeds of cultivation and other light-loving species marked the beginning of forest clearance and cultivation. Pollen analyses also suggest that Mesolithic peoples were using fire to make clearings in the forest, encouraging the growth of species suitable for human food.

Pollen diagrams show the types and amounts of pollens present in an area during different periods. This diagram of vegetation in Jutland, Denmark, covers more than 12,000 years (time periods are shown on the vertical scales at the sides). For each individual species, the thickness of the line indicates the amount of pollen—and thus the amount of vegetation—present.

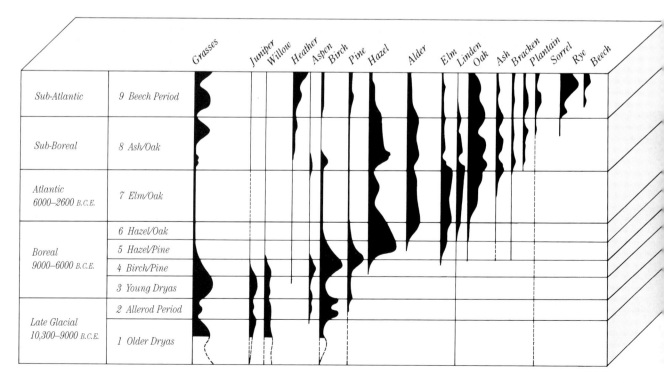

CLIMATE CHANGES OF THE STONE AGE

Since the early 19th century, archaeologists have been observing and investigating the abundant Paleolithic deposits in the caves and rock shelters of southwestern France. In the 1950s and 1960s, François Bordes, France's leading Paleolithic authority, excavated Pech de l'Azé, a cave occupied by Neanderthal people. Bordes's team included specialists from many disciplines, such as soil scientists, whose analyses provided information on the local environment in Paleolithic times.

Pech de l'Azé consists of two caves connected by a low tunnel. Pech II was first occupied in very cold, dry conditions during the Riss Glaciation (a major ice age episode during the Pleistocene era), when the local vegetation was grassy steppe with a few pine trees, inhabited by such animals as red and roe deer, horses, Merck's rhinoceros and elephants.

Later in the Riss period the climate became warmer and wetter, with more trees. Although it subsequently reverted to cold and dry, the cave was no longer inhabited. Traces of any habitation of the caves during the warm, damp interglacial period that followed the Riss have been obliterated. But in any case, in such conditions, people may have preferred to live in open-air camps.

At the beginning of the Würm Glaciation, the most recent ice age, a large section of the cave roof collapsed, and it was only somewhat later that Neanderthal people reoccupied Pech II, from which they hunted rabbits and red deer. Pech I was also occupied at this time. But due to the extremely wet climate in the main interstadial during Würm, when the ice sheets temporarily retreated, deposits in that cave were washed out, leaving only traces. Subsequently, Pech I was preferred to Pech II, and considerable deposits accumulated, full of stone tools and the bones of animals that, together with the pollen and sedimentary evidence, indicate continuing fluctuations between cold dry steppe and somewhat warmer and wetter parkland environments.

While lake and bog pollen spectra reflect regional vegetation as a whole, soil samples give a more localized picture, and so may be used to reconstruct local ecology. Buried land surfaces beneath earthworks may indicate details of local land use. As pollen in the soil is concentrated near the surface, the analysis of its distribution within earthenworks, such as banks and barrows, may help to determine details of construction.

Studying the Soil

Analysis of the soil can tell archaeologists about the conditions in which it was formed, the changes that have taken place since then and, sometimes, about the activities of early people. Soils consist of an inorganic matrix of particles of rock and minerals and organic material (humus) derived from the decay of plants growing on it. The detailed study of humus itself will give some information about local vegetation patterns in the past; this is a useful supplement to any information which has already been obtained from pollen analysis.

The presence of humus can be detected by boiling a small sample of soil in caustic soda. If it is there, the liquid will appear a deep brown color when decanted. Uncarbonized organic material will burn if a soil sample is heated, and heating will also reveal the presence and quantity of carbon and of iron compounds.

Examination of the soil's micromorphology under a microscope may reveal inclusions that indicate the original function of archaeological structures or deposits. Minute pieces of charcoal, for instance, suggest ancient fires.

Chemical tests are also used to detect important elements. Sulphates in soils in temperate climates may indicate that wood ash was at one time present. Concentrations of phosphate are usually a sign of human occupation. Localized high concentrations of manganese, visible as "soil silhouettes," are sometimes found in graves, showing the former presence of a now-vanished body.

Routine analysis of soils includes the determination of its color using what is called a Munsell chart.

A Munsell chart is used to determine the color of a sample of soil (or as in this case, pottery) by comparing it with the colored chips on the chart. A notation is used to describe the color; this may be translated into a verbal description.

Waterlogged ground, as noted earlier, is capable of preserving a wide range of organic remains, although if it is acid, as in peat bogs, it rapidly destroys shell and bone. At a number of British sites, of many periods, archaeologists are obtaining fresh pictures of earlier epochs thanks to the preservative powers of boggy soil past and present.

Tracks Across the Marshes

The Somerset Levels in southwestern England became a freshwater swamp during the 5th millennium B.C.E. Gradually this developed into peat and fen woodland. Good agricultural land and rich grazing and the wide variety of natural resources available in the marsh, lagoons and neighboring wooded slopes attracted farmers, who settled there around 4500 B.C.E. and remained until Roman times. The extensive peat deposits are today being rapidly removed for fertilizer, exposing many excellently preserved prehistoric remains.

Among the most remarkable finds has been a trackway, the Sweet Track, built in the winter of 3807–3806 B.C.E. Throughout their occupation of the area, the prehistoric peoples constructed such wooden paths to connect the sand islands in the levels with the surrounding hills.

The Sweet Track was substantial. It was built of wooden planks, laid lengthways, supported by peat, on a foundation of wooden poles held in place by pairs of cross-pegs driven into the ground. A later track, the Abbot's Way, was made of planks laid crossways, secured by pegs.

The variety of timber and brush in the tracks gives a good picture of the nearby woodlands in prehistoric times and reveals that they were being managed from the days of the first farmers. Studies of hazel and other woods employed show that the trees

were being coppiced—regularly pruned down to near ground level to provide a crop of vigorous

The Sweet Track—a wooden trackway built by prehistoric inhabitants of England some 6,000 years ago across swampy ground in Somerset—has been well preserved within a peat bog.

OPPOSITE PAGE: This schematic reconstruction of a section of the Sweet Track shows the main elements of its construction. Long wooden poles laid end to end across the swamp were held in place by pairs of cross-pegs driven into the ground. They supported a surface of planks, wedged in place by peat and anchored with pegs. Tree-ring dating (see page 130) has shown that the Sweet Track was built of timbers felled in the winter of 3807–3806 B.C.E. and that it was used and repaired for about 10 years.

young stems. Their foliage would have supplemented the diet of grazing animals, while the stems themselves made rods to be used in the tracks.

The evidence from the timber is richly supplemented by information from pollen, plant fragments and beetle remains. They show local vegetation patterns, the stages in the transformation of the Somerset Levels from open water to swamp or raised bog, and various periods of clearance and regeneration in the surrounding woodland.

Early settlers in the area were not only knowledgeable about forest management. The tracks provide a fascinating glimpse of their remarkable skill in working wood with only stone axes and flint knives. The careful selection of the timber demonstrates that they were well aware, too, of the various properties of different woods.

This schematic reconstruction of a section of the Sweet Track shows the main elements of its construction. Long wooden poles laid end to end across the swamp were held in place by pairs of cross-pegs driven into the ground. They supported a surface of planks, wedged in place by peat and anchored with pegs. Tree-ring dating (see page 130) has shown that the Sweet Track was built of timbers felled in the winter of 3807–3806 B.C.E. and that it was used and repaired for about 10 years.

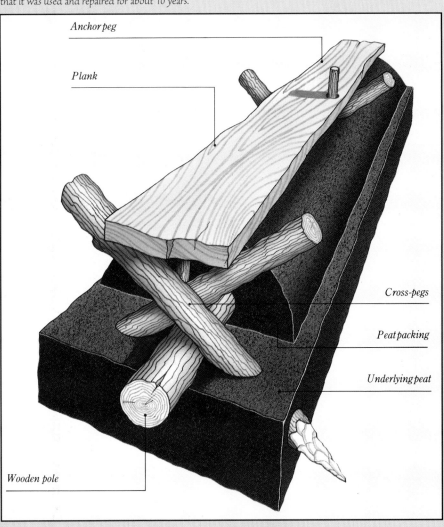

Anchor peg

Plank

Cross-pegs

Peat packing

Underlying peat

Wooden pole

PREHISTORIC DIET AND ECONOMY

Animal bones are the source of information about human diet most commonly recovered from archaeological sites, because, except in acid conditions, they are usually preserved and are easily noticed and recognized. The first stage after recovery is to identify the animal they came from and its age and sex. Other details noted include size, pathology, butchery marks and whether the bone has been adapted as a tool.

The age of young animals can be worked out by establishing which teeth have appeared, and the age of older animals by the extent to which the teeth are worn. Age is also assessed by studying the development of the limb bones. Some analysts also calculate the minimum number of individual (MNI) animals of each species from the bones found.

Analysis by age, sex and the relative proportions of each species within each period of an excavated site provides details of hunting strategies and animal husbandry methods and their evolution. For example, where domestic stock was kept mainly for meat, most of the animals will have been killed in adolescence when body growth slows down, and only a few adults kept for breeding. If milk and milk products played an important role in the diet, a greater proportion of females will have been maintained into adulthood, while the majority of animals would be slaughtered in early infancy to stop them from competing for the milk.

The relative proportions of different species also reflect the environment and people's exploitation of it, as some species are better adapted to woodland grazing while others prefer grassland. Changes in the composition of domestic stock or hunted animals may therefore reflect ecological changes, such as forest clearance or the deterioration of poor arable land into rough pasture.

Even after stock-farming began, wild animals remained an important element of many economies of the past—as a supplementary source of food, or because they provided necessary materials for clothing, tools or even fuel. In some regions, wild animals continued as the main source of meat. In North and Central America, for instance, few creatures were suitable for domestication, although domestic dogs and turkeys were kept. Most meat eaten by prehistoric farmers there came from wild animals such as deer, rabbits and birds.

Bones can also indicate the time of year at which a particular site was occupied. Those of migratory birds are particularly helpful. In cool or dry climates, most mammals have a regular birth season, so a concentration of remains of animals at a particular age is a further pointer.

Plants as Food

Little is known about the part played in people's diet by plants before the end of the most recent ice age. With the development of settled farming, however, the chances of survival of plant material greatly increased.

Occasionally, whole caches of grain are discovered, while carbonized seeds and fruits are relatively common finds. Nevertheless, the generally poor preservation of plant material and difficulties in recovering it from sites means that plants are almost always under-represented.

As with animals, the advent of agriculture did not mean that the exploitation of undomesticated resources ceased. On a number of Neolithic sites by lakes in western Europe, aquatic and other wild plants made up the bulk of the vegetable diet. Weeds associated with cultivation, such as

SHELL MIDDENS OF DENMARK

Denmark in the 6th millennium B.C.E. was an archipelago of far more islands than it is today, separated by a deeper sea. Around the islands dwelt hunter-gatherers of what is now called the Ertebølle culture, after an archaeological site in northern Jutland.

Most of the known sites of these people are shell middens, and the larger ones, such as Ertebølle itself, seem to have been occupied year-round. Despite the fact that the shell middens are composed largely of discarded shells, shellfish were in fact eaten only in fairly small quantities. The large number of shells is explained by the fact that the edible part of shellfish is fairly small compared with the shells that are discarded. Pigs and red deer provided the bulk of the diet, supplemented by fish, oysters and migratory birds. Smaller middens were probably seasonal camps, occupied to exploit resources available at particular times of the year in localities away from the main camp. These resources included sea mammals such as stranded whales, fish such as cod and mackerel, swans and other birds. Ringkloster, in central Jutland, is such a seasonal site. From the bones found there, it appears to have been occupied during winter and spring to obtain red deer antlers and to hunt pine marten for furs and baby deer for skins.

The coastal middens were composed largely of the shells of oysters, which were a critical resource during the spring. When the sea level fell, the oysters disappeared and the local people took to agriculture, abandoning the larger sites but still camping in the smaller ones to obtain seasonally available food.

Chenopodium (goosefoot), were probably harvested with the crops.

Most of the information we have on the development of agriculture relates to the cultivation of cereals and legumes. Many other important food staples, for instance, tubers like manioc and yams, decay completely, so the archaeological evidence for their exploitation is generally only indirect, from equipment used in their preparation or traces of appropriate cultivation systems.

Recent scientific developments have furthered our knowledge of diet in the past. Chemical residues on tools used for processing and on pots used to store, prepare and cook food can now often be analyzed to identify the foodstuffs involved. And amazingly, our bones tell tales: Microscopic studies of teeth show up striations produced by eating plant or animal foods, while the isotopic composition of the bones themselves can indicate the relative contribution of marine and land resources and of two major groups of plant foods in a lifetime's diet. The latter information has been used in the Americas to chart the rise of maize as a dietary staple.

Harvests from the Waters

Fish remains recovered from archaeological sites may include jaws, vertebrae, otoliths (ear stones) and scales. Sometimes the particular species or genus can be identified, but the large number of possible species and the similarities between many of them make this a hard task.

Otoliths, vertebrae and scales grow in annual rings, which means that the ages of the fish may sometimes be determined. The size of the otoliths also gives some indication of the weight.

In addition to yielding information about the local aquatic environment, discarded fish bones often help archaeologists to determine the seasons at which the site was occupied, particularly sites on coasts, where certain species shoal at known times of year. The remains can give a clue to local fishing methods and sometimes provide indirect evidence that those who caught them possessed considerable seafaring skills. For example, it is known that some prehistoric groups hunted whales and other marine mammals.

Telltale Traces

Coprolites, preserved feces, are an unusual but extremely valuable source of dietary information. They are sometimes found in waterlogged latrines in Europe, but most examples come from arid cave sites in the Americas.

For analysis, coprolites are reconstituted, using a suitable liquid such as a solution of trisodium phosphate. Their components can be surprisingly varied and give a very detailed picture of diet and food preparation.

Typical material recovered from coprolites includes tiny fragments of fish and animal bone, various plant parts, particularly seeds and pollen, and bits of edible insects and mollusks, as well as material accidentally ingested such as hair, feathers and insects (like fruit fly larvae).

Tapeworms and other parasites may also be discovered in coprolites and in cesspits—a reminder of the high levels of parasitic infestation that people of the past endured.

OPPOSITE PAGE:
The remains of a Neolithic village— more than 5,000 years old—discovered at Skara Brae on the Orkney Islands provide an excellent example of a shell midden (foreground). This heap of discarded shells indicates that the inhabitants of the village included shellfish in their diet. Shell middens are prominent archaeological sites on coasts and estuaries all over the world. They usually also contain other food debris, giving further clues to the kind of food eaten and the season at which the midden was occupied. From the remains it may also be possible to estimate roughly the size of the site's group.

HUMAN REMAINS

The object of the first analysis made of human remains found on archaeological sites is similar to that for animal remains: to determine age, sex and numbers. When, as usually happens, the remains are bones, the techniques are basically the same, too. However, when studying human remains, details about individual people are usually of interest, and establishing the minimum number of individuals (MNI) present has higher priority than in the case of animals.

The MNI is calculated by counting the total presence of bones occurring only once in an individual body, such as skulls, or occurring twice, such as thigh bones. When no other evidence is available, marked differences in the size or development of bones may imply more than one individual.

Determining the age of children and teenagers depends mainly on which teeth are present in the jaw. In adolescents and young adults, the degree of fusion between the heads and shafts of the long bones is a reliable indicator. The age of fully adult, mature and elderly individuals can be determined, though less precisely, from tooth wear and structural changes, such as those associated with osteoarthritis, in some bones.

The rate of development and skeletal change varies to some extent between races. It is also influenced by diet, health and environment. A diet of coarse, gritty plant foods causes teeth to wear rapidly, while malnutrition will retard children's growth. Nevertheless, it is generally possible to establish the age of a child's skeleton to within a year of actual age and an adult's to within 10 years.

Measurements and bone structures are the two key factors in determining a skeleton's sex. The average male human is larger overall than his female counterpart. His bones tend to be bigger and heavier and his muscle attachments to be more strongly developed. The most marked difference is in the pelvis, the only part of the body whose function differs between the sexes.

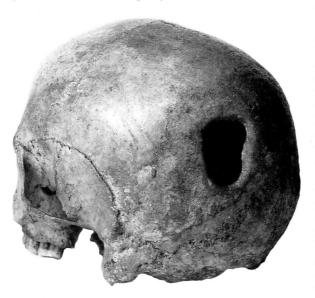

Trepanning, the practice of cutting a hole in the skull, was carried out either by scraping away the bone or more commonly, by cutting out a circle of bone with a stone knife or drill.

Differences between the male and female pelvis (below) are sufficiently marked to be a reliable means of determining the sex of a human skeleton. The female pelvis, on the left, has a wider sciatic notch than the male pelvis does; it also has a groove, or sulcus, in the pre-auricular surface (at the base of the spine).

Diseases of Antiquity

Paleopathologists, the experts who study diseases in ancient times, obtain most of their information from skeletal remains. Valuable additional data comes from soft tissues preserved in mummies and bog bodies and from representations in ancient art.

Diseases such as syphilis, yaws, tuberculosis and leprosy cause marked deformation and destruction of the bones of the head, spine and limbs. Tumors are sometimes present on bones. Osteoarthritis, too, produces characteristic skeletal changes and is found even in dinosaur skeletons.

Dental caries was less common among prehistoric peoples than it is today, but evidence of it occurs, along with gum disease and abscesses. Congenital disabilities such as clubfoot are also

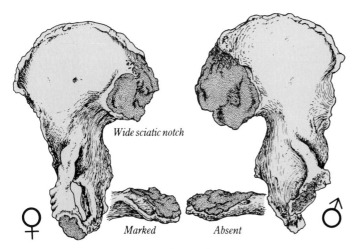

Wide sciatic notch

Marked   *Absent*

Pre-auricular sulcus

♀   ♂

known. The high incidence of a congenital condition or of genetically determined anomalies, such as minor variations in the bones of the skull, among individuals in a tomb or cemetery may imply a blood relationship between them. Such evidence is rare, however.

Lesions and deformities of bones can be informative. Abnormal wear of a particular bone or bones of an individual may suggest what the person did during life. Similarly, certain types of injury are associated with the hazards of specific activities.

Sometimes, injuries form a pattern that implies details of the environment or society. The arm and leg fractures common among Saxons probably come from frequent stumbling on rough ground; the leg was damaged by twisting and the arm was injured as the owner instinctively threw it out in falling. In ancient Egyptian skeletons, broken forearms are very common, particularly among women. Such fractures were often caused when an arm was raised to ward off a blow.

Injuries from weapons also leave characteristic traces in the skeleton. Sword cuts are narrow, while spears and other piercing weapons produce well-defined holes. Club blows produce dents with cracks radiating from them.

During childhood, while the body is still developing, periods of illness and malnutrition may be reflected permanently by lines of arrested growth in bones and bands of arrested enamel development on teeth. Rickets, a childhood ailment that is a result of vitamin D deficiency, leaves marked changes in the skeleton, including bowlegs, pigeon breast, and light and brittle bones.

Not all morphological changes are natural or accidental. Deliberate deformation was practiced among many groups as an aid to beauty. Teeth were knocked out or modified by filing, chipping or even inlaying. Some societies, such as the Maya and some native North Americans, molded babies' heads by binding or flattening them against a cradle board to produce a shape that they considered attractive. Trepanning, a dangerous operation involving the removal of a disc of bone from the skull, has been widely practiced since Neolithic times. Its purpose is uncertain, but in many cases it may have been intended to relieve pressure on the cranium due to a brain tumor or a fracture. Despite the risks involved, many individuals survived the operation, some having as many as eight or more healed or healing holes.

A man was struggling across the Tyrolean Alps when a blizzard overtook him, and he perished. His body froze where it lay, in a sheltered hollow—a common tragedy, but unique because it took place around 3300 B.C.E., and the man's intact body and all his clothes and tools survived until their accidental discovery in 1991. Ötzi, as the Iceman came to be called, has not yet yielded all his secrets, but many fascinating studies of him have already taken place. Hair found scattered around his body suggest that he was bearded. Parts of his lower body were tattooed with thin blue lines. His teeth and the one fingernail recovered show that he led a tough working life and ate a diet including coarsely ground cereals. Smoke from fires had blackened his lungs, and he had suffered from arthritis and several periods of serious illness, but a body scan showed him otherwise to have been in good health. His DNA suggests that he had come from among the people north, rather than south, of the Alps.

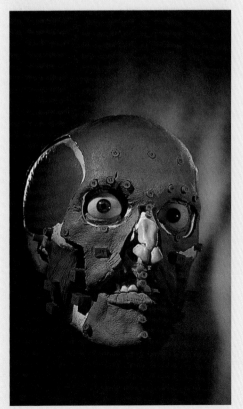

The Iceman's head and body were damaged both by pressure from the ice in which he lay preserved and by the rather brutal methods (including a pneumatic chisel) used to recover his body before the archaeologists stepped in. The original appearance of his face has been reconstructed on a replica of his skull, created using computed axial tomographic (CAT) data. Following techniques pioneered over recent years and also used to reconstruct the face of King Philip of Macedon (father of Alexander the Great), pegs were placed at key points on the skull, reproducing the normal thickness of the facial soft tissue, and muscle and skin modeled over this.

CHARRED BONES AND PRESERVED BODIES

Cremated Remains

At first sight, cremated remains may not seem to be a potential source of information, but in fact they can tell us a lot. Bones are rarely reduced completely to ash, and they can usually be recognized even when they have cracked in the fire and subsequently been broken so that they fit into a funerary urn.

The minimum number of individuals present in a group of cremated remains and their ages and sex can be established using the same criteria as those for uncremated skeletons. However, in cremations it is even more difficult to be precise about the ages of adults.

In addition, some of the circumstances of the cremation can often be reconstructed. Charred pieces of wood may be recovered, showing what type was used for the pyre. Fragments of cremated animal bone may provide details of funerary food offerings. Other such fragments, together with charred pieces of metal and orna-

ments, may give clues to the furs or other garments in which the body was wrapped.

The condition of the bones themselves can also be revealing. They may be able to indicate the position of the body on the pyre, the degree of burning and whether the cremation was of a fresh body or of collected bones.

Preserved Bodies

Corpses preserved accidentally, such as bog bodies, or deliberately, such as embalmed mummies, obviously yield far more information than can be obtained from bones alone. The soft tissue retains evidence of diseases, and the actual cause of death can often be established.

Other interesting details, such as hairstyles and body decoration, may also be discovered: A fascinating example is the elaborate tattooing on the bodies of the frozen horse-riders of Pazyryk in Siberia (see page 93). An examination of the stomach contents of a preserved body can reveal what was the last meal to be eaten. Tollund man, for instance, ate gruel containing the seeds of many plants, possibly a ritual concoction designed to ensure fertility (see page 89); Lady Li of the Chinese Han dynasty died of a heart attack shortly after eating a musk melon.

Early Egyptians buried in the hot sand have been remarkably well preserved by desiccation. Later, mummification was developed to continue this tradition of preservation. Before a mummy's elaborate bandaging is unwrapped, it is often x-rayed to check its condition and its potential interest. After it is unwrapped, the mummy, or parts of it, may be rehydrated by soaking in fluid, and an autopsy can then be performed.

Inside Information

Medical science has developed CAT (computed axial tomography) scanners and related devices to produce computer images of the bones and soft tissue inside living patients. These techniques also allow detailed information to be recovered from Egyptian mummies and other well-preserved archaeological bodies, such as the Iceman (see page 111), without having to destroy these unique remains.

The remarkable advances in knowledge of human genetics and DNA have also had their archaeological spin-off. Whereas previously it was rarely possible to demonstrate relationships

Astonishing preserved tattoos are on the body of a mummified nomadic chieftain—nearly 2,500 years old—from one of the frozen graves at Pazyryk in the Siberian steppes. The tattoos depict wild animals—some of them imaginary monsters. Part of the tattooing on his arm, a lively rendering of a spirited horse, is enlarged above.

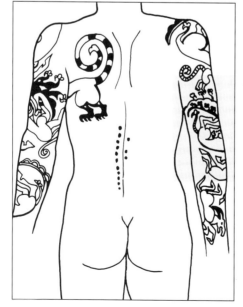

PROCESSING
THE FINDS

More than 40,000 years ago, the Neanderthal peoples began burying their dead, providing us with the first glimpse of the development of human emotions. Red ocher was often scattered over the graves, and offerings such as joints of meat and stone tools often accompanied the burial.

One individual in the Shanidar cave in northern Iraq was covered with flower heads, indicated by the pollen that remained above the skeleton. He was part of a group of seven, some of whom had died when part of the cave roof collapsed.

Another of this group was a cripple, with a withered and useless arm. He would have been unable to hunt or provide for himself, so the community must have taken care of him. His survival into old age demonstrates how strongly developed were the humanitarian instincts of the Neanderthals.

Excavations of the Shanidar cave, Iraq, in 1957, provided archaeologists with fascinating new evidence about early humans. Seven Neanderthal skeletons were found in the cave (top left), some of them victims of a rockfall 46,000 years ago. One was blind in his left eye and had a withered right arm and arthritic right ankle. When his skull was examined (bottom right), the incisors were found to be badly worn, suggesting that he may have used his teeth to supplement his good arm.

Specimens of pollen found in one of the Neanderthal burials at Shanidar (bottom left) indicate that the body was interred in a flower-lined grave. Grape hyacinths, cornflowers, groundsel and other spring flowers, some with medicinal properties, had been worked into the branches of a pinelike shrub.

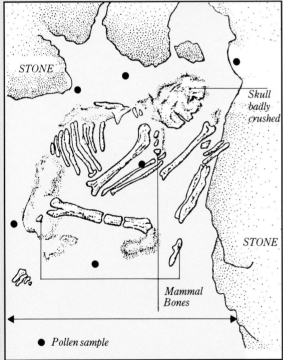

STONE

Skull badly crushed

STONE

Mammal Bones

● *Pollen sample*

between either individuals or populations, the recovery of blood protein and DNA from ancient bones is now beginning to provide such information. Genetic information also comes from studying mitochondrial DNA, which is inherited only through the female line. Results of genetic studies have supported the evidence from archaeology and linguistics of three waves of human colonization of the Americas (*see page 127*), as well as discovering that there was at least one other, unrelated group of colonists, who died out.

TECHNIQUES OF TYPOLOGY

After the artifacts recovered in field surveys or excavations have been cleaned and, if necessary, conserved, they are ready for archaeologists to use them to obtain information about the past. Their first task is to impose some order on the finds by dividing them into groups that have some meaning to them. The finds may be identified as specimens of types already known or as new types within the existing typology (classification based on a series of attributes), or it may be necessary to devise a new typology for the material.

Many criteria may be employed in this classification. First, there are obvious broad general classes into which the material can be grouped: pottery, stone tools, metal tools and weapons, jewelry and so on.

Having made these divisions, the archaeologists then look at the contents of each class in more detail. Let us take pottery as an example, as this is the most common and informative material on many sites. The pottery will probably be divided into groups on the basis of different fabrics.

Pottery fabrics depend on the degree to which the clay was worked before the vessel was formed and the kind of temper that was used. The conditions of firing and the methods used to shape the vessel are also important.

At the end of this stage, the archaeologists may have divided the pottery into groups of handmade or wheel-made wares; fine, medium and coarse wares; wares tempered with shell, sand, straw or grog (ground-up pottery); and poorly fired and well-fired wares. They will also have grouped together sherds into pieces of individual vessels.

Sorted by Shape

Within each type of ware, the pots are again subdivided, this time according to shape, into jars, bowls, dishes, vases, cups and so on. Distinguishing between different shapes is often a matter of intuition and therefore of potential disagreement. For that reason, some archaeologists now try to describe the shapes by using mathematical terms, either ratios or geometrical figures.

As well as overall shape, more specific details may be included in the classification process, such as the form of the base or rim, the addition of a spout or handle, the curve of the neck or body.

The size of the pots may also be taken into account. Differences in size frequently relate to the actual function the pot served—itself a further criterion that the archaeologist may use in constructing a pottery typology.

Finally, decoration usually gives plenty of scope for classification. Pottery is decorated in a variety of ways. Its color can be determined by the clay selected and by the firing conditions. The surface treatment that is used will also produce different colors or textures: A vessel may be slipped by applying a wash of dissolved clay, or glazed.

At various stages before firing, the surface can also be smoothed, polished or decorated. Paint, in a contrasting color or colors, is the most common form of decoration. Others include the application of clay blobs or strips; the creation of patterns on the surface by impression or incision using objects such as shells, combs, bird bones or pieces of cord; and deliberate roughening called rustification.

Piecing Together

Many of the artifacts found on a site are likely to be incomplete; pottery in particular is susceptible to breakage, leaving sherds rather than whole vessels. A single sherd, however, is enough to show the type of ware from which the vessel was made.

The shape of the vessel from which the sherd came is harder to determine, unless the sherd involved is a characteristic portion of a standardized vessel type. If the fragment is a rim sherd, the analyst can work out the diameter of the whole vessel by gauging the sherd on a chart of concentric rings of different diameters. Once

The range of artifacts recovered from an excavated site provides important clues to its date and the activities carried on there.

pottery—or any other material—has been sorted into types, it can be compared with that known from other sites.

One of the most important facts to ascertain from the material is the date of the site or of features within it. Another may be to establish the function of various parts of the site. Pieces of a storage jar, for instance, may suggest that a granary or storage area has been unearthed.

Pottery used by a particular group may imply that members of that group occupied the site or traded with its inhabitants. For example, surface finds of Roman Arretine ware at Arikamedu in southern India first suggested that the Romans had been there. Excavations by Sir Mortimer Wheeler in 1945 uncovered a major Roman trading settlement, beneath which the remains of a small Indian fishing village were discovered.

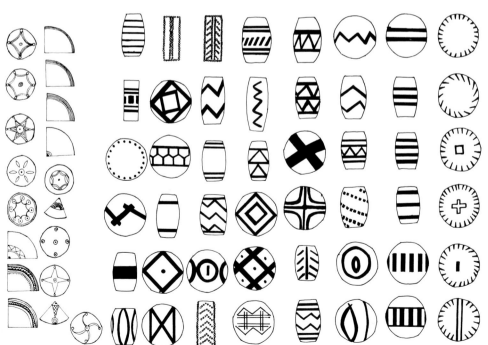

A Sumerian pottery vessel, found at Nippur in Iraq, that has been pieced together as completely as possible, is now being measured and drawn (top left).

Typological analysis is an important stage in the recording of finds from an archaeological site. Shown left is a typology of designs on shell discs (bottom left) and beads found at Iron Age Megalithic sites in south India. Designs present at a number of sites may indicate some link between them, such as membership in the same cultural group or trade between separate groups, and suggest similarity of date. This chart is an early attempt at classification of this material and its significance is not yet clear; better-known and long-studied material, such as Roman pottery, however, provides established information about the date and cultural affinities of contexts in which it is found.

PHYSICAL EXAMINATION

By simply looking at ancient artifacts and their context, we can learn a considerable amount about the culture that produced them. But often we want to know more—for example, about the raw materials used in making the artifacts, the sources of those materials and the methods of manufacture.

Microscopic examination can reveal details of an object's structure and much more. Study of thin sections of stone objects and pottery may suggest the source of the raw materials used to make them. Minute abrasions, called microwear, on the surface of stone tools give clues to the purpose for which they were used (microwear on teeth, by the same token, may provide data about diet). Examination of samples from metal objects indicates the metallurgical processes employed in making them.

Radiography

Various X-ray techniques are used to determine the chemical composition of ancient objects, although not all of their components can be detected by this means. In X-ray fluorescent spectrometry, the item to be studied is bombarded with X rays, causing it to emit secondary (fluorescent) X rays whose wavelengths are characteristic of the elements present. These can be identified and their concentration determined.

However, as the X rays cannot penetrate deeply, this technique is limited to surface examination and therefore gives an inaccurate picture of the composition of corroded or unhomogeneous metal objects. The problem can be alleviated by using an X-ray milliprobe or an electron probe microanalyzer. Both devices concentrate the X rays into a minute area that may be cleaned of corrosion without visibly altering the appearance of the object. The same is true of various methods of ion beam analysis, such as proton-induced X-ray emission,

which are also now widely used.

X rays directed at a small sample of the object under study are diffracted in directions determined by its crystal structure. The technique, X-ray diffraction analysis, provides information on the structure of the object and the mechanical and thermal treatment it has undergone during manufacture.

Information can also be obtained by infrared absorption spectrometry. Infrared rays are focused on a small sample, and the degree to which rays of different wavelengths are absorbed allows the identification of chemical compounds present.

Other Techniques

Inductively coupled plasma spectrometry is used to detect trace elements. A small sample from the specimen is electrically excited, releasing light of different wavelengths characteristic of the elements present, which allows their identity and concentration to be determined.

Small objects can be examined by neutron activation analysis. They are placed in a nuclear reactor and bombarded with neutrons, which excite the atomic nuclei to form radioactive isotopes. When these decay, they produce characteristic gamma rays that indicate the elements present and their concentration.

The concentration of individual elements can be determined by atomic absorption spectrometry. This measures the extent to which light of a wavelength characteristic of a particular element is absorbed by an atomized sample. Other techniques, including measurement of specific gravity, isotopic analysis and beta ray backscattering, are also sometimes employed.

Today, there are many scientific techniques of physical analysis that archaeologists can call upon for help. Unfortunately, they often require elaborate and expensive equipment not normally found outside laboratories. However, optical microscopes, generally used in the first stage of analyzing ancient artifacts, are not beyond the means of most people, and many archaeological laboratories have the more powerful and versatile scanning electron microscopes. A scanning electron microscope can provide valuable information about the materials used in ancient artifacts. The object to be examined is placed in the specimen chamber (behind the technician's head).

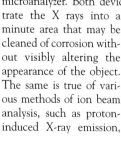

THE MOULSFORD TORQUE

Under British law, most objects found are the property of the landowner. Objects of gold or silver, however, are treated differently. Those that were placed in the ground with no intention of recovery (for example, as grave offerings) or were simply abandoned or lost remain the property of the landowner (or occasionally the finder). But if the original owner hid the objects with the intention of recovering them and the owner cannot be found, obviously the case with newly discovered ancient artifacts, then they become the property of the Crown, Treasure Trove. An inquest is therefore held to determine whether the objects were lost or hidden.

An inquest into a Bronze Age gold torque (neck band) found at Moulsford, Berkshire, in 1960 required the melted-down value of the object to be established. Several methods of physical analysis were used.

Measurement of the torque's specific gravity gave a rough indication of its gold content but showed variations between the four bars of which it was composed. Neutron activation analysis posed problems: The torque's bulk required irradiation in an unusually large atomic pile, but irradiation had to be kept to a minimum to protect the public when the torque eventually went on display.

The torque had also suffered what is called surface enrichment—that is, the silver and copper on the surface had been depleted by leaching, while the gold had not. X-ray fluorescence spectrometry, which only penetrates the surface, therefore indicated an artificially high gold content. Optical emission spectroscopy (a technique related to inductively coupled plasma spectrometry) was also employed, giving useful results but failing to detect some details.

The results of the analyses showed variation in the chemical composition of sections of the torque. This indicated that it had been made of pieces of natural electrum (gold and silver alloy) from different sources.

Neutron activation analysis yielded the best results in determining the gold content of the torque. This technique has proved very useful to archaeologists over the years, although it is less commonly used nowadays, as the nuclear reactors required in the analysis become rarer in research laboratories.

The Moulsford Torque (upper left) was analyzed by various spectrometric and other techniques to determine its gold content and hence its value. It was found that the twisted bars were not made of pure gold but of natural electrum, an alloy of gold and silver. Copper had been added, probably to make the pale electrum look more like pure gold. The surface of the end-caps of each terminal (lower left) was found to contain a high level of lead, a detail that optical emission spectros copy failed to detect.

ANALYZING STONE TOOLS

On the scree slopes below Stickle Pike in the English Lake District (center) lies the site of a Neolithic ax factory. The tools were cut from the hard, gray-green rock and roughly fashioned on-site, before being transported elsewhere for finishing.

OPPOSITE PAGE: *At Grimes Graves*, Norfolk, England, a Neolithic flint mine (upper right) was intensively worked for 300 years, around 2000 B.C.E. Miners sunk shafts up to 40 feet (12 m) deep through sand, clay and chalk; they worked by the light of lamps containing animal fat and wicks of moss to reach the high-quality flint known as floorstone, much coveted for making ax heads.

OPPOSITE PAGE: *A pick made* from a deer antler (lower right), found at Avebury, England, is typical of tools used in the Neolithic period throughout Europe to quarry flint.

The identity and arrangement of minerals in some types of stone vary according to the geological conditions under which the rock was formed. So it is often possible to match the stone used in ancient artifacts to its original source.

In thin-section examination, a small slice, approximately 4 millimeters by 15 millimeters, is cut from the artifact to be studied, ground down to a thickness of 0.03 millimeter and mounted between glass slides for scrutiny under the microscope. The minerals present are identified, and their shape, size, relative proportions and textural interrelationships are noted and compared with material from known sources.

Using such methods, British Neolithic stone axes have been divided into more than 20 groups, some subdivided, and the probable sources of most identified by comparison with known geology. Investigation of these sources has in many cases revealed Neolithic "factory" sites, such as Great Langdale in the Lake District, where the stone was shaped into rough forms that were later finished somewhere else.

Axes of greenstone probably come from a source in Cornwall, but the factory itself has not been identified and it may have been drowned by a rise in sea level since Neolithic times. Surprisingly, the products of different factories were widely distributed throughout large areas of Britain; axes from several sources are often found on the same site.

Focus on Flint

Flint lacks mineralogical variation and is therefore not amenable to thin-section examination. But it does contain trace elements, and analysis of the overall pattern of those can allow different sources to be distinguished. The trace elements are identified using neutron activation analysis, atomic absorption spectrometry and other methods (*see pages 116–117*).

Although ordinary flint was widely available locally to toolmakers in Neolithic Europe, they clearly prized particularly attractive or high-quality types, which were mined and traded extensively. Flint from the Grand Pressigny quarries in France, for example, has been found up to 500 miles (800 km) away, in areas that had good flint sources themselves.

One of the most impressive mines in Neolithic Europe is at Spiennes in Belgium. Initially, the flint was extracted by driving horizontal galleries into the flint-bearing chalk, while later more than 50 deep vertical shafts were sunk. These have yielded flint and antler picks used in the quarrying. Similar antler tools were found in the flint mines at Grimes Graves in England, also being extensively worked at that time.

From the Volcano

Obsidian (volcanic glass) was also highly valued in the past. But obsidian suitable for making tools is relatively rare and forms homogeneous deposits, so identifying its source is much easier and more reliable than with flint.

Trace element analysis by atomic absorption spectroscopy, proton-induced X-ray emission, X-ray fluorescence spectrometry and neutron activation analysis have all proved effective in locating the origins of obsidian used for artifacts. Sources can also be distinguished by their date of formation, using fission track dating (*see page 140*).

Uses of Artifacts

Traces of blood on tools may be analyzed to determine which creatures they were used to kill or butcher. Microscopic examination of the edges of stone tools may reveal microwear, polish and tiny striations resulting from use. A body of experimental data has been built up to show the wear patterns associated with specific uses and from interaction with other materials such as bone, wood or plants. By comparing that with the microwear of a particular artifact, it is possible to say what the artifact was used for. Tools for cutting plant stems, for example, often bear a silica gloss from contact with the silica present in plants.

Experiments with replicas enabled archaeologists to identify quite precisely the uses of various tools found at Pincevent in the Seine valley near Paris, a site briefly occupied in the late Magdalenian period, which ended about

TRADE IN OBSIDIAN

Finds of tools and other artifacts of obsidian provide a fascinating glimpse of the exchange networks of some ancient peoples. In the Near East, for example, obsidian sources were exploited from at least the 9th millennium B.C.E. until around 4000 B.C.E., when the development of metallurgy led to a decline in demand.

Analysis by optical emission spectroscopy reveals an interesting pattern of distribution. In sites within a radius of 150 to 200 miles (240–320 km) from the sources in Turkey and Armenia, 80 percent or more of stone tools were made of obsidian. Villages near the sources, such as the remarkable settlement at Çatal Höyük, developed considerable expertise in manufacturing a wide range of obsidian objects, including mirrors. Further away, the proportion of obsidian tools falls quite rapidly, but obsidian still reached some sites that were more than 600 miles (960 km) from its source.

Obsidian occurs widely in the Americas and was extensively traded in antiquity for use in tools, weapons, mirrors and elaborate ornaments. A major outcrop lies at El Chayal, on the outskirts of present-day Guatemala City. More than 1,000 years ago, the site was the Maya city of Kaminaljuyu. The highland Mexican Teotihuacán Empire at its height colonized or took over Kaminaljuyu, probably to control trade in El Chayal obsidian.

Another important source was at Ixtepeque on Guatemala's border with El Salvador. Studies of the distribution in lowland Yucatán of the products from both Ixtepeque and El Chayal, using neutron activation analysis, have provided information on the trade routes used, both overland and by canoe along rivers and the coast. This research also gives an indication of invisible routes along which other exports and imports were traded: these included such perishable goods as cacao, salt, cotton textiles and feathers.

10,000 years ago. The distribution of finds from the site marks out the floor area of three tents, each with a central hearth, where people sat to make stone tools, butcher animals and eat them, tossing the bones over their shoulders.

The replicas were tested on a variety of appropriate materials, and the wear patterns compared with that on the originals. The comparisons showed that Magdalenian tools included backed bladelet knives used for cutting up meat, blades for butchering, piercers for making holes in hides and for cutting grooves in antlers, a scraper for cleaning hides and, probably, a projectile point.

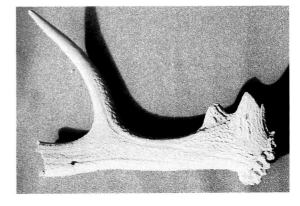

STUDYING POTTERY

Pottery was invented more than 10,000 years ago and is one of the most common categories of finds on archaeological sites, because it was a relatively cheap, everyday commodity and is a material that preserves well in most conditions. On most sites there are usually plenty of fragments (sherds) that can be spared for destructive analysis.

Much information can be gained about pottery just by examining it with the naked eye. Surface details, outside and in, and the cross section of the vessel can indicate the degree to which the clay was worked, and the nature, size and quantity of temper added. They may also reveal the techniques used in manufacture and decoration, whether the vessel's surface was wet-smoothed (self-slipped) or coated in a slip or glaze, and something about the firing conditions.

Pottery, like stone, may be studied in thin section under a microscope. However, in the sedimentary deposits from which clays come the distribution of minerals is not homogeneous, so the proportions and distribution of minerals, vital clues in the analysis of stone, are not so important with pottery. Furthermore, some minerals that were originally present may be removed when the clay is worked.

Nevertheless, characteristic mineral inclusions may still allow a clay source to be pinpointed. A fine example of this has been the analysis of Hembury F ware, a pottery type widely distributed in south and southwest Britain in the Neolithic period, often associated with stone axes of the Cornish group. The clay from which Hembury F was made closely matches gabbro clays found on the Lizard peninsula in Cornwall, and it is likely that the pottery was manufactured there.

Heavy mineral analysis relies on the fact that sands of different geological origins contain different heavy minerals (those with a specific gravity of more than 2.9). A sample of pottery is crushed and floated in a suitable liquid to extract the heavy minerals present. The identity of these may allow the clay source to be determined. The manufacture of Romano-British Black Burnished ware type 1, which contains the heavy mineral tourmaline, has been traced to the Wareham-Poole harbor area of southern England using this technique of analysis.

A prehistoric potsherd (top) found near Peterborough, England, bears a pattern of diagonal markings that is very commonly found on Neolithic pottery. The sherd was probably part of a cooking pot.

Neolithic pots (below) dating from about 3500 B.C.E., from the Lot region of France, were made before the invention of the potter's wheel; they were handmade by coiling a roll of clay into the desired shape. A fine liquid clay was used to give a smooth finish, and the pots were fired in simple but effective kilns.

Chemical Composition

The sources of clay used for ceramics may also be determined by assessing their chemical composition, using atomic absorption spectroscopy, X-ray fluorescence spectrometry, electron probe microanalysis, neutron activation analysis or other scientific techniques (*see pages 114–115*). These are particularly useful for studying fine-textured pottery or wares that have been tempered with quartz sand, which are not amenable to petrological analysis.

X-ray fluorescence spectrometry is also used in determining the constituents of glazes. Lead and alkali-silicate glazes can be distinguished by beta ray backscattering. Isotopic analysis may reveal the source of lead used in the glazes.

Details of the firing conditions of pottery, particularly temperature, can be established by a technique known as Mössbauer spectroscopy and by various thermal analyses. By observing how much weight is lost when the pottery is reheated, the firing temperature can be determined. The same information can be recovered by observing the temperature at which shrinkage of the pottery begins.

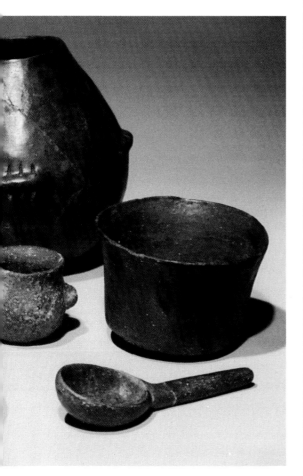

PUEBLO SURPRISE

Pecos, a large Indian pueblo in the Rio Grande area of the American Southwest, was selected for investigation by the pioneer American archaeologist Alfred Kidder in the early 20th century, because of its long occupation. As he was preparing the final report on the excavation, in the 1930s, he was approached by Anna Shepard, later to become one of the world's leading authorities on archaeological ceramics, but then a young researcher interested in testing the recently developed petrological analysis of pottery on an assemblage of archaeological pots.

Not much was expected of the study, as it was assumed that all the pottery would be locally made, but Kidder was very willing for her to try. The results were surprising.

Most of the pots were indeed locally made, as was shown by their content of local sand or sandstone temper; however, some, notably among the distinctive Rio Grande glaze paint pottery, were not of local origin. They contained rock temper not available in the immediate vicinity of Pecos.

Further investigations established the history of the pottery in Pecos. Glaze paint ware, decorated with a paint that used lead ores available in the Ortiz Mountains, was probably first made in the Albuquerque district and was traded to settlements in the Galisteo valley, where its highly unusual appearance made it popular.

Later, Galisteo settlements began producing glaze paint ware themselves and traded it to Pecos. All the glaze paint ware of the earliest type, Glaze I, at Pecos was rock-tempered. However, the people of Pecos eventually obtained the secret of producing glaze paint ware and started their own experiments, initially producing a rather degenerate version of Glaze I, which had previously puzzled Kidder and was now explained.

They soon got the hang of the technique, producing local versions of the later styles II, III and IV, distinguishable from other regional products only by their sand temper. Glaze V was an entirely local style, very flamboyant in character, and was not adopted elsewhere in the Rio Grande area. The arrival of the Spaniards in the region, in the 16th century, disrupted the supply of lead and ended the local industry; the few examples at Pecos of the latest style, Glaze VI, were all rock-tempered imports.

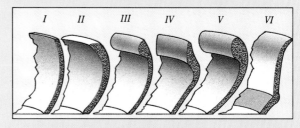

Thin-sectioning of pottery enables minerals present in the clay to be identified, giving a clue to the origin of the vessel. At Pecos, in the Southwest, glaze paint pottery of styles I and VI was found to be imported, while styles II to V were made of local materials.

METHODS WITH METALS

A naked-eye examination or inspection under a microscope usually reveals how a metal artifact was made. For microscopic study, part of the object is first polished carefully with a metal polish until a mirror finish is achieved. At this stage, any flaws and inclusions will be apparent.

Next, the polished surface is etched with a suitable reagent (certain mild acids) to reveal the structure of the metal. The shape of the grains in the metal and their patterning are modified by heating and working, so their appearance indicates what processes were used in manufacture.

Ancient nonferrous artifacts may show details of casting from molten metal, cold-working and annealing (reheating to reduce brittleness). Different techniques of minting coins, such as casting or striking from a larger metal sheet, can be distinguished by variations in grain structure. Iron and steel objects similarly reveal details of manufacture, including heating, hammering, carburization (combining with carbon to form steel) and quenching (plunging when hot into cold water to increase hardness).

Chemical Composition

Information about the composition of metal objects, such as whether they are alloys or what impurities the metal contains, can be obtained only by physical analysis. Most metals can be studied using optical emission spectroscopy or, more commonly now, atomic absorption spectrometry.

Ancient metals, particularly iron, are frequently corroded, while burial may cause surface enrichment of gold and silver. Their composition is studied by using an X-ray milliprobe or an electron probe microanalyzer on a minute area of the object, from which the surface has been removed. This is particularly useful with coins, which are generally too small and too valuable for a sample to be removed for destructive analysis.

X-ray photography can show the original form of corroded metal objects, especially those of iron, and whether they are sufficiently well-preserved to justify cleaning (see pages 100–101).

Measurement of specific gravity is a simple but limited technique enabling the relative proportions of two major components in an alloy to be calculated. It does not, however, work if there are more than two such components.

Sources of Metal

The methods of physical examination used in establishing the chemical composition of metals are also used in attempting to identify the source from which the metal ore came. Source identification of metals, however, is complicated, and subject to several limitations.

One is the problem of determining where the potential sources are. Many of those exploited in antiquity were worked out long ago and forgotten. Others may remain, but are too small to be economically viable today and can therefore be hard to trace.

Secondly, ore deposits are not chemically homogeneous in vertical section. Usually the upper layers have been leached and the bottom ones enriched, so the deposit as a whole cannot be characterized in terms of trace elements it contains. Even where some matching is possible between archaeological ores and their sources, the processes of extraction and manufacture are likely to alter the concentrations of chemical impurities. The problem is reduced if a metal object contains lead, as different sources contain the lead isotopes in different proportions, and those are not altered in manufacture. The proportions are obtained by lead isotope analysis using a mass spectrometer.

In addition, many metal artifacts are made from ores from different sources, mixed together in variable proportions. This was probably rare when metallurgy began, but as metal objects became common and widespread, scrap items were often melted down for reuse. Nevertheless, despite all the difficulties, exhaustive studies have been carried out of early metal artifacts and of ore sources known to have been worked in antiquity. They have yielded at least general information on the sources exploited by particular ancient cultures.

Other Materials

Stone, pottery and other metals account for many of the artifacts that archaeologists find and study, but there are others too, including amber (fossilized resin), glass and faience. These also are analyzed to determine three things: their chemical composition, the details of how they were made and the sources of their raw materials.

DAWN OF EUROPE'S BRONZE AGE

The earliest known copper artifacts in Europe, apart from a few isolated items made by cold-hammering from the naturally occurring pure metal, come from sites in the Balkans and date from before 4000 B.C.E. At Rudna Glava in Yugoslavia, impressive copper mines were already being worked at that date. The copper was smelted and cast in simple one-piece molds.

Many copper objects of this period have a high content of arsenic or, sometimes, antimony. These have the effect of lessening the softness of the pure metal, and it is probable that the ores containing them were deliberately chosen for that reason. Chemical analyses show that this early metallurgy was based on easily worked oxide and carbonate ores, virtually free from other impurities, except silver. Evidence shows that similar methods of copper working developed during the 4th millennium in the Aegean and southern Spain and Portugal.

By the later 3rd millennium B.C.E., the easily worked ores of the Balkans were in short supply, ironically just as innovations in metallurgy, particularly the two-piece mold for casting more complex objects, were introduced from the Caucasian region further east. However, in central Europe, exploitation of the less easily worked sulphide ores was beginning. Physical analysis shows two main groups of metal artifacts at this time, one probably derived from sources including the Harz mountains in Germany, the other coming from Slovakia or the Alpine regions. Local tin was added to produce a harder and stronger metal—bronze. Significantly, the development of pastoralism, involving seasonal movement of people and their herds into the High Alpine pastures, goes hand in hand with the first exploitation of Alpine ore sources.

By the later 2nd millennium, this area had come to dominate European metallurgy. Bronze was now widely used for everyday tools and weapons, and sophisticated technology allowed the production of elaborate forms. The replacement of bronze by iron tools during the 1st millennium B.C.E. released bronze for luxury items, and even finer bronze jewelry and vessels were created in the centuries that followed.

The remains of a copper smelting hearth dating from about 1400 B.C.E. have been uncovered at Timna, in Israel, the area of King Solomon's mines. Copper was smelted here for 1,500 years.

Gas chromatography, a purely chemical method of analysis, and infrared absorption spectrometry are used in studying amber. Differences in the botanical origins of amber and in the degree of fossilization enable a distinction to be made between sources in the Baltic, Romania and Sicily.

Infrared absorption spectrometry, X-ray diffraction and X-ray fluorescence spectrometry are widely used in the analysis of pigments. Early pigments were generally made from naturally occurring minerals such as red ocher or from chemical compounds. The use of red ocher in Neanderthal burials has been interpreted as possibly symbolizing blood.

Glass has proved difficult to analyze, as it is often poorly preserved. Even so, variations in the materials used to make and color glass have been detected using such techniques as optical emission spectroscopy, neutron activation analysis and X-ray fluorescence spectrometry.

The same techniques have also been applied to faience (a blue glassy material made from quartz sand, soda and copper ore). Segmented faience beads found in Bronze Age Europe, and originally believed to have come from Egypt, have now been shown to have been locally made.

The ancient Egyptians created elaborate bead necklaces from faience, the forerunner of glass. They also began making true glass around 1500 B.C.E.

FAKES AND FORGERIES

For more than a century scientists have been hoping to find fossil evidence of the "missing link," the creature transitional between humans and their ape ancestors. In 1912, just such a fossil was claimed to have been found near Piltdown in southern England: a skull with the expected massive, apelike jaw and large brain. Above right is an artist's impression from a London Illustrated News of that year of what Piltdown man might be supposed to have looked like. In fact, Piltdown man was one of the greatest frauds ever perpetrated on the scientific community. It was not exposed for some decades, no doubt much to the scornful amusement of the person behind it all, whose identity we shall probably never know (see page 129).

Archaeological forgeries were, until recently, comparatively rare. Those that were perpetrated tended to stem from some personal grievance against the scientific community (see page 129) or a desire for personal fame or national prestige (see page 139). Today, however, the explosion in the value of even minor antiquities has turned archaeological fakes into big business.

As the demand for antiquities has grown, so has the wanton looting and consequent destruction of archaeological sites to provide them. The frequent willingness of both private individuals and public institutions to purchase material of uncertain provenance has greatly encouraged this illicit traffic.

Ironically, the increasing skills of the forgers have proved of value to archaeologists. An awareness that an item may be a forgery has stimulated a demand for an unassailable pedigree of genuine antiquity and legal acquisition. That is making the sale of looted objects less easy.

Scientific Tests

Many of the scientific techniques applied to the analysis of ancient materials are used for authentication. So are some dating methods—dendrochronology (on wooden artifacts), radiocarbon dating (on organic materials) and thermoluminescence dating (on pottery, terra-cotta and some bronzes). Forgeries can be detected by being shown to be of the wrong date, though skillful reuse of ancient materials may fool the investigator.

Another major authentication technique involves testing for anachronistic constituents or manufacturing processes. X-ray fluorescence spectrometry and neutron activation analysis are both used for this purpose, and so are various forms of chemical analysis.

Common anachronisms in metal objects include the inappropriate use of casting techniques such as piece-mold and cire perdue (lost wax) casting, the inclusion of inappropriate alloys such as those containing zinc, or the presence of impurities that denote ore from a mine not worked at the period from which the object is supposed to date. Some forgeries are revealed by being too pure; one forger, for instance, used high-quality gold to produce "Roman" coins—unfortunately for him, he chose to imitate coins from a time when the Roman currency was actually debased.

Other forgeries convert genuine antiquities of low value into ones of higher value, usually by coating a base metal object with gold or silver. X-ray fluorescence spectrometry is valuable in detecting such fakes.

TL—THE ART SLEUTH

Thermoluminescence dating, or TL for short (*see page 138*), is of great value in authenticating antiquities. One important application has been in establishing the age of terra-cotta figures purported to date from the Renaissance period in Europe.

In the middle of the 15th century, terra-cotta became a popular and cheap substitute for stone as a medium in the making of sculptures. In addition, when sculptors worked in stone or bronze, they often made trial models from terra-cotta. A revival in the popularity of Renaissance work during the 19th century promoted a flourishing trade in forgeries. TL has been used to great effect in distinguishing these pseudo-Renaissance pieces from the genuine items.

Antique bronzes can also often be authenticated by TL dating. In the *cire perdue* and piece-molding techniques of casting bronze, a clay casting core is used and either fired before casting or in the casting process. Although this clay core is usually removed later, small pieces of fired material from it are often left in awkward angles of the finished bronze piece itself, and TL can be applied to these bits of clay for dating.

The most intriguing art forgery case in which TL has been used originated in China. In the early 1940s, terra-cotta figurines said to come from the small town of Hui Xian appeared on the market, rapidly followed by numerous forgeries. The originals were unlike any known before but were attributed to the Warring States period (c. 350 B.C.E.). TL investigations in 1972 revealed that the originals themselves were also modern.

Excavations in China have unearthed a great number of terra-cotta horses, such as this exceptionally fine one, which were used as grave offerings during the Tang dynasty (618–906 C.E.). Their desirability has resulted in widespread forgery. One way to determine the true age of such a piece is by subjecting it to thermoluminescence dating, using a tiny clay sample taken from an unobtrusive position.

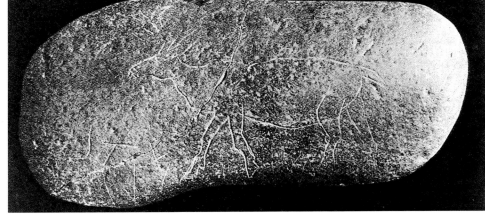

In 1924, a so-called Paleolithic find was made at Glozel, in France, by a young villager. With the help of a doctor, M. Morlet (left), from nearby Vichy, artifacts continued to be unearthed for three years. These included bones, stonemason's tools, and stones bearing carvings of reindeer-like creatures (above); the carvings were not typical of the period and aroused suspicion. Although scientific dating of the material was inconclusive and puzzling (*see page 139*), it is widely held to be a fraud.

THE IMPORTANCE OF DATING

The archaeologist today is concerned with establishing the reasons behind developments in the human past. Why did people adopt agriculture? Who built the megaliths, and what is their significance? What lies behind the extensive movement of goods and materials in prehistory?

Before such questions can be tackled at all, it is imperative to know *when* developments occurred—and the rate at which changes took place. As we saw in Part I, it was not until the advent of radiocarbon dating that it became possible to establish a firm timescale for prehistory and to place each archaeological site on it. The only exceptions were areas such as Egypt and Mesopotamia, where early historical dates are known, or those with an unusual basis for absolute dating, such as that provided by den-

drochronology in the American Southwest. To these has recently been added the Maya region of Mesoamerica, where the successful decipherment of many inscriptions is beginning to reveal the dynastic history of many Maya city-states.

The ever-increasing armory of scientific dating techniques available to modern archaeologists largely frees them from the preoccupation with chronology that characterized their predecessors. But obtaining absolute (chronometric) dates by these techniques is relatively expensive, so they define only the skeleton shape of the past. The flesh in which that is clothed is supplied by relative dating methods, some of them in use since the 19th century.

Stratigraphy and Typology

Stratigraphy, based on the principle that the most recent archaeological deposits lie nearest to ground level and deposits grow progressively earlier the deeper one digs, is one method of relative dating. But although it is helpful in many instances, there are some in which it cannot provide the information the archaeologist needs.

Deposits may not have a stratigraphic relationship. Where, for example, two pits have obviously been separately dug from the same ground surface, there is nothing in the stratigraphy to suggest which is the earlier. Similarly, excavations are often divided into trenches or squares, raising questions about the relationships between the layers exposed in different parts of the site.

In such cases, the relative dating is generally established by using typology (*see page 114*), the classification of artifacts into types on the basis of similarities in such variables as form, fabric and decoration. Pottery is most frequently used for typological dating, as it has enormous potential for variation. The relative dates of different artifact types are known from the stratigraphy of numerous excavations.

However, care is needed when single artifacts form a basis for dating. It is impossible to determine precisely how long an artifact was in circulation. For instance, grave offerings may well include both treasured heirlooms and objects made only shortly before the burial took place. Datable material (particularly small artifacts) may also appear in contexts to which it is not related at all, as a result of natural disturbances such as the burrowing of animals or the action of tree roots, or human activities, particularly plow-

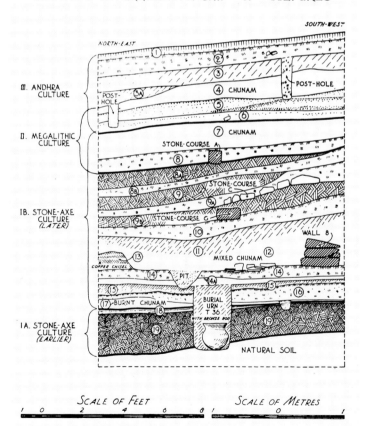

BRAHMAGIRI, 1947: SECTION BR. 21
SHOWING INTERRELATIONSHIP OF CULTURES

ing. The archaeologist must be careful to establish whether dated material is genuinely associated with the context in which it was found.

Assemblages

Groups of artifacts found together, known as assemblages, are much more useful for dating than single items are. Recurring assemblages are often called "cultures" by the archaeologist and spoken of at times as if there was a direct equation between assemblages and human groups—the so-called culture-people hypothesis. It is a convenient (though potentially misleading) way of dealing with a past known almost exclusively from material remains. What assemblages, or cultures, actually signify in human terms is an issue discussed in Part 5.

The value of assemblages over individual items for dating can be seen from the example of a Roman coin. On its own, it might suggest we are dealing with a Roman deposit. But closer examination of the associated material might show that the deposit is of post-Roman date and that the coin, lost years previously, had been turned up by post-Roman plowing.

Seriation

Stratigraphy and typology go hand in hand in dating material. Sometimes, however, there are few or no clues from stratigraphy: a cemetery where no graves intersect, or a region in which sites were never occupied long enough to build up any depth of deposit. Nowadays, we may obtain a few absolute dates—radiocarbon for some of the skeletons, TL for a few of the pots—but we cannot afford to date every grave or every vessel in that way. How do we establish the sequence of burials or of occupation of these short-lived sites?

In many cases, the answers may be provided by seriation—a method that relies on the fact that over a period of time the composition of archaeological assemblages gradually changes and certain types of artifact found in them are replaced by others. Using mathematical techniques, it is possible to put a series of assemblages into chronological order on the basis of their similarities. Some forms of seriation rely simply on the presence or absence of key artifact types, while others are concerned with the changing proportions of different types within one class of artifact.

Unfortunately, seriation has several drawbacks. First, there is the problem that the material recovered by excavation may not be fully representative of that once present. The element of chance in deposition, preservation and discovery may mean that changes observed in the assem-

blages are purely fortuitous, invalidating the seriation based on them.

Then, the presence, absence or varying proportions of key artifacts in the assemblages may signify something other than the passage of time. For example, variations in grave goods could reflect the personal wealth or social status of the occupant of the grave, rather than changes in artifacts current at the time of burial.

When Languages Change

Other techniques also give archaeologists the opportunity to establish the relative date of their material, placing it in chronological order though not establishing the absolute date. One of these is linguistic dating. When two groups of people speaking one language are divided and lose contact, for instance by the emigration of one group, the language spoken by the two groups will evolve separately, gradually becoming increasingly different. We cannot date the time of separation on the basis of the degree of dissimilarity of related languages, but a broad indication of the relative timescale is possible. Linguistic studies have provided interesting information about the early human settlement of North America.

The date of the first Americans is a question that intrigues scholars and the public alike. Archaeological evidence indicates that the extreme north was inhabited before 16,000 B.C.E. and that there was a rapid spread of people throughout the continent between 12,000 and 9000 B.C.E., after the retreat of the ice in the early postglacial period opened up an ice-free corridor through the massive North American ice sheets. Whether there was earlier colonization, however, is a matter of hot debate. Evidence for human occupation at Meadowcroft, Ohio around 20,000 B.C.E. and before 30,000 at Monte Verde in Chile has been claimed but is still controversial.

There is also evidence of two somewhat later waves of migration into the far north. Studies of tooth morphology, genetic material and Native American languages lend support to the picture derived from archaeology, indicating that the majority of Native Americans, from north to extreme south, are descended from the first colonists, speaking Amerind languages. A second wave of migrants speaking languages of the Na-Dene family settled in the north and were ancestral to the modern Athabaskans. Considerably later there was a third migration of people speaking Eskimo-Aleut languages, the ancestors of the modern people of the Arctic.

These pots found together in a grave at Kalavasos in Cyprus can be attributed to the Bronze Age because of their typological similarity to other pots already dated to this period.

THE IMPORTANCE OF DATING

RELATIVE DATING

F-U-N Dating

Three scientific techniques, often used in conjunction with one another, have proved particularly valuable in establishing relative dates for bones, teeth, antlers and ivory when items of any of those materials are found together, but when it is not clear whether they are contemporaneous and absolute dating is not possible. Such problems frequently arise in cave deposits where fossilized human material occurs with the bones of extinct fauna. The three techniques measure fluorine, uranium and nitrogen levels, and are collectively known as F-U-N.

Unlike many scientific techniques—for instance radiocarbon dating (*see page 134*)—in which a constant rate of change, dependent only on the passing of time, allows absolute dates to be obtained, changes in the level of fluorine, nitrogen and uranium depend also on other variables, such as temperature and humidity. This means that they can be used to establish the relative ages of materials found together, since within the environment of a given locality the rate of change of F-U-N levels should be the same for all contemporary material.

Fluorine dating relies on the incorporation into bone mineral of fluorine ions dissolved in groundwater—an irreversible process. Uranium dating is closely related to fluorine dating. Uranium dissolved in groundwater permeates bone and probably replaces calcium ions in bone mineral. The rate of uptake is more rapid in gravels and sands than in limestone formation and clays.

Changes in fluorine and uranium concentrations occur so slowly that they generally cannot confidently be measured in material younger than about 10,000 years. The opposite is true of nitrogen, which has virtually vanished in material of Pleistocene date. Nitrogen dating depends upon the gradual reduction of this element in skeletal material, due to the breakdown of collagen (bone protein) into amino acids, which are leached away. In freezing conditions, impermeable soils such as clays, or situations where bacteria have been excluded, the loss of nitrogen is greatly reduced.

By using the F-U-N techniques together, archaeologists reduce the risk of errors that could arise from anomalous levels of one of the three elements in certain specimens, such as occurred in the Piltdown hoax. High nitrogen and low fluorine and uranium levels suggest material of recent date, while the converse usually denotes very ancient material.

The excavated fragments of Piltdown man are represented by the black areas in this reconstruction of his skull (top right). The jaw was later found to belong to a modern orangutan.

PILTDOWN HOAX EXPOSED

The skull and jawbone of a supposed ancestor of *Homo sapiens* were sent to the British Museum in 1912 by a lawyer, Charles Dawson, who claimed to have found them in a gravel pit at Piltdown in Sussex. Dawson's discovery caused a great stir in scientific circles, coming as it did at the height of the worldwide quest for the missing link between humankind and the apes.

Piltdown man fitted then-held notions of how the missing link would look, with his humanlike skull and apelike jaw. Moreover, he was British and therefore highly acceptable to a nation that for decades had been casting envious glances at the abundant traces of early people in France.

By 1915, Dawson, working with Sir Arthur Smith Woodward, keeper of geology at the British Museum, had unearthed further fragments of Piltdown man, as well as the remains of two groups of fossil animals. However, accumulating evidence about the course of human evolution increasingly made Piltdown man seem an anomaly. When, in 1949, fluorine tests on the Piltdown bones by Dr. Kenneth Oakley of the British Museum showed these to be younger than the associated Early Pleistocene fauna, the anomaly became much greater.

These puzzling results drew the attention of Professor J. S. Weiner of the Department of Anatomy at Oxford University, who began to suspect the authenticity of Piltdown man. Together with his colleague, Professor Wilfrid Le Gros Clark, and Dr. Oakley, Weiner conducted an exhaustive examination of the Piltdown bones.

The investigators discovered that the teeth had been deliberately filed down to resemble those of humans and that both the skull and the jaw had been stained to make them appear ancient. Oakley applied an improved fluorine test to the Piltdown collection; later, nitrogen and uranium tests were also carried out. The bones of Piltdown man contained so little fluorine and uranium and so much nitrogen that they were clearly of relatively recent date, at most a few hundred years old. Careful examination revealed that the skull had belonged to a modern man who had lived around 1400 C.E., while the jaw came from a young orangutan.

Tests of relative age carried out on the animal bones associated with Piltdown man showed that they, too, were a hoax—a jumble of ancient material from various sources. Among them was the molar of an early Pleistocene elephant, *Archidiskodon africanavus*, which had an unusually high uranium content for its date. That linked it to a site in Tunisia where material, including teeth with similarly high uranium levels, had been found.

No one knows for certain who was responsible for the Piltdown fakes. Dawson, now known to have been guilty of other deceptions, seems the prime suspect, and it is difficult to imagine how anyone but Dawson could have arranged the discoveries. However, it could be argued that he was not sufficiently knowledgeable to have executed such a skilled forgery and that he could not have laid hands on the genuine fossil animal bones that were placed with Piltdown man. This points to someone within the scientific establishment who disliked and wished to discredit Sir Arthur Smith Woodward and his colleagues. Sir Grafton Elliot Smith, the eminent physical anthropologist, and William Sollas, professor of geology at Oxford, have been suggested as possible perpetrators. If this were the case, however, it is difficult to see why the hoax was not exposed earlier, to ensure the desired discomfiture of Piltdown man's supporters. The mystery still remains.

After the "discovery" of Piltdown man in a gravel pit at Piltdown, in Sussex, England, Charles Dawson and Dr. A. Smith Woodward (left) excavated further relics between 1912 and 1915. Doubts began to be cast on the claimed "missing link" as hominid fossils being found elsewhere in the world revealed that humans' large brain developed much later than other human features such as upright posture and smaller, less massive jaws. The anomalous Piltdown individual was finally proved to be a hoax in 1953.

129

PILTDOWN
HOAX EXPOSED

ABSOLUTE DATING TECHNIQUES

A breakthrough in establishing a chronology for the past came with the invention and development of radiocarbon dating (*see page 134*), in the 1940s and 1950s. Radiocarbon is still the most important technique, but science has since produced numerous other absolute dating methods, and more are still being added. The latest weapon in the armory is electron spin resonance (ESR). Recent developments have also revolutionized radiocarbon dating.

Radiocarbon remains the absolute dating method most widely applied today because it can be used on a wide range of materials and because decades of research have constantly refined its accuracy and efficiency. However, other techniques may well challenge the supremacy of radiocarbon in the future.

The range of radiocarbon dating is limited—at most 50,000 years even using the most modern techniques. The early stages of human evolution, which can be traced back several million years, are therefore dated by a number of other methods, applicable mainly to geological material and often used in combination with one another.

In addition to the major techniques, there are several of more limited scope. Though most can be used only to date certain materials, such as wood, in suitable situations they can give excellent results.

Dendrochronology

Tree-ring dating, or dendrochronology, was the first method of absolute dating applied in archaeology, and it is still of great value in environments where wood remains well preserved, such as arid or waterlogged sites. Since the 1970s it has also made a significant contribution as the basis for calibrating radiocarbon dates.

As early as the 18th century, it was known that trees develop by growing a ring of tissue each year, allowing their ages to be determined by counting the number of rings in their trunks. The future U.S. president Thomas Jefferson suggested using tree-ring dating to determine the minimum ages of ancient Amerindian earthworks from the trees on them.

Modern dendrochronology was pioneered in the early 20th century by the astronomer A. E. Douglass. While exploring the possible use of tree rings in his investigation of sun-spot cycles, he became aware of their potential for dating wooden archaeological structures, in particular those in the pueblos of the American Southwest. A 10-year investigation of Pueblo Bonito culminated in 1929 when Douglass linked a floating chronology—a series of tree rings of unknown date—to a tree-ring sequence running up to the present day. As a result of this work it was possible to date many of the major Pueblo ruins.

Complacent or Sensitive

Trees, for dating purposes, fall into two categories: complacent or sensitive. Complacent trees have annual rings of uniform width and are therefore of no use for dendrochronology. In sensitive trees, however, environmental conditions influence the width of the annual rings. Rainfall is the critical factor in arid areas, while in more humid regions, temperature is also important. Conditions such as soil depth and drainage in the immediate locality play a part, too.

Within broad limits, sensitive trees in any geographical region all exhibit the same patterns in their growth rings over the same period. By matching parts of the sequence of growth rings from living trees with those discernible in older timbers, a continuous dated regional sequence can be built up. Several such sequences now exist, including a 10,000-year-long master sequence for western and central Europe based on Irish and German oaks, and a North American sequence of more than 8,000 years using the long-lived bristlecone pine, *Pinus aristata*. A number of floating chronologies of considerable length have also been established. Although they have not been tied at any point to a precise calendar year, their approximate dates are frequently known. It has now become possible not only to date some sites with preserved wood precisely, but often also to establish the precise constructional history of structures within them.

Need for Caution

Dendrochronology provides a precise date for suitable pieces of wood in archaeological contexts and is now a major dating tool of increasing importance. However, care must be taken to establish how the piece of wood being dated

Thomas Jefferson (below), "the father of American Archaeology" and president of the American Philosophical Society, was one of the first people to suggest the study of tree rings as a means of dating burial mounds of the American Indians.

relates to the structure from which it derives. For example, timber may have been freshly cut to repair a centuries-old building; conversely, a new structure may incorporate old timbers.

Tree-ring data is best obtained from cross sections of timber, but in the case of living trees dendrochronologists have to be content with drilling out cores. The samples are sanded and polished or scraped so that the rings can be accurately measured and counted, allowing for progressive changes in width with age. The sequences of rings from different trees or archaeological timbers are matched in groups of a number of years to avoid fortuitous similarities and to overcome occasional aberrations such as missing or false rings, which may be due to extraneous factors such as frost damage.

Varves

In the period immediately after the most recent ice age, the annual summer melting of the northern glaciers fed the lakes of Scandinavia with meltwater carrying sand and clay particles. During the year, these particles gradually settled on the lake beds; at first the coarse particles formed a light layer and, later, progressively finer particles produced a dark layer.

The thickness of these annual layers, or "varves" as they are called, was determined by the amount of glacial melting that occurred that year. A sequence of distinctive annual varves from a number of deposits was built up by Baron Gerard de Geer, an eminent Swedish geologist, at the beginning of the 20th century. He linked this sequence of varves to a more recently laid-down series of estuary varves, to produce a combined dated sequence going back to about 10,000 B.C.E.

Pollen, which is preserved within the varves, provided the means of dating the pollen zones—the sequence of postglacial vegetational and climatic periods known from pollen analysis (see page 104). Archaeological material belonging to a particular pollen zone could therefore be assigned an approximate date. Though varve dating has been superseded by techniques like radiocarbon, it is now proving useful in checking the tree-ring calibration of radiocarbon dating.

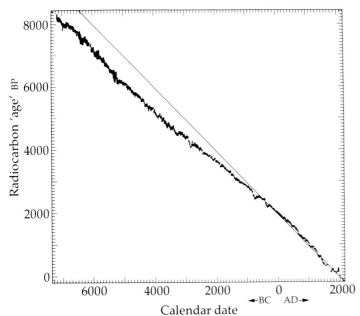

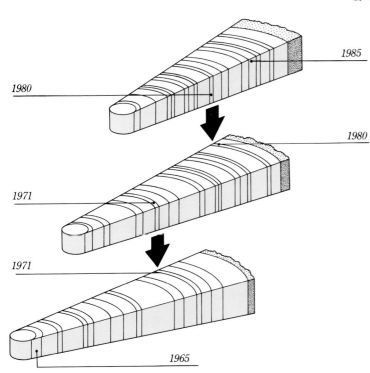

Radiocarbon years do not correspond exactly to calendar years (see pages 136–137). As wood can be dated by both radiocarbon and dendrochronology, a calibration curve has been constructed using the absolute accuracy of tree-ring dates (in this case based on Irish oaks) to indicate the true calendar age of carbon-14 dates.

The characteristic patterns of annual variation in tree-ring widths in an area allow trees of different ages to be arranged in an overlapping sequence. From these, a master sequence is built up, extending into the past. Computers aid in the laborious task of matching the rings in archaeological timbers to the appropriate place on the master sequence.

ABSOLUTE DATING
TECHNIQUES

STONES, BONES AND MAGNETISM

Until recently, typology and context were virtually the only clues to dating stone tools and rock art, although tools of obsidian could be directly dated. When a piece of obsidian is chipped to make a tool, the freshly exposed surface begins to absorb water at a rate that depends on the source (and hence chemical composition) of the obsidian, the temperature and the degree of exposure to sunlight. By examining a thin section of the tool under a microscope and measuring the thickness of the hydration layer, the date of manufacture of the artifact can be calculated, using local data on temperature and hydration rate. Obsidian hydration dating is widely used in the Americas, where many prehistoric artifacts were manufactured from this glassy volcanic rock.

Nowadays, however, using thermoluminescence (*see pages 138–139*) it is possible also to date flint tools that were heated during their manufacture, as well as other crystalline stones that were heated, for example in a fire. Stone tools with "desert varnish" should also be datable.

Desert varnish, a hard layer of minerals containing microscopic organic particles, develops on rock surfaces exposed to desert dust. In some parts of the world, such as Australia and the Americas, desert varnish has formed over ancient rock engravings. Recent advances (*see pages 136–137*) enable radiocarbon dates to be obtained from even the minute amount of organic matter found in desert varnish. Known differences in the rate at which charged atoms (cations) of certain elements leach out also allow the varnish to be dated, giving a minimum age for the art beneath it. This cation ratio dating, however, is still controversial.

Amino Acid Racemization

Amino acids, often surviving in ancient bone, exist in two forms—the L (laevo), which is synthesized in living organisms, and the D (dextro), into which the L form gradually changes. Sophisticated equipment for studying amino acids has been developed by medical and biological scientists, allowing measurement of the degree of this change in archaeological material.

The process of change, called racemization, occurs at different rates in different amino acids. Aspartic acid, which racemizes rapidly, can be used to date post-Pleistocene bone, while isoleucine and alanine, which change much more slowly, can date material probably up to 1 million years old. However, the rate of racemization also depends very much on temperature, so material can be dated by racemization only if it comes from an environment whose past temperature can confidently be determined. Older material must be from stable environments that have undergone little temperature variation, such as deep-

The position of magnetic north, which is constantly changing, is shown on the diagrams below as measured from Britain and the U.S. Southwest. Establishing the position of magnetic north at the time when a clay structure was fired allows it to be dated by matching that position with the appropriate regional sequence.

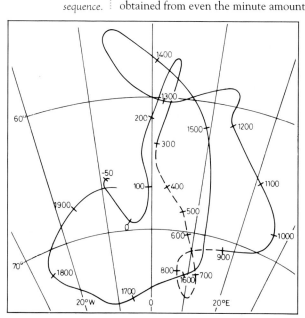

Britain

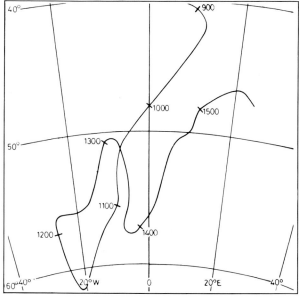

Southwestern United States

sea sediments and the deepest recesses of caves. With more recent material, the contribution of temperature can be assessed by measuring the degree of racemization in a sample of radiocarbon-dated bone. That provides a local temperature standard for calculating the age of other bones by racemization dating. Further research is being done into this technique.

Archaeomagnetism

The direction and the intensity of the earth's magnetic field are both constantly changing, due to variations in electrical currents in the earth's molten core. Records kept in London, Paris and Rome over the past four centuries have been used in conjunction with fired clay structures of known date to build up a partial picture of any changes that take place. However, because these changes will also be affected by latitude, the significance of the information is limited since it is only of regional applicability.

Clays used in pottery commonly contain the magnetic oxides hematite and magnetite. When, as happens during firing, the oxides are heated above a critical temperature (it is called the Curie point, and it varies among oxides), they lose all ability to retain magnetism. But as they cool to slightly below their Curie point, the oxides become susceptible to the surrounding magnetic field, usually that of the earth, and acquire its magnetism. At what is termed the blocking temperature, which is slightly lower again, this acquired, or thermoremanent, magnetism becomes fixed. In effect, the pottery preserves a replica of the earth's magnetism at the time and place of firing.

By comparing the remanent magnetism of archaeological material with regional records, it can be dated. A magnetometer is used to measure both intensity and direction.

Intensity may be ascertained from any fired clay for which the source (and hence the latitude) is known. Direction is composed of two elements: declination (compass direction) and inclination (angle of dip). Inclination can be ascertained in archaeological material for which the source and the position during firing can be determined—for instance, bricks stacked horizontally in the kiln. Declination can be obtained only from material still in the position in which it was fired—kilns, hearths and brick or daub structures that suffered fire damage.

Uranium Series Disequilibrium

The soluble radioactive element uranium decays into a series of insoluble daughter products

that under certain circumstances become separated from their parent. The proportions of these daughter products relative to one another and to the parent uranium, constitute the basis of a series of techniques; collectively these techniques form what is known as uranium series disequilibrium dating (USDD).

The decay of uranium is the basis of thorium/protactinium ratio dating, already established for determining the ages of deep-sea cores. Recently, similar principles have been applied elsewhere. For instance, uranium is present in cave dripwaters, which form stalagmites and travertine layers, but its daughter products are not. Their subsequent production in the cave deposits allows the date of a deposit's formation to be determined—invaluable in dating Paleolithic caves. A similar process in open-air aquatic deposits and in fossil soils may also provide dating evidence.

Electron Spin Resonance Dating

A recently developed technique, electron spin resonance (ESR), also relates to uranium radiation. Hydroxyapatite, the mineral of which tooth enamel is formed, is exposed to uranium radiation from the time when it is buried in the ground: This causes electrons in it to be displaced and trapped. Exposure to high-frequency electromagnetic radiation in the laboratory makes these electrons resonate, allowing the uranium uptake to be measured. Combined with data on local gamma radiation and on the decay of the absorbed uranium into its daughter products, these measurements allow the date when teeth were buried to be determined. ESR's theoretical range is up to a million years, so it should prove particularly useful in dating the teeth of animals found with early human remains, beyond the range of radiocarbon (*see pages 140–141*).

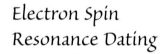

Obsidian hydration dating was used to establish the age of hundreds of artifacts, recovered by divers from the seabed off the small island of Aghios Petros, Greece, in 1981. As well as obsidian tools (above), artifacts of flint and chert (uppermost) were found on the site of a Neolithic village 7,000 years old.

STONES, BONES AND MAGNETISM

RADIOCARBON DATING

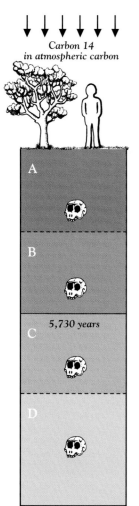

Carbon 14
in atmospheric carbon

5,730 years

A

B

C

D

Neutrons produced by cosmic radiation interact with nitrogen in the earth's stratosphere to produce C-14 (radiocarbon, or carbon 14), the radioactive isotope of carbon. Atoms of C-14 rapidly become incorporated into carbon dioxide and subsequently distributed evenly throughout the atmosphere.

As these radioactive atoms decay, they are replaced by new ones, so the proportion of C-14 in the atmosphere should remain constant. However, in modern times the balance has been somewhat affected through the burning of fossil fuels and nuclear explosions.

All living things take up C-14 during life, but the process ceases after death and the C-14 in the organism decays at a known rate. Radiocarbon has a half-life of 5,730 (plus or minus 40) years: After that period has elapsed, half of the residual C-14 will have been lost by radioactive decay; after another 5,730 years, half of the remaining amount will have been lost; and so on. Assuming that the amount of C-14 present in the atmosphere has remained constant, the amount of C-14 left in a dead organism should reflect the time elapsed since its death.

Professor Willard Libby, whose investigations of the upper atmosphere in the 1940s resulted directly in the development of radiocarbon dating, demonstrated its effectiveness by applying it to Egyptian antiquities of known historical date. The results showed a close correspondence between the historical and radiocarbon ages.

Radiocarbon dating can be used on a variety of materials, the best of which is charcoal, as that is mainly carbon. Other substances have to be reduced to their

carbon content before dating can be carried out. Wood also yields excellent results, particularly if only the cellulose fraction is used. However, as in dendrochronology, there is the risk that the sample being analyzed may not be contemporary with the associated archaeological material unless it has been carefully chosen. Shorter-lived plant material is also very suitable and does not present such sampling difficulties.

Dating of human and animal bones has to be performed on their protein fraction, collagen, of which a relatively large amount is required. Shells pose problems, as they are easily contaminated. Iron can be radiocarbon dated if charcoal or wood was used in the smelting, the method that was common practice in the past. Occasionally, pottery will contain enough carbon to allow it to be dated by C-14.

Analyzing the Sample

A sample for radiocarbon dating is first treated to remove any contaminants, usually by repeated washing in dilute acid and alkali, then reduced to pure carbon and combined in a suitable carbon compound. If a gas counter is being used to measure radioactivity, that will be carbon dioxide, methane or acetylene. Alternatively, when a liquid scintillation spectrometer is employed, the carbon will be converted to some form of liquid, such as benzene.

A few routine tests must be performed on the sample. Sometimes, the carbon isotopes C-12, C-13 and C-14 separate out (fractionate) instead of remaining uniformly distributed. Measurement of the C-12:C-13 ratio using a mass spectrometer allows the scientist to determine whether fractionation has taken place. The background radiation of the counting device is also measured, and this is subtracted from the count rate of the sample—the result of this final calculation is its net count rate.

Both the gas counter and the liquid scintillation spectrometer measure the sample's present rate of radioactive decay over a period of hours or days, and from that its C-14 content can be calculated. The device also counts the activity of an artificial control standard, usually NBS oxalic acid (NBS are the initials of the U.S. National Bureau of Standards that formulates it), which represents the C-14 activity of living tissue before changes in atmospheric levels of C-14 took place in modern times. Dates are calculated from the ratio of the net count rate of the sample to that of the standard, allowing for the rate of decay.

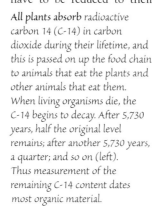

All plants absorb radioactive carbon 14 (C-14) in carbon dioxide during their lifetime, and this is passed on up the food chain to animals that eat the plants and other animals that eat them. When living organisms die, the C-14 begins to decay. After 5,730 years, half the original level remains; after another 5,730 years, a quarter; and so on (left). Thus measurement of the remaining C-14 content dates most organic material.

THE ORIGINS OF AGRICULTURE

The revolutionary impact of radiocarbon dating can clearly be seen in the transformed picture it has given us of the origins of agriculture.

The earliest historical dates in the Near East are around 3000 B.C.E., when civilized societies were emerging in Mesopotamia and Egypt. Both civilizations were founded on sophisticated agricultural technology, involving irrigation, and so it was apparent that agriculture was already no longer in its infancy. When had it begun?

Until the advent of radiocarbon dating, scholars generally agreed that agriculture was a radical innovation, readily embraced because it offered a secure way of life in place of the uncertainties of a hunter-gatherer existence. They considered that its development was rapid and suggested a date of around 4500 B.C.E. for its inception.

The accepted view was that postglacial climatic changes brought man into closer contact with plants and animals, leading to an awareness of the economic potential of controlling them. Once that awareness dawned, agriculture quickly spread.

Radiocarbon dating drove the first nails into the coffin of this theory. The initial dates obtained for the impressive early farming settlement at Jericho, 6250–5850 B.C.E., raised a considerable storm. They were strongly challenged to begin with, but soon similar and even earlier dates were obtained for this and other agricultural sites in the Near East. These indicated not only that farming was well established in the Levant, Turkey, Iraq and western Iran 9,000 years ago, but that the first steps toward it had been taken long before, in the final millennia of the Ice Age.

In caves such as those of Mount Carmel and at open-air sites like Ain Mallaha, the appearance of sickles and pestles and mortars for harvesting and preparing cereals and other plants indicates an increasing interest in plant foods. In the early postglacial period, settlements such as Jericho began to emerge in areas beyond the natural range of wild cereals. Their economies were partly based on the cultivation of cereals on well-watered land, although the inhabitants continued to gather and hunt, too. Gazelle were the main source of meat among these Near Eastern peoples, but gradually that role came to be filled by domesticated sheep and goats.

Some implications of this new information about the origins of agriculture are clear. The cultivation of plants and animal husbandry both began far earlier than was previously thought. However, they did not go hand in hand; in the Near East, plants were cultivated long before animals were domesticated.

Furthermore, food production was not a sudden discovery that was immediately acceptable, but the culmination of a series of changes in the relationship between people and their food sources (*see pages 108–109*).

Excavations of the ancient city of Jericho have revealed an impressive farming community indicating that agriculture was well established there 10,000 years ago. A substantial wall with a massive watchtower surrounded the settlement at that time. Other agricultural sites in the Near East have been dated even earlier. Farming spread gradually across Europe, reaching Britain around 6,000 years ago.

ADVANCES IN RADIOCARBON DATING

Older Samples

The radioactivity of samples more than 40,000–50,000 years old is so weak that it is very difficult to measure. However, by passing the sample through thermal diffusion columns for several weeks, it is possible to concentrate the C-14 in the sample. This technique extends the date range to 70,000 years, but it is expensive and time-consuming and requires large samples, rarely obtainable from material of this age.

Advances in the 1980s, using an accelerator mass spectrometer (AMS), permit dating back to at least 50,000 years. The AMS directly measures the amount of C-14 present and needs carbon samples of only 1–5 milligrams, as opposed to 1–5 grams with the other techniques. Samples can be freed from possible sources of contamination much more effectively, as suspect portions can be discarded. And the AMS yields accurate results in a few hours.

After pretreatment, the sample is converted to graphite on tantalum wire. This is suspended in a cesium sputter ion source, and the ions produced are accelerated through large electrical and magnetic fields. Ions of different mass are separated and counted in the process.

AMS is expensive, but it represents a major step forward and several laboratories now use it. In the future, it may extend the range of radiocarbon dating even earlier, though this now seems less likely than was first thought.

Striving for Precision

Libby originally calculated the half-life of C-14 as 5,568 years. Later, it was more accurately determined as 5,730 years, but by then many dates had been published on the basis of the earlier figure. It was therefore decided to retain the original for calculation and publication. These dates can easily be converted to their correct determination on the new half-life simply by multiplying by 1.03.

Radiocarbon dates are quoted in years "before present" (BP). Convention dictates that *present* in this context is the year 1950 C.E., so a radiocarbon date of 2976 BP represents (2976 - 950) = 1026 B.C.E. (more correctly, this should be *bc* [bce]—*see under "Calibration"*).

Even the updated figure for the half-life of C-14 is based ultimately on statistical probability. Radioactive decay is a random process and cannot be predicted with certainty. So in giving radiocarbon dates, archaeologists qualify them according to accepted statistical practice, with a standard deviation (σ) such that in most cases two in every three readings will fall within it.

For our date of 1026 B.C.E., for example, if the standard deviation is ± (plus or minus) 120 years, the chances are two in three that the object dates from between 1146 and 906 B.C.E.

Normally, radiocarbon date ranges are calculated to one standard deviation. If this is increased to two standard deviations, however, the probability of the date lying within this range rises to 95 percent (99 percent for three standard deviations), but the date range then becomes excessively large. In our example, for instance, there is 95 percent chance that the object dates between 1266 and 786 B.C.E. The size of the deviation may be reduced, and the accuracy of the mean date improved, by dating a number of samples from the same deposit. This is recommended practice, as clearly, the greater the number of consistent dates obtained from a context, the greater the confidence that can be placed in them.

Calibration

It was initially assumed that the ratio of C-14 to C-12 in the atmosphere had remained constant. But disquieting discrepancies between some radiocarbon dates and historical dates eventually caused this assumption to be called into question, and the accuracy of C-14 dates was therefore tested using dendrochronology.

A sequence of datable trees was assembled in America, first using the long-lived giant redwood, *Sequoia gigantea*, and then living and dead bristlecone pines, *Pinus aristata*, which enabled the sequence to be extended to 8200 BP. By comparing tree rings (in 25-year blocks) with their radiocarbon date, it became apparent that the radiocarbon dates were consistently younger than the true dates of the wood before about 1000 B.C.E. The discrepancy increases with time; new data from deep-sea cores dated beyond the present range of dendrochronology indicate a discrepancy

THE MEGALITH BUILDERS

Since the days of the earliest antiquarians, scholars have been puzzled by the many megalithic tombs of Neolithic date and impressive architecture around Europe's Atlantic seaboard. Although there are considerable regional variations in their form, there is a general overriding similarity in design and, particularly, in their use of massive stones.

The construction of such large and architecturally complex collective tombs by European barbarians struck prehistorians as anomalous. The seafaring civilizations of the Bronze Age Aegean, among whom collective burial and a diversity of stone-built tombs were known, seemed a probable source of inspiration. It was suggested that Aegean people had visited Iberia in search of metal ores and had introduced the idea of collective burial in massive tombs, which then spread northward to Brittany, Britain, North Germany and Scandinavia.

Radiocarbon dates for the fortified settlement of megalith-builders at Los Millares in Spain appeared to confirm this picture, though dates for megaliths in Brittany seemed too early. When calibrated, however, it became clear that the radiocarbon dates were universally too early to support a Bronze Age Aegean origin. The oldest tombs in Brittany are now dated to the early 5th millennium B.C.E., while megalith building became well established elsewhere on the Atlantic seaboard during the 5th and 4th millennia. It is now clear that the megaliths are a western and northern European invention, not an introduced idea, and recent theories consider them in this light (*see pages 160–161*).

Massive stone tombs such as this one near Plouharnel, Brittany, have been discovered in several areas around the coast of northwest Europe. The tombs have been dated to 5000–1500 B.C.E. and were generally used for the collective burial of many individuals.

of some 3,000 years between radiocarbon and true dates by 18,000 B.C.E.

No one is certain what caused the changes in C-14 levels in the past, but it may be related to variations in the intensity of the earth's magnetic field. It has been suggested that this magnetic field around the earth acts to deflect radiation arriving from outer space and that a decrease in its intensity sometime in the past had permitted an increase in the flux of cosmic radiation reaching the upper atmosphere. That in turn would have resulted in an increase in the C-14 atoms produced.

In addition to the broad divergence, there were also apparently minor fluctuations known as wiggles. The wiggles have yet to be explained but may relate to changes in solar activity. Recent work on European tree-ring sequences, particularly on oak trees from Irish bogs, has been used by scientists to establish a wiggle curve.

Data obtained through dendrochronology from many sources has made it possible to construct a calibration curve, which is now accepted back to 6000 B.C.E. By comparison with this, radiocarbon dates can be converted to calendar years (*see figure, page 131*). This is done by reading off the true calendar values for the dates at either end of the date range given by the standard deviations: The calibrated date will lie between them.

It is now archaeological convention to write uncalibrated radiocarbon dates with the notation bc (bce) and the calibrated dates (now equivalent to calendar dates) as BC (B.C.E.).

THERMOLUMINESCENCE DATING

Thermoluminescence (TL) is the dating technique archaeologists have long hoped for—the one that can date pottery. It can date material over a very long time range, from very recent times to 70,000 or more years ago. Despite more than two decades of research, however, it still suffers from problems that seriously limit its precision.

TL relies on the presence in clay of tiny quantities of radioactive matter, which emits alpha and beta particles that in turn bombard quartz crystals, knocking electrons out of place. The displaced electrons become trapped in irregularities in the clay lattice.

If fired clay is reheated to a temperature above 380°C, or 716°F (most pottery is fired at more than 500°C, or 932°F), the electrons pop back into their original place. Light is also emitted. By measuring the amount of such light given off and the quantity of radioactive material present, TL can establish the time that has elapsed since the clay was fired.

The technique applies to most clay heated to more than 380°C, and not just to pottery. So it can be used to date Paleolithic clay figurines that were either accidentally or deliberately baked, and clay hearth surrounds. TL has also been used successfully on flint tools heated accidentally or during manufacture.

Testing the Samples

The first step in preparing a sherd for TL analysis is to grind it to powder and to extract the quartz grains from it using laboratory separation techniques. The grains are then heated on a graphite plate in an airtight chamber, and the light that is given off is measured using a photomultiplier. A chart recorder prints out details of the temperature and the glow curves of the TL.

The material is heated again, when all the TL has been given off, to measure the background emission of the plate. The comparison of the two glow curves allows the amount of TL to be calculated. The radioactivity of the material is also measured with a counting device.

An important consideration in TL dating is where the pottery comes from. Radioactive elements in the environment emit gamma particles that vary in intensity according to local conditions. Although most of the TL that is measured is caused by the clay's internal alpha and beta particles, some may be due to the external influence of these gamma particles. If the source of the pot-

tery is known, the level of gamma irradiation can be allowed for in the dating. If not, the dates obtained may not be very accurate.

TL Completes the Picture

TL has been used to date several important archaeological cultures for which there are few or no radiocarbon dates, or for which the C-14 dates are of disputed reliability. One recent example is the investigation of the Neolithic and Chalcolithic cultures of Portugal.

To a large extent, these cultures are represented by a variety of megalithic burials, but there are also hilltop settlements. On the basis of the finds, it was possible to work out a general picture of the stages in the development of the tomb architecture, but the actual dates involved were uncertain. Were the Portuguese megaliths as early as their counterparts elsewhere in western Europe? When did the settlements begin?

TL was called upon to answer such questions, and 55 sherds were analyzed, from nine sites. The TL dates for the earliest tombs with pottery, the passage graves at Gateira and Gorginos, were around the middle of the 5th millennium B.C.E.— a good match with the radiocarbon dates for the earliest Breton passage graves.

Right through the sequence, TL dates from Portugal fitted radiocarbon dates elsewhere in western Europe, even to the surprisingly early rock-cut tomb at Carenque, which has exact parallels in Malta at the same date, around 4000 B.C.E.

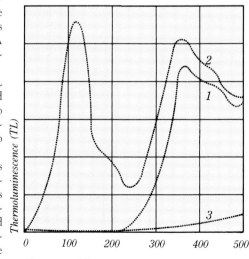

Thermoluminescence dating measures the emission of light from a sample that is heated in an airtight container in a special apparatus (above). The light emitted at different temperatures is plotted on a graph (right). The glow curve, line 1, represents the light emitted by the sample—the archaeological thermoluminescence. Line 2 indicates the pottery's sensitivity to radiation. Line 3 represents the background light emitted from the chamber, which must be taken into account when calculating the TL of the sample.

SURPRISES AT GLOZEL

In 1924, a young Frenchman, Émile Fradin, accidentally discovered a medieval glass furnace at Glozel, near Vichy, France. The local schoolmistress excavated it, while the schoolmaster encouraged Émile's enthusiasm by lending him books on archaeology. This newly acquired knowledge would lead to interesting events connected to Fradin.

Over the next three years, some very curious things appeared from Glozel: tools and carvings of prehistoric type, inscribed clay tablets and extraordinary vases with human faces.

Opinion on the authenticity of the artifacts was sharply divided, but in 1927 an international commission investigated the site and reported it to be a hoax.

In 1974, an international team of scientists decided to subject some of the Glozel artifacts to TL dating. To everyone's amazement, the dates obtained were neither modern, as the anti-Glozelians had supposed, nor very ancient, as the Glozelians had hoped, but clustered between 700 B.C.E. and 100 C.E. What was going on? The TL scientists were certain that there was nothing wrong with the TL dates. On the other hand, many of them were just as convinced as the archaeologists that the material must be forged.

Various suggestions were made. One was that the objects were originally undistinguished material of genuine antiquity but modified by the forger: old bones with modern "Paleolithic" carvings, modern "writing" on tablets of genuine ancient fired clay. More recent TL tests gave some support to this theory, since some of the pieces proved to be of medieval date.

Glozel remains a mystery. At present most experts believe that it was a fraud, but there are still some who disagree.

A clay brick (left) found at Glozel bears a selection of written characters resembling the Minoan and Phoenician scripts but making no sense. Archaeologists declared the Glozel finds to be a hoax in 1927 but digging at the site continued, as shown in the above photograph taken in 1928.

The settlements were shown to have begun at the period of the largest megalithic tombs.

Related Dating Methods

Sedimentary deposits of archaeological interest, for example, sands containing artifacts or silts accumulating in ditches, can now be dated using optical dating, a technique similar to TL. Electrons displaced by radiation and caught in the electron traps of many minerals are released by short periods of exposure to sunlight. However, when these minerals are deposited as sediments and no longer exposed to the sun, the electrons begin to accumulate again. Measurement of the light given off (the optically stimulated luminescence) when a sample of such a sediment is again exposed to light allows the date of deposition to be calculated.

Electron spin resonance (see page 133) is also dependent on measuring trapped electrons that accumulated due to radiation.

DATING EARLY HUMANS

Human ancestry extends back far beyond the range of radiocarbon dating. Attempts to date our earliest ancestors depend on various other techniques, most of which apply to geological strata. Usually, archaeological remains occur in deposits above or below such strata rather than within them, so dating is indirect. However, electron spin resonance, TL, amino acid racemization and optical dating (*see preceding pages*) all promise some hope of directly dating Pleistocene material in the future.

Potassium-Argon Dating

The volcanic material from which igneous rock is formed contains both potassium (K) and an argon isotope (Ar-40). At the time of formation, all the argon is released. However, the potassium still present has a radioactive isotope, K-40, part of which becomes the inert argon isotope Ar-40 as it decays. The process of decay takes place at a known rate, so by measuring the Ar-40 now present, it is possible to gauge its age.

One method of doing this (known as laser-fusion argon-argon dating) involves irradiating a sample with fast neutrons, converting the K-39 isotope to the argon isotope, Ar-39. By measuring this, it is possible to calculate the original K-40 content. The amount of argon present is measured with a sensitive mass spectrometer.

Samples for potassium-argon (K/Ar) dating must be carefully selected, avoiding contaminated rock and strata from which argon has been lost through diffusion. The most reliable results are obtained by dating several crystal types from the same deposit and samples from scattered localities in the same geological stratum.

Fission Track Dating

The spontaneous fission of the uranium isotope U-238 produces submicroscopic damage trails in certain rocks containing uranium impurities, particularly volcanic "glasses" such as obsidian. As U-238 decays at a known rate, the density of these fission tracks is proportionate to the age and to the amount of uranium present. When the rock is heated beyond a certain temperature, the fission tracks fade and disappear. It is therefore necessary to select materials for dating that have a high "fading temperature." The date obtained from these will be the date of formation of the rock.

The fission tracks can be observed in a thin section under a microscope and counted, particularly if they are enlarged by etching with hydro-fluoric acid. The uranium content can be calculated by irradiating the sample to induce the fission of U-235 (which does not undergo spontaneous fission), producing a number of new damage trails proportionate to the uranium content.

Fission track dating can be used over a very considerable time range, from as little as 20 years to more than 1 billion. Although it has mainly been applied to volcanic rocks, it can also be used to date human-made glass and pottery that contains suitable crystalline minerals.

Paleomagnetism

In addition to short-term variations in the intensity and direction of the earth's magnetic fields, discussed previously, there have been longer periods when the earth's magnetic polarity has been completely or partly reversed. They have been identified in volcanic and sedimentary rocks and, more particularly, in deep-sea sediments, which contain a continuous record datable back to about 5 million years ago. This paleomagnetic information provides a useful control for other dating techniques.

Ocean Sediments

Seawater contains the stable oxygen isotopes O-18 and O-16. Water molecules containing O-16 evaporate more readily than those with O-18 and are therefore preferentially incorporated into polar ice during glacial periods, altering the ratio between the two isotopes in the sea.

Planktonic foraminifera, minute ocean creatures, reflect this ratio in their composition. After death, the shells of foraminifera accumulate on the ocean floor, where they form a major component of the sediments. These sediments therefore provide a continuous record of fluctuations in global temperature.

Radiocarbon, K/Ar, fission track and thorium protactinium (USD) dating techniques are all applied to ocean sediment samples.

Biostratigraphy

Intensive work by paleontologists has produced a widely accepted family tree for a number of animals, such as the ancestors of horses, pigs and elephants. Certain of these can be used as "index fossils," providing a reliable date range for a geological deposit. Index fossils should be species that can easily be identified and that were abundant over a wide geographical area but existed for a short period of geological time.

Zinjanthropus, "Man of East Africa," (far right) found in Tanzania by Louis Leakey in 1959 has been scientifically placed in the Australopithecine group and is believed to be between 1.7 and 1.9 million years old. The jaw has been reconstructed.

The skull of Homo habilis, found at Lake Turkana, Kenya, by Richard Leakey (below) in 1972, has been dated to 1.8 million years ago. Recent reassessments of hominid fossils suggest that this may actually belong to a new and somewhat different hominid species, named Homo rudolfensis.

THE ANTIQUITY OF OUR ANCESTORS

In 1972, Richard Leakey discovered an impressive skull of *Homo habilis*, referred to by number 1470, at Lake Turkana, Kenya. This lay in a deposit below a volcanic tuff, KBS, dated 2.6 million BP by K/Ar. Leakey therefore dated 1470 to 2.9 million BP. As previous discoveries of *Homo habilis* had been in deposits dated 1.8 to 1.5 million BP, there was a considerable stir in scientific circles.

Eventually, Basil Cooke, a distinguished paleontologist, presented evidence that the type of pig (*Mesochoerus*) present in the same deposit as 1470 could not be older than 2 million years. The remains of forerunners of horses and elephants suggested the same.

Consequently, fission track dates of 1.8 million BP were obtained from a tuff below KBS. Very carefully selected uncontaminated samples finally yielded K/Ar dates of 1.8 and 1.6 million BP for the KBS tuff. Thus 1470 was securely dated to the same period as the other *Homo habilis* remains.

A similar combination of dating techniques was applied at Hadar, Ethiopia, where the bones of Lucy, *Australopithecus afarensis*, and her relatives were discovered above and below a layer of black basalt, for which a date of 3 million BP was obtained. However, at Laetoli in Kenya, similar hominid remains had been found between tuffs dated 3.59 and 3.77 million BP. Could they be the same species at such different dates, or were the dates wrong?

The paleomagnetic evidence showed that the Hadar fossils belonged to a period of reverse polarity, which the associated fauna, particularly the pigs, indicated should be the so-called Gilbert reversal of 3.8–3.4 million BP. Very careful collection of material for further K/Ar testing yielded a date of 3.75 million for the basalt, closely matching the Laetoli evidence, and permitting the classification of all these hominids as a single species, *Australopithecus afarensis*.

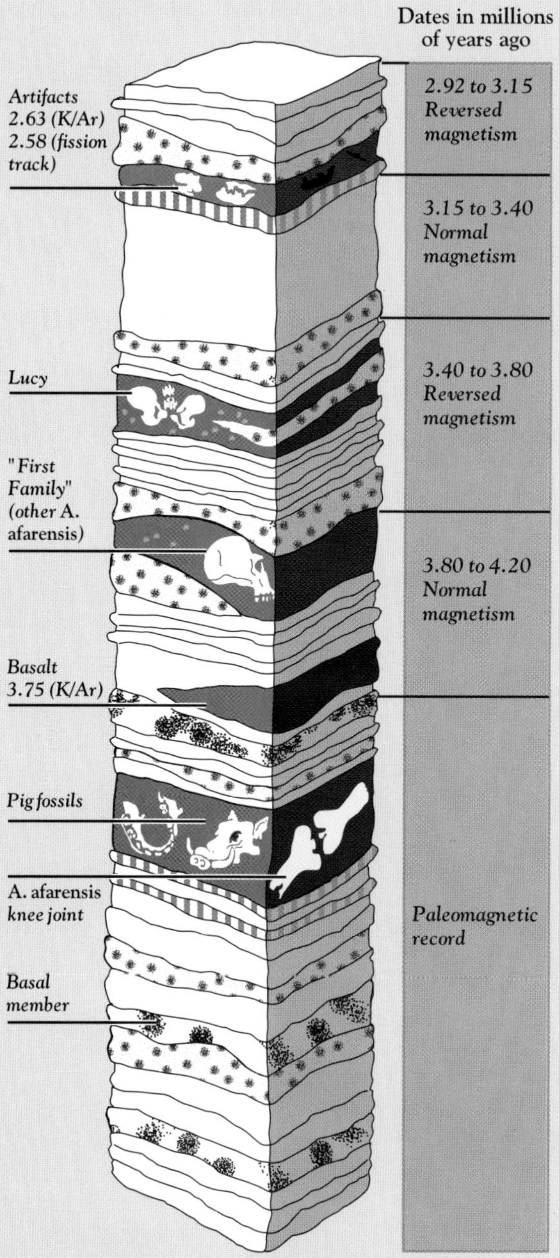
Dates in millions of years ago
Artifacts 2.63 (K/Ar) 2.58 (fission track)
Lucy
"First Family" (other A. afarensis)
Basalt 3.75 (K/Ar)
Pig fossils
A. afarensis knee joint
Basal member
2.92 to 3.15 Reversed magnetism
3.15 to 3.40 Normal magnetism
3.40 to 3.80 Reversed magnetism
3.80 to 4.20 Normal magnetism
Paleomagnetic record

FAR LEFT: **Five dating techniques** were used in the 1970s and 1980s to determine the age of the newly discovered fossils of our early ancestor *Australopithecus afarensis*, including the famous well-preserved skeleton nicknamed Lucy. Relative dating was possible using the geological stratigraphy of the site. The evidence of pig fossils of known date (via biostratigraphy) allowed the sequence of normal and reversed magnetic polarity identified in the strata to be tied to a dated segment of the paleomagnetic record. Potassium-argon and fission track dating were also used, giving a final date of 3.5 million years for Lucy.

Excavation seasons are short, and every moment is precious. This team
has been digging all day in a sweltering Middle Eastern desert, and they
continue their work even as the last light fades

PART

5

UNDERSTANDING THE PAST

UNDERSTANDING THE PAST

In a now-famous paper that appeared in *American Anthropologist* in 1954, Christopher Hawkes discussed the kind of inferences we are able to draw about the past. He concluded that they can be made at four levels.

The simplest inferences, in which we can place great confidence, concern ancient technology. Generally, it is easy to deduce from the physical examination of ancient artifacts how they were made. We have already seen the ways in which archaeologists tackle this relatively straightforward topic.

According to Hawkes, the second level concerns subsistence economics—how people have satisfied their basic needs for food, shelter, clothing and tools. Again, we have already seen that some information about that may be gleaned from physical analysis of archaeological remains. The movement of raw materials can be discovered, and the study of food remains gives clues about what people ate and at what time of year. Further indications of how past economies operated can be deduced using the methods of the economic prehistorian (*see page 152*). Considerable confidence may be placed in the conclusions.

Hawkes's two remaining levels concern social and political organization and religion. They pose much harder problems. The organization of human societies is extremely varied, so how can we attempt to deduce the organizational patterns of the past? Even more difficult, how do we recognize prehistoric religion and attempt to reconstruct it? Can we, in fact, do so?

All these aspects of the past are static, dealing with what a given society was like at a given time. But archaeologists are also concerned with how such societies interacted and changed. What mechanisms were operating, and were they the same as those that operate today?

It is to such questions, and the methods that archaeologists use in attempting to answer them, that this section is devoted.

Present into Past

Many theories have been put forward to explain observed archaeological phenomena, derived ultimately from the imagination, knowledge and experience of archaeologists themselves. But most of those archaeologists live in technologically advanced societies very different from the ones they are trying to reconstruct. Two important techniques in use today test their theories to see if they are rea-

sonable or even possible, and may also yield information to extend the range of theories. They are experimental archaeology and ethnoarchaeology.

Experimental archaeology aims to test hypotheses—particularly, though not exclusively, those associated with function, technology or economic matters—about specific aspects of the past. Ethnoarchaeology entails the study of contemporary societies from an archaeological viewpoint for the light they may shed on their ancient counterparts.

Archaeological Experiments

Ethnographic information is often the source of inspiration for archaeological experiments. For example, pits are a common feature of prehistoric sites. Frequently, they now contain rubbish, but it is assumed that their original function was, in many cases, storage—in particular of grain, but also of pulses, nuts, green vegetables and other foodstuffs.

Further alternative uses can be suggested by examining the functions of similar pits among present-day groups. In parts of Africa, for instance, some pits are used in the manufacture of indigo dye. By experimenting with various uses in the environment inhabited by the prehistoric group under study, archaeologists can assess which of the uses are most likely.

Experimental archaeology can be used to demonstrate that explanations rejected in theory as impossible may not in fact be so—although, of course, practical proof that something is feasible does not prove that it actually occurred. One of the most famous experiments of this kind was the daring voyage of the balsa raft *Kon-Tiki* in 1947.

Across the Pacific

For many years, scholars speculated that the Polynesian islands of the Pacific might originally have been colonized from South America. However, the idea was generally rejected, because the boats available to the South Americans at the time colonization was supposed to

OPPOSITE PAGE:
Following his daring *Kon-Tiki* voyage, the Norwegian anthropologist Thor Heyerdahl (top right) later made a voyage across the Atlantic in a papyrus-reed boat, the *Ra* (below right), to show that people from the Mediterranean could have sailed to Central and South America in similar vessels. Heyerdahl's journeys personally challenged previously held beliefs that such voyages were impossible. Such archaeological experiments can test the feasibility of suggested explanations and ideas and may point the way to new avenues of research.

have taken place were not considered capable of long ocean voyages.

The Norwegian anthropologist Thor Heyerdahl decided to challenge the received wisdom. He and his crew set sail from South America on a balsa wood raft of traditional design, the *Kon-Tiki*. Despite the gloomy prognostications of all who saw the raft depart, the *Kon-Tiki* landed safely about three months later, on the Pacific island of Tuamotu.

Heyerdahl's achievement demonstrated that South American colonization of Polynesia could not be discounted on the grounds of impossibility. He did not, however, prove that such colonization took place. Indeed the weight of archaeological evidence is still against it and overwhelmingly in favor of settlement from Southeast Asia.

Exposing Flaws

The voyage of the *Kon-Tiki* exposed a false assumption. Experiments also sometimes reveal flaws in archaeological reasoning. For example, the accepted picture of food production methods in Iron Age Britain had to be revised dramatically when proper tests were carried out on storage pits of the period.

For starters, it had been believed that a typical pit could hold 5 bushels (0.18 m³) of grain. Exper-

iments showed that their capacity was actually no fewer than 44 bushels (1.58 m³), indicating that the scale of Iron Age farming was far greater than had been supposed.

Archaeologists had also reasoned that the pits would have been lined with clay or basketry to protect the grain inside them and that they would have a limited life—say, 10 years—before the soil soured and they were used for rubbish disposal. Work by Peter Reynolds, the British experimental archaeologist, demonstrated otherwise.

Grain stored over winter in unlined pits, dug in a variety of subsoils and well sealed with a clay capping, quickly became dormant. The germination rate after storage was high, between 60 and 70 percent. The pits were easy to clean for reuse and showed no signs of souring.

Finally, the tests revealed a hitherto unrecognized fact. Careful study of the edges of such pits can provide clues about what they were used for. Although the idea seems obvious, it needed Reynolds's work to show that the pit edges should not be neglected or treated superficially—exemplifying another role of experimental archaeology.

RECONSTRUCTING THE PAST

Archaeological experiments are today an important means of advancing our scientific knowledge of the past. They enable archaeologists not only to test established hypotheses, but also generate new ones, which in turn can be tested.

One successful example of an experiment leading to a new hypothesis concerns the function of the notched ribs commonly found on sites of the American Indians of the Basketmaker period. It was initially thought that they might have been used for scraping hides, but when that was tried they broke. Further investigation revealed, however, that the ribs were very effective combs for extracting fibers from the leaves of yucca plants. It was known that ropemaking from these fibers was a major industry among the Indians, so it seemed reasonable to assume that the ribs were used in the process. The assumption was justified when a notched rib was found with yucca fibers and sap caught in it.

Most archaeological experiments relate to technology or to subsistence economics. They include such activities as: forest clearance, agriculture and food preparation; the reconstruction of buildings, earthworks and ships; manufacturing tools and weapons; pottery, weaving and painting; and the making of musical instruments. Recently, the American Egyptologist Robert Brier was even able to assess ancient Egyptian techniques of mummification by experimenting with a modern corpse.

Replicas for Research

Experimental reconstructions that are made of ancient objects and activities can be done on several levels. These range from simple copies, or reproductions, of ancient artifacts, perhaps for museum display, to reproductions made using only the technology, tools and materials available at the time the original was produced. A further stage is to test the reproduction in simulated ancient conditions. Nowadays, certain experimental simulations can also speedily and cheaply be undertaken by computer, allowing many possibilities to be tested.

At the Lejre research center in Denmark, for example, a replica of an Iron Age plow, or ard, found in a peat bog was used in experimental plowing, yielding useful information. The researchers discovered that the original ard accidentally lacked a vital wedge between the plowshare and the beam. They were able to study the ard's effectiveness in breaking ground, the wear on the share and the shape of Iron Age plow-

Basketmaking (bottom right) has been practiced by Native Americans for thousands of years and was particularly important in the Basketmaker period in the Southwest, before the development of pottery in the area. The descendants of the Basketmaker people lived in cliff settlements similar to these (top right) at Mesa Verde, Colorado. Ethnographic observation of modern craftsmanship is important in providing the archaeologist with data on techniques that may also have been used in the past.

UNDERSTANDING
THE PAST

MILLIE'S CAMP

A fascinating and important extension of the experimental approach applies it to the interpretation of remains. In a pioneering study in the 1970s, the Canadian archaeologist Robson Bonnichsen examined a Canadian Indian camp that had been abandoned relatively recently; he interpreted the archaeological evidence he recovered in terms of the activities that took place there and the number, ages and sex of the inhabitants.

Bonnichsen then asked an Indian woman, Millie, who had once lived in the camp to tell him about the actual inhabitants and what they did. Bonnichsen's interpretations were shown to be erroneous in many respects, but the exercise was valuable in highlighting potential problems in such interpretations.

The approach used at Millie's camp combined experiment with ethnography, and the two are often closely connected in archaeological research. Many of the experiments made on archaeological material stem from ideas and possibilities derived from ethnographic data.

marks. Experiments similar to the Danish ones have been carried out by Peter Reynolds at Butser Farm in Britain.

Reconstructions of incomplete remains of the past provide a fruitful area for experiment. Ancient houses, in particular, are often reconstructed on the basis of surviving postholes and other structural traces. They can then be tested for structural soundness and to gain information on the time they must have taken to build originally and the materials used. By allowing the reconstructions to decay naturally, or even destroying them by fire, archaeologists can obtain valuable insights into the signs such decay or destruction may have left.

In another series of experiments, several bank and ditch earthworks have been dug and then left to decay. Periodically, a portion is excavated to observe the changes that have taken place.

Testing the Tools

Besides giving an insight into prehistoric technology, experiments allow us to appreciate the skill and organization that went into a variety of activities, the time and manpower required and the relative efficiency of evolving versions of early tools—the comparative felling power of stone, bronze and iron axes, for example.

One constraint, however, is possible lack of proficiency by those carrying out the experiment. Incompetent or unpracticed use of tools will obviously increase the time taken to perform a task and reduce the quality of the work, inviting a risk of drawing erroneous conclusions. Despite that potential drawback, much has been achieved.

Replication of ancient artifacts is invaluable in providing information about methods of manufacture and the time and effort involved. A detailed insight into stone tool manufacture can also be gained by refitting the flakes in the order in which they were removed thereby reversing the process of knapping the tool in order to understand the stages involved in producing it (the "chaîne opératoire"). Experiments in working different materials with stone tools have provided the essential background data for microwear analysis, where minute wear marks on ancient tools are examined under a microscope to reveal the uses to which they were put.

Among the most impressive achievements has been the demonstration, in many parts of the world, of the ability of experimenters using simple technology and large teams to carve, transport and erect huge stone monuments such as Stonehenge and the Easter Island statues. Their work shows that such feats were within the capabilities of ancient people and that neither supernatural nor extraterrestrial beings need to be called upon to account for these works.

Enormous figures, such as the above bird, created by moving dark stones to reveal light soil beneath, are a remarkable feature of the desert around Nazca, Peru. As they can only properly be viewed from the air, they have provoked much speculation, including claims that they were made by beings from outer space. Experiments have shown, however, that it is easy to create such figures as hugely scaled-up versions of small line drawings. Their purpose seems to have been closely tied in with Nazca religious practices.

ESTABLISHING RELATIONSHIPS

Analogies between the present and the past have been drawn since the earliest days of archaeology. The realization in the 17th century that ancient stone tools were indeed human artifacts was largely due to observation in the Americas of the native Indians using similar tools. By the 19th century, direct comparisons were being made between ancient peoples and contemporary groups such as the Australian aborigines, who were looked on as surviving relics of Paleolithic life.

Gradually, however, the idea of such complete correspondence between ancient and present-day societies was abandoned. It has been replaced by a more specific and less generalized use of analogies.

Today, the value of ethnographic analogies is a matter of debate. Some archaeologists argue that by drawing them to suggest elements in a picture of past lifestyles, we are limiting ourselves, because human culture is infinitely variable and nothing in the past need be mirrored in the present. The opposite view is that a comprehensive examination of present-day societies will provide us with a range of possibilities that broaden our outlook when considering the past.

Both contentions are valid. Ethnography provides a spectrum of ideas about how things may have operated in the past, but we must not allow ourselves to be limited in our reconstruction of that past by considering only those things we know to be true of the present day or of historical times. That is particularly important when looking at the eons before the emergence of modern humans. The behavior of our hominid ancestors was probably very different from anything with which we are familiar from our own time.

Many archaeologists, however, believe that the value of ethnographic studies is greater when they are used to compare present and past groups in the same area.

The Tsumkwe Bushmen (below) inhabit the Namib Desert. Their nomadic hunter-gatherer lifestyle provides helpful insights into that of prehistoric people, though groups such as the Bushmen cannot be regarded merely as living relics of the Stone Age. Every human group is unique although there are also some regularities in human behavior. Ethnographic studies by archaeologists have also provided important data on what happens to food remains, artifacts and structures after they have been discarded or abandoned.

A New Approach

In recent years, a new approach to the use of ethnographic data has been adopted; it is known as ethnoarchaeology. Some scholars believe that information about all the activities and interactions of ancient societies is encapsulated in the artifacts and other evidence uncovered by archaeologists—if only we can find ways of unlocking their secrets. Others are less optimistic, but no one disputes the fact that archaeological evidence can reveal valuable things about the past.

Many experts, among whom the eminent American professor Lewis Binford is the chief exponent, are seeking to establish the relationship between the static archaeological remains we study and the dynamic activities of the peoples of the past. It is a common assumption, for instance, that the pattern of artifacts recovered from a locality represents the activities that have taken place there. But do people really just leave things lying around, to be unearthed by their descendants?

PREDATORS OR VICTIMS?

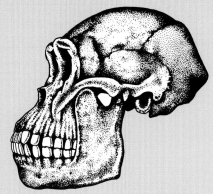

Much of the debate about whether certain of our early forebears qualify as hominids or as ancestors of the apes centers on their behavioral patterns. Raymond Dart's battle from the 1920s to have his *Australopithecus* accepted as a hominid *(see pages 10–11)* encouraged him to search for evidence of specifically human behavior, in particular the manufacture of tools and the regular consumption of meat.

Baboon skulls discovered in caves near the *Australopithecus* sites in southern Africa had depressions in them that Dart considered to have been caused by blows from clubs. That implied to Dart that *Australopithecus* had hunted and killed game. Furthermore, the caves did not contain complete baboon skeletons, but only certain bones. Dart concluded that those had been retained because of their potential usefulness as tools.

In the 1960s, a South African archaeologist, C. K. Brain, tried to test the validity of Dart's assumptions and to find out whether there were other ways in which the baboon bones could have accumulated. Brain studied a Hottentot village where the inhabitants kept and ate goats and where dogs scavenged the food remains discarded by the villagers. The results showed a pattern that has subsequently been found to be generally characteristic of the combined operations of carnivores and scavengers—the bigger and heavier bones tend to survive their attentions, while the smaller and lighter ones do not.

Dart's baboon bones matched this pattern. In addition, the damage observed on them closely matched that inflicted by leopards on the bones of their prey. It seems therefore that *Australopithecus* was not the hunter of the baboons. Indeed recent studies indicate that Australopithecines themselves were at times also victims of the leopards.

The Australopithecines, who lived from about 5 to 1 million years ago, had a similar sized brain to that of a modern ape, but they walked upright and may have used tools. Their teeth resemble those of other primates; they probably ate mainly fruit, berries and wild plants, and they were not hunters, although some species may have eaten lizards and other small creatures. The place of the Australopithecines in the human family tree is still debated, and recently discovered fossils only make the picture seem more complex.

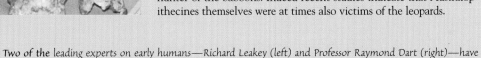

Two of the leading experts on early humans—Richard Leakey (left) and Professor Raymond Dart (right)—have devoted much of their life to unraveling the mystery of human origins.

To answer this and many other questions, archaeologists are increasingly studying ethnography directly, rather than relying on the accounts of anthropologists. Ethnoarchaeology is one of the most promising fresh approaches to understanding the past.

The Garbage Project

In 1972, William Rathje and a group from the University of Arizona began trying to determine the extent to which variable factors influence the types of ordinary refuse that people discard. With the help of the health department in the city of Tucson, Arizona, the team analyzed the contents of the trash cans of more than 600 households and related the information to socioeconomic data, such as the size of the household, the age of its members, their income and their ethnic group.

Among other things, the researchers found there were similarities in the material discarded by young and old people, and that considerably more food was thrown away by middle-class whites than by other ethnic groups. Much of the food wasted by the whites was not even unwrapped—and there was evidence that many households spent as much as $100 a year on steak that they never actually ate.

The archaeological implications of the study have still to be assessed fully. But it did establish that the archaeological premise that people make sensible economic use of the resources available to them is not always valid.

ARTIFACT VARIATION

We have already seen (page 127) the part that artifact assemblages may play in dating. They are also among the basic data from which archaeologists reconstruct the past.

Early antiquarians began to use variations both in the form and material of artifacts and in their associations to divide the past into chronological periods. By the early 20th century, scholars like Oscar Montelius and Paul Reinecke had refined and elaborated C. J. Thomsen's basic Stone Age–Bronze Age–Iron Age chronology into a detailed sequence of subdivisions, on the basis of variations in the forms of swords, pots, jewelry, axes and other artifacts.

In addition to chronological changes in the forms of artifacts and the composition of assemblages, variations between artifacts or assemblages found in different locations were also considered. The idea that geographically distinct archaeological assemblages denote separate cultural groups came to be one of the major assumptions underlying archaeologists' views of the past.

Cultures and Peoples

This so-called culture-people hypothesis derived from geographical variations still underpins much archaeological thinking, but today there are also many who question its validity, believing that other factors must also be considered, such as the availability of raw materials. This has encouraged the ethnographic examination of variations in artifacts and assemblages.

As long ago as 1939, Donald Thomson published a paper outlining the seasonal aspects of an Australian aboriginal economy, in which he noted that a single group occupied several widely separated sites in the course of a year. There were marked differences between the tools used at the different sites, as each season involved different activities.

The standard interpretation of Thomson's findings according to the "culture-people" hypothesis would be that each site was occupied by a different cultural group. Nevertheless, despite the flaws in the hypothesis, ethnographic and historical data and our knowledge of present-day Western societies clearly demonstrate that the expression of cultural differences through preferences in style of dress, hairstyles and body adornments, personal possessions, architecture and so on is a trait that recurs throughout humankind's history and spans not only geographical but also cultural boundaries.

Australian aborigines, who move across the country as the seasons change, varying their lifestyle, demonstrate the limitations of the "culture-people" hypothesis. While their tools and other objects differ from site to site, the artifacts all belong to the same cultural group.

TOOLS OF THE MOUSTERIAN

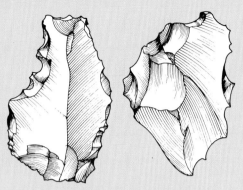

The great French scholar of the Paleolithic era, François Bordes (1918–1981), made an intensive study of stone tools from caves, rock shelters and open-air sites, particularly in southwest France. From them, he built up a generally accepted typology of tools of the Mousterian (Middle Paleolithic) period. Assemblages from different deposits on these sites varied considerably in the proportions they contained of different types of tools.

Bordes divided the assemblages into four main groups. The so-called Mousterian of Acheulean Tradition contained hand axes (as in earlier Acheulean assemblages), rare or absent in the other three groups. Denticulate Mousterian contained many toothed and notched tools, while the Charentian group (subdivided into Quina and Ferrassie) was abundant in scrapers. What Bordes termed Typical Mousterian had relatively few backed knives, but fairly balanced proportions of other types of tools. Bordes attributed each group to a different tribe, and the presence of all four groups on many sites to occupation by all of the tribes at various times.

Nevertheless, many archaeologists found the tribal explanation unacceptable. Was it likely that four cultures could repeatedly occupy the same sites, apparently at random, without influencing one another? One suggestion was that the varia-

tions were, at least in part, chronological. Another, by Professor Lewis Binford, proposed that Mousterian man constructed basic "tool kits" that varied according to the specific task to be performed.

Binford and his wife, Sally, used a computer to analyze which artifacts tended to be regularly associated with each other, forming the tool kits. Bordes's four groups, it was suggested, each represented a different combination of the tool kits and reflected the activities taking place at the site during each period of occupation. The Binfords first studied Mousterian tools in the Near East, where they had isolated five main tool kits. These they interpreted as relating to toolmaking, butchering animals, processing food, hunting and specialized plant food processing. At the important French site of Combe Grenal, they isolated no fewer than 14 tool kits, suggesting a considerable range of activities had taken place. It should be possible to check their interpretation of the tool kits' functions using microwear analysis. Many of the tools analyzed so far, however, seem to have been used for working wood and relatively few for other tasks.

Dr. David Clarke suggested that, as well as functional variation, chance may have played some part in determining the composition of Mousterian assemblages. The material recovered by archaeologists is only a fraction of what was once in use. Only some of the tools used at a particular location are likely to be discarded there, and of those only some will survive where they were left, while others are cleared away by humans or removed by natural agencies. Of those that do survive, only a proportion will be found by archaeologists digging a small part of the site.

Mousterian tools were often designed for very specific purposes. Sawing tools (left and center) had notched edges. Boring tools (right) with sharp points were used like awls.

Tools of the Mousterian period (left0—the age of the Neanderthal people—were fashioned from flint, chert, fine-grained igneous rocks and other raw materials. Some variation in the assemblages of this period may be related to the raw material selected to make the tools. Although concentrated in southwest France, Mousterian tools occur throughout western Europe and the circum-Mediterranean region.

ECONOMIC PREHISTORY

Certain factors are common to all forms of economic organization. People must obtain enough food and drink to sustain life and to reproduce, without expending as much energy in the quest for food as they get from the sustenance it yields. This means that subsistence economies must be efficiently organized to exploit productively the resources available within the limits of their technology. Societies may indeed indulge in "uneconomic" behavior, but if they do so to any significant extent they are unlikely to survive for very long.

Inevitably, the requirements of subsistence are reflected in the locations chosen for the settlements of small-scale, simple societies of hunter-gatherers, pastoralists and farmers who are self-sufficient in food. As societies become more complex, communities become increasingly interdependent economically, and the locations of their settlements reflect considerations other than subsistence alone. In attempting to reconstruct the organization of these more complex societies, archaeologists may use the techniques of locational analysis (see pages 154–155). The theory and methods of economic prehistorians are generally confined to subsistence economies, although they can be adapted to advanced economies, too.

Limits of Distance

Ethnographic and historical studies show that within subsistence economies, settlements are located to minimize the travel and effort involved in exploiting staple resources. As accessible distance depends on the nature of the terrain, the presence or absence of natural barriers such as rivers or mountains, and the transport available to the community, it is best thought of in terms of time.

A hunter, for example, generally operates within an area no more than two hours distant from his base. Pastoralists in general spend less time than that on the move each day, to keep down the energy used by their animals in traveling. Arable agriculture imposes a general limit of about one hour's traveling-time from the settlement. Within this, a radius 10 minutes distant from the site may enclose the area of intensive cultivation, growing important crops that require considerable labor, such as frequent watering or the application of manure. The gathering of plant foods, too, usually takes place within a one-hour radius. The considerable energy needed to collect and open shellfish, and their low calorific value, similarly restricts the distance at which

Cave paintings dating from around 20,000 B.C.E., in the French Pyrenees, may show bison wounded by arrows. Such hunting scenes are rare, but the evidence from bones shows the importance of meat in the diet.

UNDERSTANDING
THE PAST

they can effectively provide a food source.

Territorial Analysis

With these considerations in mind, analysis of the immediate environment of an archaeological settlement should suggest the economic reasons for the choice of location. Allowing for other constraints, such as the availability of water or the risk of flooding, sites tend to be located to exploit efficiently those natural resources—wild plants and animals, pastures, arable land—appropriate to the economy of the community. The resources considered to be of greatest importance are those most easily accessible from the site.

Site territorial analysis is a method devised to investigate the immediate environment of a settlement. The investigator makes four walks from the site, each two hours long and in a different direction, noting such things as soil types and vegetation.

The recent development of computer GIS (Geographic Information Systems, *see pages 168–169*) has made it possible to consider simultaneously many different relevant factors in the location and exploitation of site territories. To some extent it is possible to replace actual walking with computer simulations based on detailed topographical maps of the area.

Any environmental change since the site was occupied must be taken into account. For instance, in many areas, alluvial deposits have been laid down in comparatively recent times, so the present-day environment is not that exploited by the people of the past.

Seasonal Changes

Agricultural communities are dependent for most of their daily subsistence on the stored fruits of their labors—grain and other plants for themselves, and fodder for their animals if that is not available locally all the year round. If they can lay down such stores, they can occupy their settlements permanently.

Except in a few rare cases where suitable food sources are available throughout the year, the

changing seasons force hunter-gatherers and pastoral communities to move periodically. Hunter-gatherers may migrate between different ecological zones in which particular foods are available at different seasons. Pastoralists in Europe and elsewhere drive their flocks upland in summer and lowland in winter, or between inland and coastal pastures. Groups who largely depend for food on the hunting of large herbivores follow a similar seasonal pattern of movement between pastures. Often, the flocks kept by a settled farming community are also moved to seasonal pastures; some members of the community accompany them, while the rest remain at home.

When studying a settlement, therefore, economic prehistorians consider whether such seasonal migration was necessary. They reconstruct not only the economic potential of a site, but also the annual territories of its inhabitants, by looking for similar sites in complementary environments.

Because archaeological dating is relatively imprecise, it is not possible to link two or more sites together as successive habitations of a particular community. But archaeologists can identify the sites as part of the same economic system, and they have successfully predicted the likely location of complementary seasonal sites using this approach.

The Tsumkwe Bushmen of Namibia are nomadic hunter-gatherers whose lifestyle has changed little over thousands of years. Studies of prehistoric hunter-gatherer communities need to take into account the whole area exploited during the year (the "annual territory"), not just individual camp sites and their immediate environs.

SOCIAL ORGANIZATION

What can be discovered about social organization in the past? One approach is through studies of pottery styles—so-called ceramic sociology. The American archaeologists James N. Hill and William A. Longacre, working from the ethnographic observation that women are the potters in many societies, suggested that the patterns of distribution of individual pottery styles should reflect the social movement of women. In the pueblos they investigated, different pottery styles appeared in different parts of the sites, suggesting that each family or residential group had its own, the tradition of which was handed down from mother to daughter.

Ceramic sociology has been strongly criticized by both archaeologists and anthropologists who emphasize the complexity of kinship patterns and the fact that pottery styles are not necessarily transmitted from mother to daughter but may reflect many other influences. Nevertheless, this approach may still have potential.

Locational Analysis

Another significant method of approach to reconstructing social organization is through locational, or spatial, analysis. Some aspects of settlement patterns, as we have seen, relate directly to economic factors—the availability of essential resources such as water, food or fertile land. But others are based on social considerations, the interactions within and between societies.

To choose an obvious example, a preference for easily defensible sites would seem to imply that conflict was an ever-present threat to the builders of the settlements. The proliferation of fortified settlements across central Europe during the 6th century B.C.E. may reflect growing competition and warfare in the face of environmental

Changing pottery styles at an American Indian site in South Dakota during the 18th century, recorded in the chart at right, have been interpreted by the American archaeologist James Deetz as reflecting changes in patterns of social organization. The jug shown is a typical example of Indian "black-on-white" pottery.

154

UNDERSTANDING
THE PAST

deterioration; in the east of the area, it also reflects the need for defense against nomad incursions from the steppes.

The models used by economic geographers have been extensively borrowed by archaeologists as a way of looking at the human landscape. These allow the archaeologist to investigate whether sites are deliberately placed to make efficient use of certain interactions: the movements of goods in trade, access to centrally placed resources, control by centers over lesser centers through a hierarchy of settlements, and communications networks linking centers to each other and to settlements that are subordinate to them.

This approach has successfully been applied to the archaeological evidence of many different times and places—Roman Britain and Near Eastern and Central American civilizations, for instance.

A major problem facing the archaeologist investigating the distribution of sites lies in knowing whether the picture he or she obtains is complete or even representative. Many sites have been destroyed entirely, while others remain undetected under modern towns, deep soils or thick forests. Another difficulty is that archaeological dating is generally too imprecise to give a definite picture of the distribution of settlements at a particular time. In many instances, sites considered to be contemporary with each other could easily be consecutive, making the interpretation of their relationship very different.

Distribution of Artifacts

Much information can be obtained by plotting the distribution of certain classes of artifacts and other remains on a site. Areas where artifacts of known, or at least highly probable, function are clustered could well have been used for specific tasks; for example, a series of heavy stone implements associated with large animal bones would suggest a butchering area. It may be possible to identify the homes of separate families. Within a structure,

spatial analysis may yield information about the social organization of its occupants and the functioning of its different parts.

Mathematics plays a large part in the study of archaeological distribution on all scales, as the object is to ascertain whether the distribution is random or contains a pattern, and, if so, what that pattern is.

Trade and Exchange

Another insight into the workings of ancient societies can be gleaned from studies of patterns of trade—a field where, again, ethnographic research provides models. There are several contrasting mechanisms of exchange.

The first is based on reciprocity and is conducted between individuals and communities of equal status. Often, such exchanges are between members of a kin group and are more in the nature of gifts to smooth the workings of the kinship network than economic transactions. In general the concentration of such items in archaeological sites falls with increasing distance from the source. The second exchange mechanism is redistribution. In complex societies, kinship exchanges are overlaid by politically controlled movements of goods and raw materials from their sources of origin to political centers, from which they are then redistributed. Concentrations of commodities appear in the centers, with lesser quantities in settlements lower in the hierarchy.

Market economies based on mercantile and, generally, monetary exchange seem to have emerged relatively late in the archaeological record. Markets may develop in various types of location—particularly at important nodes in a communications network, at sites where a wide range of goods is easily obtainable, or on safe neutral ground at the frontiers or boundaries dividing separate groups or societies. In contrast, the location of political centers tends to depend on many factors of which trade is only one.

In common with other forms of spatial analysis, exchange networks are often studied with the help of models borrowed from geography. These can be used, for instance, to predict the size of a center or an industry that exported materials known to archaeologists from findings on "client" sites. Similarly, the models can identify cases where the distribution of a commodity is either wider or more localized than might be expected, and assist in constructing possible explanations.

Many Pueblo Indians of the U.S. Southwest lived in cliff villages such as this one at Mesa Verde, Colorado, dating from about 1200 C.E. The shift from plateau settlements to cliff dwellings reflects a developing need for defense. Major pueblos, such as Pueblo Bonito in Chaco Canyon, were probably political, religious and economic centers within a hierarchy of settlements, connected over much of the area by impressive straight roads that facilitated trade and communications.

Spatial analysis in settlements like the pueblos can be used to investigate the use of space between and within structures, providing clues about the organization of groups living there and social interactions among them. Such analyses may reveal the dwellings of individual families at one end of the spectrum and a whole hierarchy of social distinctions, from king to peasant, at the other.

FROM THE GRAVE

Archaeological assumptions about the significance of burials have included a belief that formal disposal of the dead and the provision of grave goods indicates a belief in an afterlife, and that the richness of grave goods reflect the wealth and social standing of the person buried.

Peter Ucko, professor of archaeology at London University in England, set out to test these assumptions by examining a range of ethnographic data. He discovered that some societies dispose of their dead merely to get rid of them. Others believe in an afterlife but do not practice burial; one group, for instance, requires the corpse to be eaten by hyenas. The type and variety of grave goods proved to relate to many factors. Similarly, the method of disposal of bodies and the form of the tomb or grave varied widely between the societies for which Ucko had data. He therefore concluded that there are severe limitations to the information that can be deduced from the study of burials.

In America, Professor Lewis Binford took a more optimistic view, after he, too, had examined the ethnographic literature, and other scholars followed his lead. They found the form of disposal and the accompanying ritual are frequently of symbolic significance within the community, giving expression to the position held by the dead person within the society.

Binford isolates three important aspects likely to be given expression in funerary rites. First, there is what he calls the "social persona" of the deceased, a sum of all the roles played by the person in his or her lifetime. Important variables in the social persona may include age, sex, kinship affiliations, rank and social position. Second, there is the size and composition of the social unit to which the dead person had belonged. The third criterion is the mode of death; distinctions may be made, for example, between the treatments accorded to suicides, executed criminals and heroes slain in battle.

Complex Variations

There is a considerable variety of ways in which a corpse can be disposed of and in the associated rites. Variables include the location and form of the grave, the position of the corpse within it, the treatment of the body (cremation or mummification, for example) and the selection of grave goods.

Recent ethnoarchaeological work, notably by Dr. Ian Hodder of Cambridge University, England, indicates that the relationship between funeral arrangements and social structure are even more complex than Binford suggested. Religious beliefs, ideology and attitudes toward death all play a part in determining details of funerary practices, rites and offerings, which do not therefore simply provide a mirror of social organization. Where social dimensions are expressed, they often reflect an idealized picture rather than the contemporary reality. Nevertheless, there is still

Inca mummies, bound with rope and buried in a sitting position with the knees drawn up to the chest, have been found in caves near Cuzco, Peru, the ancient Inca capital. The bodies have been naturally preserved for more than 500 years by the dry conditions of the area.

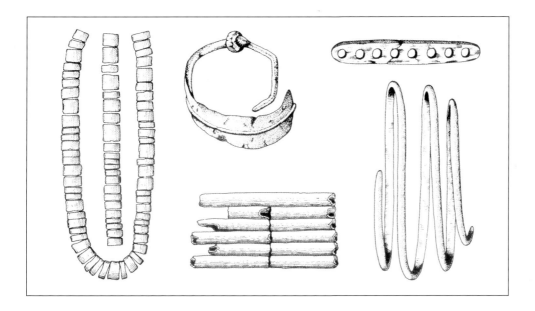

guarded optimism among archaeologists that burials can reveal something about the way in which early societies were organized.

A Slovakian Cemetery

The value of cemeteries in the reconstruction of prehistoric societies was elegantly demonstrated in a paper by Sue Shennan, at the time a research student at Cambridge University, England, about a cemetery of the early Bronze Age Nitra group at Branč in southwest Slovakia.

Shennan analyzed the grave goods in 274 burials that, on the basis of radiocarbon dates from the Nitra group, were made over a period of no more than 200 years, between about 2400 and 2200 B.C.E. Anthropological data on the age and sex of the skeletons were available, and Shennan was able to isolate elements associated with these variables. Men and boys were generally buried on their right sides, lying southwest/northeast or west/east. Women and girls were interred on their left sides, lying east/west or northeast/southwest.

Many of the associated grave goods were obviously part of distinctive clothing and personal ornamentation. Women wore necklaces and garters of bone beads, and copper willow-leaf earrings. Men wore copper daggers, willow-leaf knives, whetstones and a stone ax around their waist, presumably on a belt. Children wore willow-leaf rings as arm bands and had miniature vessels instead of the full-sized pots buried with the adults.

Shennan divided the graves into groups similar in their content and assessed the wealth of each burial according to three criteria: the variety of grave goods, the quantity of particular artifact types and the objects' value. The value was determined by allocating points according to the distance of the source of the raw material, the difficulty of obtaining it and the time needed to make the object.

Rich and Poor

Shennan thus isolated some graves that were "rich" according to all three criteria, and various grades that were less rich. She then looked at the age and sex distribution in the different grades. She found that both adult and child males were in some cases given wealthy burials, while among women wealthy burials were mainly confined to adults and adolescents. More female graves were wealthy than those of males, and in overall terms the female graves were wealthier, too. Shennan used these observations to make tentative suggestions about social organization at Branč.

It was clear that the status of individuals was to a large extent indicated by what they wore. Wealth among the men seemed to be hereditary, but the women could either have possessed hereditary wealth or have acquired it through marriage.

Since the community probably consisted of only 30–40 individuals at any one time, the complexity of its social organization implied that it must form part of a much wider social group. That conclusion was reinforced when similarities with other contemporary cemeteries in the region were noted.

Grave goods found in an early Bronze Age cemetery at Branč, Slovakia, included items of normal dress that varied according to the age and sex of the individual. Women were buried wearing bead necklaces, copper earrings and other jewelry; children wore copper arm rings, and men carried a range of tools. Other grave goods, however, were found with only some of the bodies, and were indicative of the status of the individual. From these, it was possible to build a picture of the social organization of the Nitra group to which the people of Branč belonged.

IRON AGE FARMERS OF SOMERSET

In the 15 years following the discovery of the Glastonbury lake village in England's Somerset Levels in 1892, excavation revealed a waterlogged settlement built on artificial mounds beside the lake. The village, inhabited some 2,000 years ago, had been defended on the landward side by a palisade and had contained a number of timber buildings. Preservation of plant and other organic remains was excellent, due to waterlogging.

In 1972, the brilliant British pioneer of "new archaeology," Dr. David Clarke, brought together the ideas of many of his students and colleagues in a book entitled *Models in Archaeology*. Clarke's own contribution to the volume was a study of the Glastonbury site, beginning with the individual buildings and working outward to view Glastonbury within the context of the British Iron Age.

Clarke isolated a "modular building unit" that occurred throughout the site, linked by lanes. This consisted of a pair of large round houses, a small house and several subrectangular structures.

From the remains within these buildings, Clarke was able to suggest their functions. The pair of large houses faced each other across a courtyard. They contained artifacts relating to almost all the activities undertaken on the site, and from those it seemed likely they served as central stores as well as dwellings. Near them were one or two workshop huts, with additional outside workfloors that could be used in fine weather.

structures near the smaller house was a bakery hut containing a row of hearths and an abundance of artifacts associated with female activities, suggesting that the women of the group congregated here to conduct their day-to-day activities, making clothing and preparing food.

The site also had a guard hut beside each of the two gates through the stockade. The gates and palisade bore impaled skulls, following Celtic custom.

A combination of different lines of evidence suggested each modular unit housed an extended family or lineage group of about 15–20 adults and children. Although the social status of each household appeared about equal, a unit at the center of the village seemed possibly wealthier than the others. It was flanked by two units rather poorer than average; perhaps these were the homes of families who were dependent upon a headman who lived within the central unit of the settlement.

Marriage and Migration

Clarke went on to make tentative suggestions about other aspects of social organization at Glastonbury. Certain imported items in the settlement could have been the property of women who had married into the community. They included the occasional spindle whorl of unattractive, nonlocal material.

Clarke next looked beyond the settlement to see it in the context of local economy and soci-

Segregation at Work

The material recovered from the workshop huts had been used to produce tools and weapons, including lathe-turned objects of wood—male activities. The courtyard between the large houses also contained items associated with male tasks, including manufacturing, threshing and dealing with horses.

The third, smaller house in each group resembled the larger ones but was set at some distance from them. The material from the small houses seemed exclusively associated with women and their activities—jewelry, and tools for spinning, leather and fur working and food preparation. Among the

The "modular building unit" identified by David Clarke at Glastonbury lake village probably housed an extended family of 15–20 adults and children. Men apparently worked in the buildings around the courtyard; women worked separately around the minor house. Not everyone accepts Clarke's interpretation.

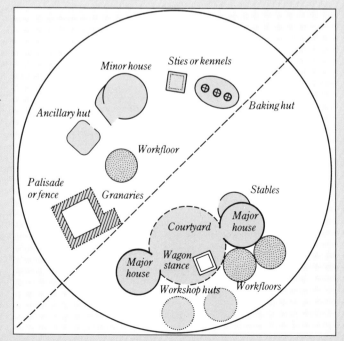

ety. Glastonbury was set in low-lying marsh, subject to annual flooding but otherwise rich in arable land, pastures and wild resources. Clarke outlined two ways in which such an environment could have been exploited: by small-scale, independent communities adapting to the constraints of flooding and by farmers who grazed their flocks there in summer, moving elsewhere during the seasonal floods.

He argued from the data that the inhabitants adopted the second course and had formed part of an extensive network linking the fenland with the nearby Mendip Hills. In particular, the material from Glastonbury showed close links with the large hillfort at Maesbury in the Mendips and its surrounding territory, from which Glastonbury obtained, among other things, stone for handmills and fine pottery. The slopes around Maesbury probably provided hilly pastures for the flocks from Glastonbury during the winter. The exploitation of the two zones allowed the area to sustain far larger flocks than could have been supported in either one alone.

Cloth and Crops

The evidence collected from Glastonbury indicated a well-developed textile industry. Woolen cloaks were a famous British export to the Roman world, and their manufacture could well have been an important activity at Glastonbury. Certainly, the flocks were large—perhaps as many as 1,000 sheep.

Plant remains suggested that barley was cultivated in the area immediately around the settlement that did not flood in winter, while the main crop of wheat and Celtic beans was sown in spring on the more extensive summer lands. The

A wooden god, probably a fertility figure, shows the classic features of a hermaphrodite. This came from the excavations of Neolithic Sweet Track in the Somerset Levels area, several thousand years earlier than the Glastonbury lake village. Because of waterlogging, the area has been a rich source of prehistoric wooden artifacts, otherwise rarely preserved.

inhabitants of Glastonbury could also draw on the rich natural resources of the fenland—fish and fowl, animals and plants.

Finally, Clarke examined the wider Celtic tribal area of Dumnonia, to which Glastonbury belonged. Maesbury, on the basis of the available evidence, fulfilled the role of local center within the Glastonbury district. It would have provided goods such as luxury metalwork, as well as affording political protection to the smaller settlements.

The lake village at Glastonbury was an agricultural community that adapted itself to the changes caused by seasonal flood patterns. Below, at left, we see one possible yearly pattern. The whole site consisted of the infield, on the highest ground and within which the village lay; the outfield; and sedge wasteland, low-lying and subject to the greatest flooding. To make best use of the natural cycle of flooding alternating with rich grazing and farming land, the sheep would have been brought in to graze in the outer sedge area in July and taken out in November, before the floods. This would have happened slightly later in the outfield.

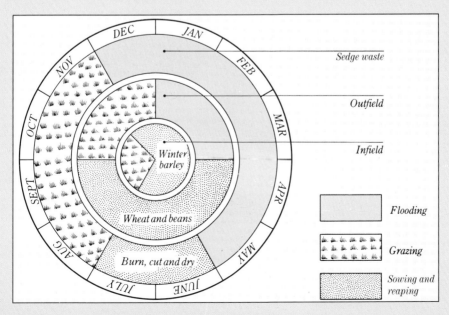

Sedge waste

Outfield

Infield

Winter barley

Wheat and beans

Burn, cut and dry

☐ Flooding

Grazing

Sowing and reaping

SILENT SENTINELS
OF STONE

It is now generally accepted that the megalithic tombs of western and northern Europe *(see page 137)* have nothing to do, as was once thought, with Mycenaean metal prospectors but are the products of indigenous inhabitants of the region. Even so, they are still a subject of speculation and inquiry. What induced their builders to invest massive efforts in erecting such monumental tombs? How was the necessary labor force assembled? What underlies their striking similarities?

One answer to the last question was proposed by Professor Grahame Clark, one of Britain's greatest prehistorians. Investigating the megaliths of southern Sweden, he noted that one group was concentrated in coastal locations from which deep-sea fish such as cod, haddock and ling could have been caught in winter. Historically, much of the Atlantic was linked by the travels of fishermen and this could well have provided a mechanism by which the "megalithic idea" and fashions in the style of tomb architecture spread between coastal Iberia, Brittany, Ireland, western England and Scotland, and Scandinavia. The high concentrations of megaliths on coasts, and the surprising numbers on small islands, may support a connection with fishing.

Professor Colin Renfrew of Cambridge University, England, however, views the similarities as similar responses to similar needs. At the structural level, the passage that forms a major element of many graves could have been devised independently in different areas to meet the need for repeated access to the interior of these communal tombs.

Other structural resemblances could be due to similarities in the raw materials available. In answer to the question of why the idea of building monumental tombs should arise independently in a number of areas, he cites the similarities in their backgrounds.

Territorial Markers?

Most megaliths occur in areas inhabited in the postglacial period by Mesolithic hunter-gatherers. The adoption of agriculture through contact with Neolithic farmers, Renfrew argues, led to a population explosion in the region and consequent competition for farmland between neighboring groups. In the face of potential conflict, the groups may have found it desirable to define and emphasize their territories and boundaries. The construction of megalithic tombs could have arisen in response to this need.

Renfrew has studied two circumscribed areas, the Scottish islands of Arran and Rousay, to examine this premise more closely. He found that

Massive slabs of stone some weighing as much as 50 tons, were dragged by teams of workers and shaped with stone hammers to build this megalith at Carnac, Brittany (above right). Dating from around 3000 B.C.E., it is one of numerous similar stone tombs found scattered throughout Atlantic Europe, built perhaps as territorial markers.

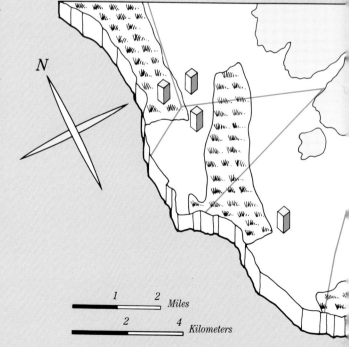

N

1   2 Miles

2   4 Kilometers

a division of the arable land into territories, each containing one megalithic tomb, results in units that correspond in size to the individual crofting communities of recent times in the same area. Each unit supported between 10 and 50 people.

The labor needed to put up a megalithic tomb would probably be beyond the capabilities of a community of this size. But Renfrew argues, by ethnographic analogy, that the cooperation of other communities could be secured by some form of recognized social incentive—perhaps a period of feasting at which communal building was one of several activities.

Bones of the Ancestors

Most megalithic tombs contain collective burials. Complete bodies were placed in some tombs, while in others only defleshed bones were deposited. Sometimes the bones from earlier burials were swept aside when new bodies were added, but often they were neatly tidied in an order that was far from arbitrary. Different tombs used different arrangements: In West Kennet long barrow, for example, many of the bones were grouped by age or sex, while at Isbister in Orkney, mixed bones from a number of individuals were arranged in small heaps, each with one skull. Despite the differences, there seems to have been an underlying theme: People deposited in these tombs were representative of their society, but their identity as individuals was not important. The tombs belonged to the ancestors, through whom the living society laid claim to their land. This interpretation reinforces Renfrew's view of the megaliths as territorial markers.

West Kennet long barrow, England (above left), a huge collective tomb, consists of a long central stone corridor with four side chambers off it, built into the east end of an enormous long earthen mound that was begun around 3500 B.C.E. Inside, the remains of 46 people, men, women and children, have been found as well as beads, pottery and arrowheads.

This map of the southern portion of the island of Arran, Scotland, shows the distribution of megalithic tombs. Hypothetical boundaries indicated on the map by straight lines divide the area into territories, each of which contains one megalith. Many archaeologists believe that megaliths served as territorial markers for farming communities, and as can be seen here, many of them were located in close proximity to arable land.

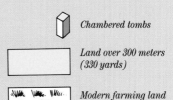

Chambered tombs

Land over 300 meters (330 yards)

Modern farming land

ANCIENT BELIEFS

Remaintsof a *shrine* (right) at the Neolithic village of Çatal Höyük, Turkey, date from about 6000 B.C.E. Such shrines alternated with domestic rooms within the settlement and were probably devoted to a cult in which bulls played an important role. An artist's reconstruction (below) shows the shrine as it may have looked. The bulls' heads were modeled in clay over the skulls of actual animals and set with real horns. A scene painted on the wall probably shows a corpse being devoured by vultures. Human skulls on the floor may be linked with the skull cult widespread in the Neolithic Near East.

OPPOSITE PAGE: A seated figure carved in white marble, found in a Neolithic shrine at Çatal Höyük, was probably a cult statue. It is wearing a leopard-skin cap and multiple armlets.

Religion is the last refuge of the troubled archaeologist. There is a well-known tendency for anything that seems otherwise inexplicable to the excavator or prehistorian to be interpreted as "ritual" in intent. The problems of reconstructing past beliefs are twofold: to identify the material symbols and to understand the system of belief that these symbols represent. The diversity of human thought and imagination is infinite, and it is probably unrealistic to hope ever to unravel the beliefs of people of the past from archaeological data.

In many instances, though, some attempt may be made to identify ritual structures and objects. It seems reasonable to interpret the fish-faced stone sculptures in the Yugoslavian Mesolithic hamlet of Lepenski Vir as cult figures, and rooms decorated with plastered bulls' heads in the vast Anatolian Neolithic village of Çatal Höyük as shrines. Large accumulations of fine Iron Age bronzes in rivers appear more likely to be votive offerings than the results of exceptional carelessness, and sacrificial victims like Tollund man (*see page 89*) similarly point to Iron Age veneration of watery places.

Where there is some historical continuity of practice or belief, the interpretation is less speculative. The magnificent temples of the ancient Near East can be traced back to their inception as small shrines. In India, there are striking similarities between some of the representations on Indus seals and the iconography of later Hinduism, allowing us to draw tentative conclusions about the beliefs of the earlier civilization.

On occasion, evidence has been found in Europe of an unbroken veneration of a particular locality despite official changes of religion. Christian churches are built over the remains of pagan

sanctuaries, and Celtic shrines lie beneath the two Roman temples at Frilford in southern England.

The clues to ancient ideologies and creeds are elusive and piecing them together must always be largely a matter of guesswork, but the results of religious inspiration are among the most glorious relics of the past. Magnificent temples all over the world and exquisite religious art creations attest the strength of human imagination and beliefs. Even though we may not understand, we can appreciate the feelings that inspired them.

Penetrating the Paleolithic Mind

Ever since their discovery in the 19th century, the magnificent Paleolithic cave paintings of bison, horses and other animals in France and Spain have provoked speculation about their purpose and meaning. The explanations offered include several drawn from ethnography—that the paintings were associated with totemism, hunting magic or fertility magic. It can be argued that fertility magic is unlikely, as explicit representations of sexual activity or of pregnancy are rare. By contrast, frequently found sculptured representations of pregnant women, so-called Venus figurines, were also a feature of Paleolithic art right across Europe.

The idea that the art was intended to ensure success in hunting also seems improbable. The animals upon which the painters mainly depended for food (reindeer in southwest France, for instance) are rarely represented. A few beasts are depicted with lines or dots on their bodies, which some people interpret as spears or wounds. But the rarity of these again argues against hunting magic as a universal explanation.

Recent work suggests that we should not in any case seek a single, all-embracing reason behind the cave art. Several different ones may apply to different aspects of it. Detailed and careful studies of the distribution, layout and execution of the paintings and engravings have revealed interesting common features. Traces are now being found of such art in the mouths of other caves and rock shelters where Paleolithic people once lived. The greater part of this art has been destroyed by the elements and by later inhabitants, but enough remains to suggest that it was originally common. That may imply it was intended as decoration of the home, although that does not preclude a ritual significance, too.

Rites of Passage

At the opposite extreme, many of the paintings are located in the utter depths of the caves, extremely difficult and often dangerous to reach.

One suggestion is that penetration of this hostile region may have played some part in initiation ceremonies, when children underwent rites transforming them into full adult members of their community. Sculptured clay bison deep in the Tuc d'Audoubert cave are reached by a tortuous route. Near the bison are the deep heelprints of children's feet. The evidence from many such caves indicates that the art was visited only rarely.

A pattern has also been detected in the way in which certain animals are regularly depicted in the same parts of different caves. Annette Laming and André Leroi-Gourhan, pioneers of this investigation of the spatial distribution of art, initially interpreted it entirely in terms of opposing male and female principles, represented chiefly by the bison and the horse (the animals most frequently shown) that take pride of place in the designs. Although that interpretation seems unsatisfactory, it appears that the paintings were often executed to an overall formula, the purpose of which was to divide the available space in a cave.

As data accumulates about the diversity of artistic representations in the Paleolithic, so the complexity of the subject increases. Microscopic examination, by the American scientist Alexander Marshack, of engravings on a bone has revealed minute representations of animals characteristic of the spring; other scenes and tally marks have been found on other pieces. He interprets these as evidence of recording of the seasons and other intervals of time, a primitive calendar. Like the other theories, this is hard to prove or disprove. We are left with a mystery that will continue to fascinate and stimulate people for many years to come.

Clay models of bison (uppermost) probably dating from around 15,000–10,000 B.C.E., at Tuc d'Audoubert, France, are among the finest of the many spectacular examples of Paleolithic cave art found in France and Spain. Bison and horses were the most common subjects in the cave paintings. Other sculptures included magnificent bears. There may have been magicoreligious reasons behind such artwork.

163

FORCES OF CHANGE

One of the most fascinating series of questions that archaeologists are incessantly striving to answer is what factors lie behind changes in the past. Principal among these are what Binford calls "the Big Questions"—the transformation of society by the development of agriculture and the emergence of civilization. But change is of interest at every level, right down to the appearance in an area of a new style of pottery or an alteration in burial practices.

One school of thought approaches these topics by assembling data on the sequence of changes and studying it to try to discover the mechanisms involved. A rival school attempts to employ an explicitly scientific approach, by proposing a theory, assembling data to test it and discarding or modifying it if it is disproved. Recently, some archaeologists have rejected this approach, arguing that it fails to take into account the uniqueness of individual cultures and that it cannot adequately explain the less concrete aspects of life, such as religion. Alternative methodologies are currently being developed.

The first approach generally seeks to explain change in terms of mechanisms familiar from history and ethnography or predicted intuitively. Some exponents look to the internal workings of society, seeing cultural change as a natural human propensity. It can be due to random, almost accidental "cultural drift," to progressively more complex cultural adaptations that have the appearance of inevitability, to shifts in fashion or to the inspired inventions of geniuses. Although individuals have undoubtedly shaped historical development, archaeology can rarely, if ever, recover evidence of such influences; nevertheless, modern approaches place more emphasis on attempting to do so and on penetrating the thoughts as well as the actions of people of the past.

External factors are also cited. One is environmental change, for which independent evidence may be sought, for example, through pollen analysis or geological study. A second is the influence of other human groups, by trade, migration or invasion. Criteria used to identify migration are the sudden appearance of traits new to the area, their previous existence in an identifiable source area and subsequent modifications of some of the indigenous traits by the newcomers. Invasions show the same characteristics, with, in addition, evidence of conflict, such as the destruction of settlements or skeletons showing signs of violent death, and of the imposition of aspects of the alien culture. Though in principle these rules sound straightforward, they are not always easy to apply to archaeological data.

Archaeology as Science

In contrast to the traditional approach, which begins with a body of archaeological data and then attempts to draw conclusions from it, the "scientific" approach begins with a set of theories and then sets out to prove them. Archaeologists propose a series of mechanisms that may have operated in a given situation in the past and outline the kind of evidence that would show whether these had done so. They then explicitly seek this evidence and discard any theories that are refuted by the data obtained. They adopt as provisional explanations those theories that seem most consistent with the evidence but continue to refine old hypotheses and formulate new ones, and seek new data by which to test them. Another approach that archaeologists have borrowed from science is the General Systems Theory, which proposes that any organization can be studied as a system of interrelated parts. Using this approach, the operation and interrelationship of different portions of the social system are examined to establish how they function, and the impact on them of new elements is studied. Explanations of changes that occur can then be advanced in the light of the results.

The Olmec of the Gulf coast of Mesoamerica built their first ceremonial center at San Lorenzo around 1200 B.C.E. and began carving colossal human heads such as this one from the later center at La Venta, apparently wearing helmets for the dangerous ritual ball game. The Olmec's distinctive culture laid the basis for all the later civilizations of Mesoamerica. Understanding the factors involved in the emergence of civilization is one of the "Big Questions" of archaeology.

THE GERMANS IN BRITAIN

In the later days of the Roman Empire, from the 4th century C.E., problems of defending its extensive frontiers induced the Romans to employ free German barbarians from outside the empire as mercenaries. Many of them subsequently settled within Roman territory, which then, of course, would have included Britain.

The British archaeologist, Giles Clarke, carried out a study in the 1970s to see whether the presence of these German mercenaries could be identified by looking for features of German origin among those of the native British culture of the time.

Clarke considered various aspects of the lifestyles of the immigrants as possible sources of such evidence. Many of those aspects, he argued, would have changed for purely practical reasons: The immigrant groups would be likely to adopt the locally available pottery, weapons and houses, for example.

Clarke turned therefore to burials. He reasoned that the method of disposing of the body and the type of tomb would conform to local customs, but the clothing and grave goods would reflect the beliefs and customs of the Germans.

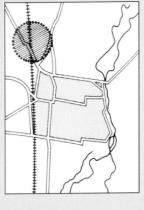

He therefore studied 450 burials in a late Roman cemetery (310–410 C.E.) at Lankhills in Winchester. Most contained few or no grave goods. In addition, many of the skeletons wore hobnailed boots. But two small groups of graves showed a different pattern.

One group, of 16 graves dating from about 350 to 400 C.E., held an abundance of personal possessions including ornaments, and the skeletons did not have hobnailed boots. Many of the grave goods bore a strong resemblance to material found in graves in southern Bavaria. The six graves in the second group, dating from around 390 to 410, were diverse in their contents, but each had general Germanic affinities. Clarke concluded that both groups belonged to the Germans and confirmed that the appearance of immigrants in an area can be detected by archaeology.

A Roman cemetery at Lankhills, England (left), contained the graves of several German immigrants who served as mercenaries in the Roman army in the 4th century. These German graves held an abundance of burial goods, a factor that distinguishes them from Roman graves. The skeleton of a German soldier (below) is accompanied by an iron knife (1), a bronze buckle (6), a bronze crossbow brooch (3) and other unidentified objects of bronze (4), silver (2) and glass (5).

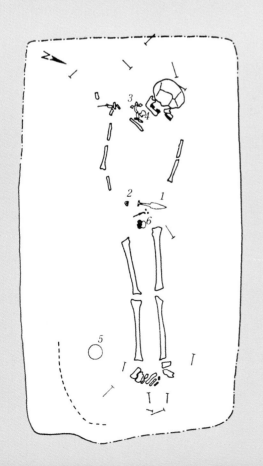

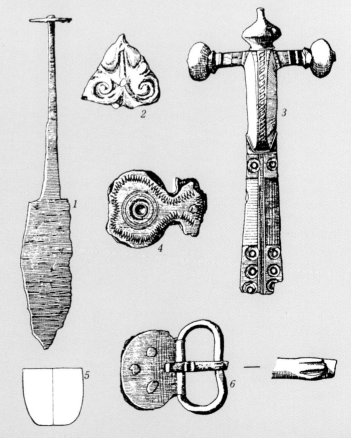

CIVILIZATIONS OF THE AEGEAN

The causes behind the emergence of the Minoan and Mycenaean civilizations in the Aegean during the late 3rd and 2nd millennia B.C.E. have intrigued scholars for years. Until recently, most explanations attributed Aegean development to outside influence, either in the form of invasion of the area or by diffusion.

Civilization had emerged in Mesopotamia by 3000 B.C.E., and, some archaeologists argued, Mesopotamian trade introduced civilized ideas and technological innovations into nearby, less advanced areas. Others postulated an invasion of the Aegean from some adjacent region, of which Anatolia seems the most probable.

Professor Colin Renfrew approached the problem from a different viewpoint. He contended that the scanty available evidence for invasion or immigration from Anatolia into Greece in the early Bronze Age showed that, at most, such incursion was limited, and that it could not be deemed responsible for the transformation of society there. Trade, though clearly documented, was also an inadequate explanation in itself.

To understand the major changes in social organization and complexity that took place, it was necessary, said Renfrew, to study the workings of late Neolithic society in the Aegean, to examine the fresh variables that emerged in the early Bronze Age and to determine the impact these may have had on every interrelated aspect of the local social system. The two major new developments he considered were changes in the subsistence economy and the introduction of bronze metallurgy.

Renfrew examined the resultant impact of both of these developments on population growth, economics, craft technology, social organization, trade and communications.

From Subsistence to Surplus

The subsistence economy of Neolithic Greece was based on mixed farming. In addition to wheat and barley, pulses and flax were cultivated, while sheep were the main animal raised.

Early in the 3rd millennium B.C.E., cultivation of the vine and olive also became important in southern Greece and the Aegean Islands. Both crops were eminently suitable for storage, in the form of olive oil and wine, and for trade. They were grown on the lower slopes of hills, within easy reach of the villages, on land that was not suitable for arable farming. Their cultivation required work at a different time of year from that needed by cereal crops, and much of this work, such as harvesting, was light enough to be done by children.

As a result, agricultural yields were substantially increased without disrupting established agricultural practice. That in turn allowed, or stimulated, population growth, and for the first

Shaft graves within the citadel at Mycenae (right) house the magnificently furnished burials of warrior kings or chiefs and their families. Heinrich Schliemann, who excavated the graves in 1876, fancifully identified this death mask of beaten gold (above) as the face of the legendary Mycenaean king Agamemnon.

UNDERSTANDING
THE PAST

time there was enough demand for specialized crafts and services to justify the existence of full-time craftspeople, who could be supported from the extra agricultural output.

The Coming of Bronze

Some copper artifacts were made during the 4th millennium B.C.E., but there were not many of them and they had little economic or social significance. When, in the 3rd millennium, copper began to be mixed with tin to produce the relatively hard alloy bronze, demand for metal goods grew. Bronze could be used to make a range of useful new tools and weapons and a variety of impressive ornaments. The demand for metalwork stimulated specialization in crafts such as metallurgy and jewelry-making, while the new tools promoted the development of other crafts, like carpentry and shipbuilding. Competition for prestigious or useful craft products and for control of their producers helped to heighten both social differences within communities and conflicts between them, resulting in the emergence of local chieftains, who were also in many instances warriors.

These chieftains regulated agricultural and craft production, operating a redistributive system through which the farmers could obtain tools or ornaments they needed or wanted. The organizational demands of controlled redistribution made it necessary to develop methods of measurement and recording, which culminated in the emergence of writing.

Renfrew argued that any single innovation would have had a limited or negligible effect on social organization, because the inherently conservative nature of societies acts to minimize change. However, the interaction of several simultaneous developments created a "multiplier effect." In the Aegean, increased agricultural productivity provided the means to support craft specialization, while bronze metallurgy supplied the motive, setting in motion a series of changes in other subsystems of society.

Those changes in turn resulted in what, in a term borrowed from the jargon of electronics, are called "positive feedback loops"—alterations in the workings of a social system that serve to reinforce themselves. Thus Aegean society was transformed from one consisting of basically self-sufficient, equal and egalitarian farming villages to one of prosperous, hierarchical chiefdoms, with palace-dwelling rulers, actively competing with one another both at home and in international trade.

The royal palace at Knossos (above) was the heart of the Minoan civilization of ancient Crete in the 2nd millennium B.C.E. As well as being the home of the king and queen, the palace was a religious center where priests and priestesses lived. It was decorated with elaborate wall paintings reflecting the Minoans' love of nature.

This snake goddess (left) from the palace of Knossos probably represents the Minoan mother goddess. She was a major focus of Minoan worship, along with a male deity represented by bulls and bulls' horns, probably the forerunner of the Greek god of the sea, Poseidon. Effigies of the goddess, such as this one in faience (a glassy material), come from domestic shrines and mountain sanctuaries.

167

CIVILIZATIONS OF THE AEGEAN

ARCHAEOLOGY IN THE COMPUTER AGE

Archaeology, like so many other fields of modern life, has been radically affected by the rapid advances in computer technology. At the simplest level, computers can store vast quantities of data, making it feasible to create national databases of sites, monuments and other archaeological discoveries. Although such records have been built up over decades and could previously be consulted, computers have greatly facilitated access to the information they contain. Excavations are now routinely recorded on computer databases, allowing easy manipulation.

In many scientific analyses, computers have enabled archaeologists to perform complex or laborious mathematical operations (for example, seriation) quickly, easily and in great numbers. This has transformed the potential information output of an individual archaeological site. Similarly computers have greatly facilitated the task of matching tree-ring sequences for dendrochronology. Use of computers imposes a requirement to use standardized recording systems and has made archaeological analyses much more rigorous. Artifacts that were once classified largely by intuition can now be assessed according to mathematically derived criteria.

Aerial archaeology has been another beneficiary of computer developments (*see page 45*). Scanning devices and computer programs have superseded the laborious techniques formerly used to map information from air photos. Computer enhancement and manipulation of photographs have also produced admirable results, both for air photo interpreters and for others, for instance those studying growth rings on ancient human or animal teeth.

Layered Landscapes

Archaeologists regularly borrow techniques from sister disciplines such as geography in the interpretation and manipulation of their data. The latest addition to this armory has been Geographic Information Systems (GIS). It has always been of interest to archaeologists to map different variables in order to compare their distribution and look for meaningful correlations. For example, someone studying the development of farming in a region would be interested in comparing the distribution of agricultural settlements with that of water sources, various soil types, forest, high ground and so on. However,

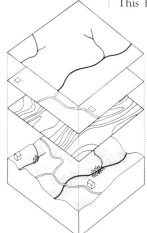

Geographic Information Systems allow many different spatial variables to be recorded, compared, manipulated, analyzed and interpreted. They may include data from aerial photographs, a range of maps, geophysical surveys, sites and monuments records, field surveys and excavations.

the simultaneous presentation of all these variables on a single map makes it far too cluttered to read easily; the task of making a number of maps is time-consuming, and the job is exacerbated if changes through time are under consideration. By using one of the GIS programs developed for geography and modified for archaeologists and others, it is possible to generate nests of elegant maps that present a number of different variables and to do so at the touch of a button. Not only does GIS allow the clear simultaneous presentation of a number of spatial variables, but it can also be used to generate maps to answer a number of questions.

One may cite the example of British megalithic tombs. Archaeologists studying them now consider that they acted as territorial markers (*see pages 160–161*). If this was indeed the case, the visibility of these monuments will likely be of importance. Using known data on the topography of the region, several archaeologists have used GIS to plot out the areas from which individual megalithic monuments would be visible and have studied the patterns of intervisibility, in order to define the extent of the territory to which each monument might have related.

GIS has proved an invaluable tool for looking at spatial relations on land and underwater. It is particularly useful for predicting the location of archaeological sites and other areas of human activity on the basis of past distributions. The GIS plots are extremely elegant and attractive, and perhaps because of this, some archaeologists are tempted to see them as an answer in themselves rather than merely a sophisticated means of examining data. This is a danger that is often associated with the computer: It is easy to forget that the computer is not intelligent and that the quality of the material it produces is only as good as the data that is fed in. It is still the responsibility of the archaeologist to frame the questions, choose the data and interpret the results.

Modeling the Past

GIS builds a static picture of past landscapes. Computers can do much more, however, given the appropriate set of variables. For example, archaeologists are interested in finding out what construction techniques were used in creating the enormous stone monuments that were raised in the past in different parts of the world—Stonehenge, the Pyramids of Egypt, the massive Inca walls, the Easter Island statues. To test in person the techniques that

Australia, therefore, came by sea. Were they accidentally carried there when fishing off the Southeast Asian coast, or did they deliberately colonize this land that may have been visible on a clear day? One way to attempt to answer this question is by looking at the number of people required to found an island population. Computer simulation allows the investigator to use ocean currents to indicate likely places for chance or deliberate landfalls and to "breed" from a founding population of various sizes, finding out how many people of suitable age and sex would be required to establish a viable and expanding population, and whether this could be achieved by chance castaways. The answer seems to be no. There is a strong possibility that Australia was deliberately colonized. If the computer simulations are correct, these surprising results would greatly enhance our appreciation of the remarkable capabilities of our distant human ancestors.

Inside Vanished Buildings

As "virtual reality" becomes an everyday feature of computer games and an essential tool for architects, archaeologists have also begun to harness this useful and informative method of bringing the past to life. Where detailed information on the ground plan of a structure is available and its superstructure can be predicted, it is possible to produce a three-dimensional computer model of the vanished building, through which the computer user may wander at will. Fine examples produced in recent years include collapsed Egyptian tombs, the spectacular Anatolian Neolithic village of Çatal Höyük, the great ruined medieval abbey of Cluny in France and the ceremonial center of the Aztec capital Tenochtitlán. As well as providing an excellent impression of what vanished structures would originally have looked like, virtual reality can for example test the feasibility of different reconstructions of structures for which the data is not complete or assess the costs, effects and other factors involved in various plans to reconstruct the original.

may have been used may require huge teams of helpers and considerable periods of time; given all the appropriate data, a computer can test a number of such techniques very quickly.

Computers may also be used to simulate things that cannot be tested with real human experiments. For instance, Australia was colonized by ancient humans around 60,000 B.C.E. Despite fluctuating sea levels in the past, the region of Australia and New Guinea has always been separated from Southeast Asia by at least 36 miles (60 km) of open water. The first humans in

Tenochtitlán, the Aztec capital destroyed in 1521 by the Spanish conquistadores, lies buried beneath modern-day Mexico City. Construction work has revealed traces of it, including a sculpture of a principal Aztec goddess, the uncovering of which led to a full-scale excavation at the site. This in turn revealed remains of the Templo Mayor, or Great Temple (left), which was located in the heart of the Aztec city and where human sacrifices were performed. Computer virtual reality that incorporates the excavated remains of the temple and its modern surroundings can render a reconstruction of the center of Tenochtitlán (above).

ARCHAEOLOGY TODAY

The past has always been destroyed by the people of the present, and in many ways our age is more conscious of the need to preserve our heritage than ever before. But at the same time, our means of destruction and the demands behind them have also grown to unprecedented proportions. Adequate food, housing, transport and leisure pursuits are generally seen as reasonable requirements, but the world's daily population expansion and the wealth of the affluent area of the globe mean that meeting these requirements makes a significant daily impact on the world's physical and cultural environment.

The response to this problem in many countries has been to introduce or tighten up legislation to ensure that what is destroyed is adequately investigated first. This has led to a great increase in rescue, or salvage, archaeology, often carried out by a burgeoning number of contract archaeological teams. There is a danger, however, that the gap is widening between the active uncovering of the evidence of the past and the theoretical understanding of such evidence. The story of the past has to be extracted from the material remains—it is not an open book—and so the unstructured collection of data because it is under threat does not necessarily advance our knowledge.

Another response to the rapid rate of destruction has been to make far more explicit what stands in need of preservation or protection. Such awareness has resulted in more detailed surveys of surviving remains, tighter legislation to protect these and increased financial penalties for their destruction, ideally linked to the commercial value of the related development.

But the risk even of death can seem a reasonable price to pay for great potential wealth. Looting of monuments such as the *huacas* (sacred burial mounds in South America), which may yield gold and silver objects or valuable richly decorated pottery, is a major problem in a world where the gap between rich and poor is so great. Harsh penalties and official vigilance in the countries of origin must be matched by responsible attitudes in the wealthy

Living museums in many countries bring the past to life. In settlements of reconstructed or restored early buildings, people can be observed working in authentic ancient ways and are often happy to talk about aspects of life at the time. At Colonial Williamsburg in Virginia, a man dressed in 18th-century work clothes is laboring in a charcoal yard.

countries that provide a market for such plundered material. Most museums today will not buy objects that are offered without an impeccable record of legal acquisition, but many private collectors are not so scrupulous, and between buyer and original "finder" there is a network of international criminals, often operating with impunity, who run few risks and make the greatest gains. Occasionally they are brought to justice, but archaeological looting is now a major growth area of international crime. Prevention of this criminal and destructive looting and smuggling of antiquities will only occur when developed nations unite in taking steps to curb the activities of rapacious collectors and those who supply them.

Whose Past Is It Anyway?

In addition to protecting and preserving our heritage, there is a desire in the developed world to investigate our antecedents and uncover the human story. The efforts of institutions like the Jorvik Viking Centre in England or Colonial Williamsburg in the United States to make archaeologists' knowledge of the past accessible and intelligible have stimulated public interest on a growing scale. This interest continues to be fueled by popular television programs, readable and lavishly illustrated accounts of exciting discoveries, or reconstructions and reenactments of past events and lifestyles. There is a danger, however, that the attempt to make information about the past attractive and accessible may lead to oversimplification and trivialization, turning a quest for knowledge and an understanding of our origins and antecedents into a way of passing the time agreeably —"edutainment," with the emphasis on entertainment rather than education.

Not all societies share these attitudes toward the past. Just as the Christian Church in the 19th century often appropriated prehistoric skeletons for "decent" Christian reburial, fundamentalist believers of several religions today seek to control and appropriate archaeological investigations and materials on the grounds, often mistaken, that all the people of the past in their country must have been their coworshipers. The attempt to mold the past to underwrite and reinforce the regimes of the present is not a new phenomenon—it was notoriously practiced in Nazi Germany, for

Archaeologists' ultimate goals of reconstructing what happened in the past and why will only be achieved if we carefully and meticulously integrate modern theoretical approaches with strictly controlled scientific excavations and investigations. The work of the great American archaeologist, Lewis Binford (above right, with friends), exemplifies this vital marriage of theory and practice.

instance—but it remains a significant abuse of archaeological investigation.

On the other hand, the desire for knowledge of the human past has led in former times in many parts of the world to an insensitive and roughshod attitude to the acquisition of data relating to native peoples, running alongside more general abuses. In the present more enlightened and sensitive climate, the legitimate grievances of native North Americans, Australian aboriginals, New Zealand Maori and other ethnic groups are resulting in major "repatriation" programs by which the skeletons and artifacts of past indigenes are being handed back to their descendants, the skeletons to be accorded appropriate funerary rites and the artifacts often to take their place with other important cultural and sacred materials of the groups in question.

Undoubtedly, such programs are justified. The issues, however, are by no means clearcut. Land rights, for instance, present a knotty problem, the claims of farming settlers whose forebears have perhaps cultivated a given region for many generations coming into conflict with the claims of indigenous peoples to control access to the lands that supported their ancestors and that are often full of places of important cultural meaning and sacred significance.

Archaeology has demonstrated the complexity of the record of human settlement across the globe. Ultimately we are all descended from primates who evolved some 6 million years ago in Africa. To whom, then, do the remains of early people (such as a 30,000-year-old skeleton) belong? To the present indigenous inhabitants of the regions in which they were found, who may not in fact be their lineal descendants? (DNA and other studies have demonstrated that some groups in the past have entirely died out.) Or to humanity in general? And if the latter is the case, is it appropriate that the Western quest for knowledge of the past through archaeological investigation be preferred to the contrasting attitudes of other societies? For the native North Americans, for instance, the past needs no material demonstration, being adequately accounted for in traditions. These are vexed questions to which there is as yet no satisfactory answer.

Lessons from the Past

It would be wrong, however, to go to the extreme of viewing archaeology as a self-indulgent and unjustified exercise. A knowledge of the past has much to teach us, both generally—about who we are and how we got where we are—and more specifically. There is a tendency to view progress as an inevitable, desirable process, bringing constant improvement to human society. A glance at the human record shows that this is not the case. Societies not only rise but fall, and the lessons of the past may alert societies of the present to potential pitfalls and dangers. Advanced technology is not always better than the simpler technology of the past, as archaeology has successfully demonstrated. Two well-known examples of this come from the Andean region of South America.

In one, experimental reconstruction of ancient raised field systems around Lake Titicaca proved not only to be highly fertile but to provide extra protein from the fish in their drainage channels and, unexpectedly, to have a microclimate that protected the crops against the major local problem of frost damage at night. In the other example, excavations at Cusichaca (Peru) revealed an Inca canal network that formerly brought much needed irrigation waters to the arid local valley. Restoration of the canals was achieved by archaeologists and local villagers working side by side. In both cases, the ancient system has now been adopted locally, with the result that productivity has been raised while labor and equipment costs have been cut, and the lessons learned here are being applied elsewhere. Examples of such valuable lessons from the past can be multiplied.

Archaeology Today

Today our picture of the past is very much clearer than it was a few hundred years ago or even a few decades ago. A great deal of the "thick fog" in which Nyerup (the 18th-century antiquarian) lamented that it was wrapped has now been dispelled. More than two centuries of excavations have yielded directly a picture of the technological and artistic achievements of the past and the inspiring story of humanity's ever-increasing control over nature, from the earliest days when our ancestors began using tools to extend their biological capabilities, through their colonization of hostile environments made possible by their development of shelter, fire and clothing, to the awe-inspiring situation of today when we hold in our hands the means to destroy the earth entirely. The development of dating techniques has enabled us to trace the course of human history, giving both the sequence of events and their absolute age. The exponential rate of change, so rapid today, can be traced back through progressively slower stages until we reach the period some 6 million years ago when humans, like other creatures, were evolving through biological rather than cultural adaptations.

The battery of scientific techniques now at the disposal of archaeologists allow them to supplement the information they can extract from traditional studies. Many of the material aspects of society can be reconstructed from these data: details of their dwellings and clothing, the tools they used, the food they ate, where they obtained their raw materials.

But ultimately we would like to know much more about the people of the past. What did they believe and think? How were their societies organized socially and politically? What was life actually like? What stimulated people to change their lifestyles? We look across the millennia, fascinated alike by the human similarities and the striking differences between us and them, and eager to know more. Much, alas, seems inaccessible by archaeological, or by any other, means. We have only the slightest indications of the beliefs and ideologies of preliterate people of the past and their view of the world around them. But some answers are now available to these challenging questions, and methodologies are being developed that may enable others to be answered in part. Ultimately we hope to achieve a clear picture of the world of the past, the challenges it presented, the responses people made and their interactions with each other.

SUGGESTED FURTHER READING

Aitken, M. J. *Physics and Archaeology*. Oxford: Clarendon Press, 1974.

Alcock, Leslie. *"By South Cadbury Is That Camelot. . ." The Excavations of Cadbury Castle, 1966–1970*. London: Thames and Hudson, 1972.

Bahn, Paul, ed. *The Cambridge Illustrated History of Archaeology*. Cambridge: Cambridge University Press, 1996.

Bahn, Paul, and Jean Vertut. *Journey Through the Ice Age*. London: Weidenfeld and Nicolson, 1997.

Barker, Philip. *Techniques of Archaeological Excavation*. 3rd ed. London: Batsford, 1993.

Binford, Lewis. *In Pursuit of the Past*. London: Thames and Hudson, 1983.

Bordes, François. *A Tale of Two Caves*. New York: HarperCollins, 1972.

Brothwell, Don, and Eric Higgs, eds. *Science in Archaeology*. London: Thames and Hudson, 1969.

Coe, Michael D. *Breaking the Maya Code*. London: Thames and Hudson, 1992.

Coe, Michael, Dean Snow, and Elizabeth Benson. *Cultural Atlas of Ancient America*. New York: Facts On File, 1986.

Coles, Bryony, and John Coles. *People of the Wetlands: Bogs, Bodies and Lake-Dwellers*. London: Thames and Hudson, 1989.

———. *Sweet Track to Glastonbury: The Somerset Levels Project*. London: Thames and Hudson, 1986.

Cunliffe, Barry. *Fishbourne Roman Palace*. Stroud/Charleston: Tempus, 1998.

Cunliffe, Barry, ed. *The Oxford Illustrated Prehistory of Europe*. Oxford: Oxford University Press, 1994.

Daniel, Glyn. *150 Years of Archaeology*. London: Duckworth, 1975.

Delgado, James, ed. *British Museum Encyclopaedia of Underwater and Maritime Archaeology*. London: British Museum Press, 1997.

Dimbleby, Geoffrey W. *Plants and Archaeology*. 2d ed. Atlantic Highlands, N.J.: Humanities Press International, 1978.

Dixon, Philip. *Barbarian Europe*. Oxford: Elsevier Phaidon, 1976.

Dowman, E. A. *Conservation in Field Archaeology*. London: Methuen, 1970.

Dymond, David. *Archaeology and History: A Plea for Reconciliation*. London: Thames and Hudson, 1974.

Evans, Angela Care. *The Sutton Hoo Ship Burial*. London: British Museum Publications, 1986.

Evans, John G. *An Introduction to Environmental Archaeology*. Ithaca, N.Y.: Cornell University Press, 1978.

Fleming, Stuart. *Dating in Archaeology: A Guide to Scientific Techniques*. London: Dent, 1976.

Forte, Maurizio, and Alberto Siliotti, ed. *Virtual Archaeology*. London: Thames and Hudson, 1997.

Fowler, Peter. *Approaches to Archaeology*. New York: St. Martin's Press, 1977.

Gelling, Margaret. *Signposts to the Past: Placenames and the History of England*. London: Dent, 1978.

Gowlett, John. *Ascent to Civilization: The Archaeology of Early Humans*. 2d ed. New York: McGraw-Hill, 1992.

Greene, Kevin. *Archaeology—An Introduction: The History, Principles and Methods of Modern Archaeology*. 3rd ed. London: Routledge, 1996.

Hadingham, Evan. *Lines to the Mountain Gods: Nazca and the Mysteries of Peru*. Norman, Okla.: University of Oklahoma Press, 1988.

———. *Secrets of the Ice Age*. London: Heinemann, 1980.

Hagen, Victor von. *Search for the Maya: The Story of Stephens and Catherwood*. n.p.: Saxon House, 1983.

Hall, Richard. *Viking Age York*. London: Batsford/English Heritage, 1994.

Hodder, Ian. *The Present Past, an Introduction to Anthropology for Archaeologists*. London: Batsford, 1982.

Hudson, Kenneth. *World Industrial Archaeology*. Cambridge: Cambridge University Press, 1979.

Johanson, Donald, and Blake Edgar. *From Lucy to Language*. New York: Peter Nevraumont/Simon and Schuster, 1996.

Lloyd, Seton. *Foundations in the Dust: The Story of Mesopotamian Exploration*. Rev. ed. London: Thames and Hudson, 1980.

Mithen, Steven. *The Prehistory of the Mind*. London: Thames and Hudson, 1996.

Renfrew, Colin. *Before Civilization*. London: Jonathan Cape, 1973.

Renfrew, Colin, and Paul Bahn. *Archaeology: Theories, Methods and Practice*. 2d ed. London: Thames and Hudson, 1996.

Renfrew, Colin, and E. Zubrow, eds. *The Ancient Mind: Elements of Cognitive Archaeology*. Cambridge: Cambridge University Press, 1994.

Roaf, Michael. *Cultural Atlas of Mesopotamia and the Ancient Near East*. New York: Facts On File, 1990.

Robinson, Andrew. *The Story of Writing*. London: Thames and Hudson, 1995.

Rudenko, Sergei. *Frozen Tombs of Siberia*. London: Dent, 1970.

Scarre, Christopher, ed. *Past Worlds: The Times Atlas of Archaeology*. New York: Random House Value Publishing, 1995.

Scarre, Christopher, and Brian Fagan. *Ancient Civilizations*. London: Longman, 1997.

Schele, Linda, and David Freidel. *A Forest of Kings*. New York: Morrow, 1990.

Sharer, Robert, and Wendy Ashmore. *Archaeology: Discovering Our Past*. 2d ed. Mountain View, Calif.: Mayfield Publishing, 1993.

Tattersall, Ian. *The Fossil Trail*. Oxford: Oxford University Press, 1995.

Vita-Finzi, Claudio. *Archaeological Sites in Their Setting*. London: Thames and Hudson, 1978.

Weiner, John. *The Piltdown Forgery*. Oxford: Oxford University Press, 1955.

Wells, Calvin. *Bones, Bodies and Disease*. London: Thames and Hudson, 1964.

SUGGESTED
FURTHER READING

ACKNOWLEDGMENTS

This book was originally designed and produced by The Paul Press Ltd, 41-42 Berners Street, London W1P 3AA

Art Editor: Antony Johnson
Project Editor: Elizabeth Longley
Editorial: Mike Groushko, Christopher Mole, John Burgess
Art Assistant: David Ayres
Illustrations: Alan Suttie, Antony Johnson (maps)
Art Director: Stephen McCurdy
Editorial Director: Jeremy Harwood

Typeset by Wordsmiths, Street, Somerset
Origination by South Sea International, Hong Kong
Printed in Singapore through Print Buyer's Database

The author wishes to thank the staff of the Department of Archaeology, University of Cambridge, for the use of library and computer facilities in the preparation of the first edition; Paul Croft, Rog Palmer and Pat Carter for helpful advice on and criticism of the manuscript; and Dr. Joan Weir for proofreading the final text of the first edition.

Picture research: Liz Eddison
Key: (t) top; (b) below; (l) left; (r) right; (c) center
Thanks to the followong persons and organizations, to whom copyright of the photographs noted belongs:
vi Vision International; 2 Salisbury and South Wiltshire Museum; 3 The Illustrated London News Picture Library; 4(t)(b) The Mansell collection; 4(c), 5 C.M. Dixon; 6 The Mansell Collection; 7 French Government Tourist Office; 8 Ann Ronan Picture Library; 9 The Mansell Collection; 10 The Illustrated London News Picture Library; 11 Bruce Coleman; 12 The British Library; 13(t) Ronald Sheridan; 13(b) The Illustrated London News Picture Library; 14(tr)(tl) BBC Hulton Picture Library; 15(c) Michael Holford; 15(bl) Kevin Schafer/Corbis; 16 The Mansell Collection; 17(t)(br) BBC Hulton Picture Library; 18(t)(b) The Mansell Collection; 19(bl) Ronald Sheridan; 19(cr) Michael Holford; 20, 21(t) Robert Harding Picture Library Ltd; 21(b) Kevin Schafer/Corbis; 22(t)(b) Paolo Koch, Vision International; 23 Robert Harding Picture Library Ltd; 24 Werner Forman Archive; 25(t)(b) Salisbury and South Wiltshire Museum; 26 The Illustrated London News Picture Library; 27 Stephanie Colasanti, FIIP; 28–29 Royal Commission of Historical Monuments of England; 28(bl) Griffith Institute, Ashmolean Museum; 30(tr) Topham Picture Library; 30(br), 31 Robert Harding Picture Library Ltd; 32 Dr. Georg Gerster, John Hillelson Agency; 33 Planet Earth Pictures; 34 Dr. Georg Gerster, John Hillelson Agency; 36–37 Michael Holford; 38 Michael Holford; 39 The Public Record Office; 40 crown copyright: reproduced permission of Historical Scotland; 42 Aerofilms; 43 The Mansell Collection; 44 Dr. Georg Gerster, John Hillelson Agency; 45 Aerofilms; 46 Thames & Hudson Ltd; 47 Robert Harding Picture Library Ltd; 48 B. Norman, Sheridan Photo Library; 49 Jane McIntosh; 50 Academic Press, Inc.; 51 Jane McIntosh; 53 Gwil Owen; 55 Daily Telegraph Colour Library; 56 Ronald Sheridan; 58, 59(b) Robert Harding Picture Library Ltd; 59(t) Michael Holford; 62, 63 Mike Duffy, York Archaeological Trust; 64–65 Dr. Georg Gerster, John Hillelson Agency; 68, 69 Leslie Alcock, Camelot Research Committee; 70 Museum of London; 71 Michael Holford; 72, 73, 74, 75, 76 Museum of London; 77, 78 Robert Harding Picture Library Ltd; 79 Cambridgeshire Country Council; 80, 81 Museum of London; 84(r) Museum of London; 84(tl)(bl) Gwil Owen; 85 The Illustrated London News Picture Library; 86 Topham Picture Library; 87 Michael Holford; 88 Conservation Dept, Museum of London; 89 The Illustrated London News Picture Library; 90(t) Cambridgeshire County Council; 90(b) Ronald Sheridan; 91 Fishbournc Roman Palace, Sussex Archaeological Society; 92 Michael Holford; 93 Photoresources; 94 Planet Earth Pictures; 95(t) S.J.K. Photographic; 95(b) Institute of Nautical Archaeology; 96 Dr. Brian Bracegirdle; 98, 100, 101(b) Consevation Dept, Museum of London; 101(tr), 102(tr) Daily Telegraph Colour Library; 102(b) C.M. Dixon; 103 British Museum; 105 Museum of London; 106 Rog Palmer; 108 C.M. Dixon; 110(t) Wellcome Institute; 111 Kenneth Garrett/NGS Image Collection; 112 C.M. Dixon; 113(tl)(br) The Illustrated London News Picture Library; 114 Robert Harding Picture Library Ltd; 115 John Hillelson Agency; 116 Science Photo Library; 117(t)(b) Reading Museum and Art Gallery; 118–119 C.M. Dixon; 119 Ronald Sheridan; 120–121 Ronald Sheridan; 120(t) Michael Holford; 122 Nathan Benn/NSG Image Collection; 123(bl) Museum of London; 123(t)(c) Ronald Sheridan; 124 Tohpam Picture Library; 124(b), 125(b) The Illustrated London News

Picture Library; 125(t) Victoria and Albert Museum, John Sparks Ltd; 127(t) Jane McIntosh; 130 Topham Picture Library; 131(t) Topham Picture Library; 131(b) The Illustrated London News Picture Library; 133 S.J.K. Photograhic; 135 Topham Picture Library; 136–137 Ronald Sheridan; 138(l) Topham Picture Library; 138(r) The Illustrated London News Picture Library; 140, 141 Bruce Coleman; 142 Vision International; 144, 145 Topham Picture Library; 146(b) Tropix; 146(t) Werner Forman Archive; 147 H.R. Dörig, Vision International; 148–149 Bruce Coleman; 148(b), 150(l) Robert Harding Picture Library Ltd; 150–151 Michael Holford; 152 C.M. Dixon; 153 Robert Harding Picture Library; 154, 155 Werner Forman Archive; 156 H.R. Dörig, Vision International; 159 Michael Holford; 160 Jane McIntosh; 161 Michael Holford; 162, 163(b) The Illustrated London News Picture Library; 163(t) Robert Harding Picture Library Ltd; 164 Kevin Schafer/Corbis; 166(t) Photoresources; 166(b) Michael Holford; 167(b) Ronald Sheridan; 167(t) C.M. Dixon; 168 Thames & Hudson Ltd; 169 Taisei Corporation; 169(b) David Hiser/Photographers Aspen; 170 David G. Houser/Corbis; 171 Lewis Binford. **Illustrations** 54 Leslie Alcock, © Camelot Research Committee; 60–61 Prof. Keith Branigan for his technical assistance; 83 Museum of London; 115 Jane McIntosh; 126 Mortimer Wheeler, © Archaeological Survey of India; 132 BT Batsford Publishers Ltd; 154 from *Stylistic Change in Arikara Ceramics*, by James Deetz (Illinois Press); 165 (The Antiquaries Journal 1970) The Society of Antiquaries London

Note: The publishers have made every effort to trace copyright holders for illustations that appear in this volume and wish to offer their apologies for any unintentional errors or omissions.

Front cover: U.K. edition: Main photograph—Brain Brake, John Hillelson Agency; Bottom left—Museum of London; Bottom right—Michael Holford. Original U.S. edition: Main Photograph—Michael Holford; Bottom left—Museum of London; Bottom right–Michael Holford

ACKNOWLEDGEMENTS

INDEX

thermoremanent magnetism 133
thin section examination 116, 118, 120, 121, *121*, 132, 140
Thíra 19, 92, *102*
tholos tombs 18
Thomsen, Christian J. 6, 150
Thomson, Donald 150
thorium/protactinium ratio dating 133, 140
three-age system **6–7**, 150
three-dimensional recording 25, *25*, 82, 83, 94
Thucydides 4, *4*
thunderbolts 4, 5
Tiahuanaco 21
Tikal 46
timber *See* wood
Timna *123*
tin 123
Tintagel ware 69
Tiryns 18
Titicaca, Lake 172
TL dating 124–25, *125*, 127, 132, *138*, **138–39**, 140
Togidubnus, King 91
Tollund Man **89**, *89*, 112, 162
Toltecs 21
tombs 92, 156–57, 160, *160*, 165, 169
tools
 excavation 73, *73*, **76–77**, *76*, *77*, 92, 94
 grave goods 157, *157*
 importance of 172
 kits 151
 Mesolithic 93
 Mousterian 151, *150–51*
 preserved 111
 testing 118–19, 144, 146–47
 See also individual materials,
 e.g., flint
topography 5, 67
top soil, removing 69, 72, 73
torques 117, *117*
tortoiseshell 100
totemism 163
Toulouse 41
town planning 22, 71
town plans **38–39**, 49
trace element analysis 118, 122
trackways 38, 53, 106, *106–7*
trade 33, 42, 71, 118–19, **155**, 164, 166
Trajan 98

treasure hunters *31*, 60
treasure hunting 24
treasure trove law 117
tree ring dating *See* dendrochronology
tree ring sequences 130, *131*, 168
trees 103, 105
 pollen analysis 104
 See also dendrochronology
trenches
 excavation 67, *67*, 68, 69
 foundation 36, 69
 trial 68, 68
trepanning *110*, 111
trial trenches 68, *68*
triangulation **78–79**, *79*, 82
troweling 73, 74, 76, 80
trowels 73, 74, 76, 77, 92
Troy 18, *18*, 19, 25, 29
Troyes *See* Chrétien de Troyes
Tsumkwe Bushmen *148*, 153
Tuamotu 145
Tuc d'Audoubert *163*, 163
Turkana, Lake *11*, *140*, 141
Turkestan 23, 25
Tutankhamun, King 2, *3*, **13**, *13*
Tyler, Sir Edward 7
Tylissos 15
type fossils 27
typological change 26–27, 127
typology **114–15**, *115*, 126, 127, *127*, 132

Uaxactún 46
Ucko, Peter 156
Uhle, Max 21
Uluburun 95
underwater archaeology *31*, 32–33, *33*, *55*, 101, **94–95**, 168
uniformitarianism **8–9**
Ur 4, *4*, 17
uranium dating **128**, 133
uranium series disequilibrium dating (USDD) 32, **133**, 140
urban archaeology 38–39, **49**, 56, 63, 72, 96
urbanism 31
USDD *See* uranium series disequilibrium dating
Ussher, Archbishop James 8
Uxmal 21

Valley of the Kings 13
Vandals 41
varves 104, 131
vegetation *See* environmental reconstruction
Ventris, Michael 15
Venus figurines 163
Vespasian 59
Vesuvius *2*, *5*, 5, *24*, 24, 36
video cameras 94
Vija Tai *vi*
Vikings *5*, 20, 39, **63**, *63*
 colonization 40
villages 38, 95, *155*
 deserted 38, 40
Vindolanda 103
Virchow, Rudolf von 10
Virginia 24
virtual reality (VR) 90, 169, *169*
Visigoths 41
vitrified forts 58
volcanic eruptions 92
 Thíra 19, 102
 Valley of Mexico 71
 Vesuvius *2*, *5*, 5, *24*, 24, 36
votive offerings 162
VR *See* virtual reality

Wales 41
Wallonia 41
walls
 on aerial photographs 44
 excavated *55*, *61*, *66*, *67*, 68
 in geophysical surveys *52*, 52
 quarrying 59
 site features 58, 60, 75
 surviving 49, 95
Wareham 120
warriors *166*, 167
waste flakes 48, 82, 85
waterlogging
 preservation and decay 92, 103, 106
 waterlogged sites *63*, 92, **95**, 130, 158–59
weapons 6, 27, 150, 157, 158, 165, 167
weather, coping with 76–77
weaving *61*, 95, 146
Weiner, J.S. 129

Wessex from the Air (Crawford) *28*, 29
West Kennett long barrow 161, *161*
wet sieving 84
wheelbarrows *73*, 76
Wheeler, Sir Mortimer 25, 29, 62, 66, 115, *126–27*
Winchester 42, 165
wood 105, 151
 artifacts *92*, *93*, 100, *103*, 124, 158, *159*
 conservation 100
 dating 130, 134, 136
 excavation 92
 structures 58, 62, 91, 92, 106, 130, 158
 waterlogged 86, 92, 101, 109
woodland management 106
Woolley, Sir Leonard 17
Wor Barrow 25
workshops 60–61, 158
Worsaae, J.J. 6, 24
wrecks 33, 55, 95, 101
writing 167
 decipherment **14–15**, 22, 47
Wroxeter 62
Würm Glaciation 105

X-ray analysis 100, 101, 116
X-ray diffraction 116, 123
X-ray fluorescent spectrometry 116, 117, 118, 121, 123, 124
X-ray milliprobe 116, 122
X-ray photography 100, 122

Yangshao 23
York 56, **63**, 63
York Archaeological Trust 63
Yuan Kang 4
Yucatán 21, 46, 47, 119
yucca fibers 146

Zeus 18
Zhou 23
Zhoukoudian 10, *10*, 20, 23
Zinjanthropus ("Dear Boy") 11, *140–41*
Zoroastrian religion 15